Building Machine Learning Projects with TensorFlow

Engaging projects that will teach you how complex data can be exploited to gain the most insight

Rodolfo Bonnin

BIRMINGHAM - MUMBAI

Building Machine Learning Projects with TensorFlow

First published: November 2016

Production reference: 1181116

Published by Packt Publishing Ltd.
Livery Place
35 Livery Street
Birmingham
B3 2PB, UK.
ISBN 978-1-78646-658-7

www.packtpub.com

Credits

Author

Rodolfo Bonnin

Reviewer

Niko Gamulin

Commissioning Editor

Veena Pagare

Acquisition Editor

Namrata Patil

Content Development Editor

Siddhesh Salvi

Technical Editor

Danish Shaikh

Dharmendra Yadav

Copy Editor

Safis Editing

Project Coordinator

Nidhi Joshi

Proofreader

Safis Editing

Indexer

Mariammal Chettiyar

Graphics

Disha Haria

Production Coordinator

Arvindkumar Gupta

About the Author

Rodolfo Bonnin is a systems engineer and PhD student at Universidad Tecnológica Nacional, Argentina. He also pursued parallel programming and image understanding postgraduate courses at Uni Stuttgart, Germany.

He has done research on high performance computing since 2005 and began studying and implementing convolutional neural networks in 2008,writing a CPU and GPU - supporting neural network feed forward stage. More recently he's been working in the field of fraud pattern detection with Neural Networks, and is currently working on signal classification using ML techniques.

To my wife and kids and the patience they demonstrated during the writing of this book. Also to the reviewers, who helped give professionalism to this work, and Marcos Boaglio for facilitating equipment to cover the installation chapter. Ad Maiorem Dei Gloriam.

About the Reviewer

Niko Gamulin is a senior software engineer at CloudMondo, a US-based startup, where he develops and implements predictive behavior models for humans and systems. Previously he has developed deep learning models to solve various challenges. He received his PhD in Electrical Engineering from University of Ljubljana in 2015. His research focused on creation of machine learning models for churn prediction.

I would like to thank my wonderful daughter Agata, who inspires me to gain more understanding about the learning process and Ana for being the best wife in the world.

www.PacktPub.com

For support files and downloads related to your book, please visit www.PacktPub.com.

Did you know that Packt offers eBook versions of every book published, with PDF and ePub files available? You can upgrade to the eBook version at www.PacktPub.com and as a print book customer, you are entitled to a discount on the eBook copy. Get in touch with us at service@packtpub.com for more details.

At www.PacktPub.com, you can also read a collection of free technical articles, sign up for a range of free newsletters and receive exclusive discounts and offers on Packt books and eBooks.

Mapt

https://www.packtpub.com/mapt

Get the most in-demand software skills with Mapt. Mapt gives you full access to all Packt books and video courses, as well as industry-leading tools to help you plan your personal development and advance your career.

Why subscribe?

- Fully searchable across every book published by Packt
- Copy and paste, print, and bookmark content
- On demand and accessible via a web browser

Table of Contents

Preface

In recent years, machine learning has changed from a niche technology asset for scientific and theoretical experts to a ubiquitous theme in the day-to-day operations of the majority of the big players in the IT field.

This phenomenon started with the explosion in the volume of available data: During the second half of the 2000s, the advent of many kinds of cheap data capture devices (cellphones with integrated GPS, multi-megapixel cameras, and gravity sensors), and the popularization of new high-dimensional data capture (3D LIDAR and optic systems, the explosion of IOT devices, etc), made it possible to have access to a volume of information never seen before.

Additionally, in the hardware field, the almost visible limits of the Moore law, prompted the development of massive parallel devices, which multiplied the data to be used to train a determined models.

Both advancements in hardware and data availability allowed researchers to apply themselves to revisit the works of pioneers on human vision-based neural network architectures (convolutional neural networks, among others), finding many new problems in which to apply them, thanks to the general availability of data and computation capabilities.

To solve these new kinds of problems, a new interest in creating state-of-the-art machine learning packages was born, with players such as: Keras, Scikyt-learn, Theano, Caffe, and Torch, each one with a particular vision of the way machine learning models should be defined, trained, and executed.

On 9 November 2015, Google entered into the public machine learning arena, deciding to open-source its own machine learning framework, TensorFlow, on which many internal projects were based. This first 0.5 release had a numbers of shortcomings in comparison with others, a number of which were addressed later, specially the possibility of running distributed models.

So this little story brings us to this day, where TensorFlow is one of the main contenders for interested developers, as the number of projects using it as a base increases, improving its importance for the toolbox of any data science practitioner.

In this book, we will implement a wide variety of models using the TensorFlow library, aiming at having a low barrier of entrance and providing a detailed approach to the problem solutions.

What this book covers

`Chapter 1`, *Exploring and Transforming Data,* guides the reader in undersanding the main components of a TensorFlow application, and the main data-exploring methods included.

`Chapter 2`, *Clustering,* tells you about the possibility of grouping different kinds of data elements, defining a previous similarity criteria.

`Chapter 3`, *Linear Regression,* allows the reader to define the first mathematical model to explain diverse phenomena.

`Chapter 4`, *Logistic Regression,* is the first step in modeling non-linear phenomena with a very powerful and simple mathematical function.

`Chapter 5`, *Simple Feedforward Neural Networks,* allows you to comprehend the main component, and mechanisms of neural networks.

`Chapter 6`, *Convolutional Neural Networks,* explains the functioning and practical application, of this recently rediscovered set of special networks.

`Chapter 7`, *Recurrent Neural Networks,* shows a detailed explanation of this very useful architecture for temporal series of data.

`Chapter 8`, *Deep Neural Networks,* offers an overview of the latest developments on mixed layer type neural networks.

`Chapter 9`, *Running Models at Scale – GPU and Serving,* explains the ways of tackling problems of greater complexity, by dividing the work into coordinating units.

`Chapter 10`, *Library Installation and Additional Tips,* covers the installation of TensorFlow on Linux, Windows, and Mac architectures, and presents you with some useful code tricks that will ease day-to-day tasks.

What you need for this book

Software required (with version)	Hardware specifications	OS required
TensorFlow 0.10, Jupyter Notebook	Any x86 computer	Ubuntu Linux 16.04

Who this book is for

This book is for data analysts, data scientists, and researchers who want to make the results of their machine learning activities faster and more efficient. Those who want a crisp guide to complex numerical computations with TensorFlow will find the book extremely helpful. This book is also for developers who want to implement TensorFlow in production in various scenarios. Some experience with C++ and Python is expected.

Conventions

In this book, you will find a number of text styles that distinguish between different kinds of information. Here are some examples of these styles and an explanation of their meaning.

Code words in text, database table names, folder names, filenames, file extensions, path names, dummy URLs, user input, and Twitter handles are shown as follows: "We can include other contexts through the use of the include directive."

A block of code is set as follows:

```
>>> import tensorflow as tf
>>> tens1 = tf.constant([[[1,2],[2,3]],[[3,4],[5,6]]])
>>> print sess.run(tens1)[1,1,0]
5
```

When we wish to draw your attention to a particular part of a code block, the relevant lines or items are set in bold:

```
>>> import tensorflow as tf
>>> tens1 = tf.constant([[[1,2],[2,3]],[[3,4],[5,6]]])
>>> print sess.run(tens1)[1,1,0]
5
```

Any command-line input or output is written as follows:

```
# cp /usr/src/asterisk-addons/configs/cdr_mysql.conf.sample
     /etc/asterisk/cdr_mysql.conf
```

New terms and **important** words are shown in bold. Words that you see on the screen, for example, in menus or dialog boxes, appear in the text like this: "Clicking the **Next** button moves you to the next screen."

Warnings or important notes appear in a box like this.

Tips and tricks appear like this.

Reader feedback

Feedback from our readers is always welcome. Let us know what you think about this book—what you liked or disliked. Reader feedback is important for us as it helps us develop titles that you will really get the most out of.

To send us general feedback, simply e-mail feedback@packtpub.com, and mention the book's title in the subject of your message.

If there is a topic that you have expertise in and you are interested in either writing or contributing to a book, see our author guide at www.packtpub.com/authors.

Customer support

Now that you are the proud owner of a Packt book, we have a number of things to help you to get the most from your purchase.

Downloading the example code

You can download the example code files for this book from your account at http://www.packtpub.com. If you purchased this book elsewhere, you can visit http://www.packtpub.com/supportand register to have the files e-mailed directly to you.

You can download the code files by following these steps:

1. Log in or register to our website using your e-mail address and password.
2. Hover the mouse pointer on the SUPPORT tab at the top.
3. Click on Code Downloads & Errata.
4. Enter the name of the book in the Search box.
5. Select the book for which you're looking to download the code files.
6. Choose from the drop-down menu where you purchased this book from.
7. Click on Code Download.

Once the file is downloaded, please make sure that you unzip or extract the folder using the latest version of:

- WinRAR / 7-Zip for Windows
- Zipeg / iZip / UnRarX for Mac
- 7-Zip / PeaZip for Linux

The code bundle for the book is also hosted on GitHub at https://github.com/PacktPublishing/Building-Machine-Learning-Projects-with-TensorFlow. We also have other code bundles from our rich catalog of books and videos available at https://github.com/PacktPublishing/. Check them out!

Errata

Although we have taken every care to ensure the accuracy of our content, mistakes do happen. If you find a mistake in one of our books-maybe a mistake in the text or the code-we would be grateful if you could report this to us. By doing so, you can save other readers from frustration and help us improve subsequent versions of this book. If you find any errata, please report them by visiting http://www.packtpub.com/submit-errata, selecting your book, clicking on the Errata Submission Form link, and entering the details of your errata. Once your errata are verified, your submission will be accepted and the errata will be uploaded to our website or added to any list of existing errata under the Errata section of that title.

To view the previously submitted errata, go to https://www.packtpub.com/books/content/support and enter the name of the book in the search field. The required information will appear under the Errata section.

Piracy

Piracy of copyrighted material on the Internet is an ongoing problem across all media. At Packt, we take the protection of our copyright and licenses very seriously. If you come across any illegal copies of our works in any form on the Internet, please provide us with the location address or website name immediately so that we can pursue a remedy.

Please contact us at copyright@packtpub.com with a link to the suspected pirated material.

We appreciate your help in protecting our authors and our ability to bring you valuable content.

Questions

If you have a problem with any aspect of this book, you can contact us at questions@packtpub.com, and we will do our best to address the problem.

1
Exploring and Transforming Data

TensorFlow is an open source software library for numerical computation using data flow graphs. Nodes in the graph represent mathematical operations, while the graph edges represent the multidimensional data arrays (tensors) passed between them.

The library includes various functions that enable you to implement and explore the cutting edge **Convolutional Neural Network** (**CNN**) and **Recurrent Neural Network** (**RNN**) architectures for image and text processing. As the complex computations are arranged in the form of graphs, TensorFlow can be used as a framework that enables you to develop your own models with ease and use them in the field of machine learning.

It is also capable of running in the most heterogeneous environments, from CPUs to mobile processors, including highly-parallel GPU computing, and with the new serving architecture being able to run on very complex mixes of all the named options:

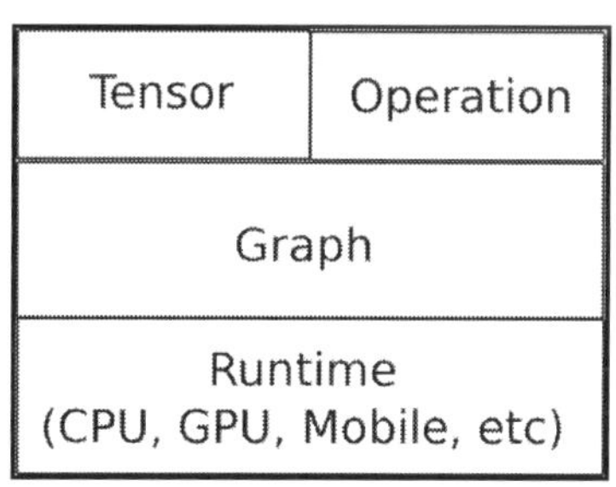

TensorFlow's main data structure – tensors

TensorFlow bases its data management on **tensors**. Tensors are concepts from the field of mathematics, and are developed as a generalization of the linear algebra terms of vectors and matrices.

Talking specifically about TensorFlow, a tensor is just a *typed, multidimensional array, with additional operations, modeled in the tensor object*.

Tensor properties – ranks, shapes, and types

As previously discussed, TensorFlow uses tensor data structure to represent all data. Any tensor has a static type and dynamic dimensions, so you can change a tensor's internal organization in real-time.

Another property of tensors, is that only objects of the tensor type can be passed between nodes in the computation graph.

Let's now see what the properties of tensors are (from now on, every time we use the word tensor, we'll be referring to TensorFlow's tensor objects).

Tensor rank

Tensor ranks represent the dimensional aspect of a tensor, but is not the same as a matrix rank. It represents the quantity of dimensions in which the tensor lives, and is not a precise measure of the extension of the tensor in rows/columns or spatial equivalents.

A rank one tensor is the equivalent of a vector, and a rank one tensor is a matrix. For a rank two tensor you can access any element with the syntax *t[i, j]*. For a rank three tensor you would need to address an element with *t[i, j, k]*, and so on.

In the following example, we will create a tensor, and access one of its components:

```
>>> import tensorflow as tf
>>> tens1 = tf.constant([[[1,2],[2,3]],[[3,4],[5,6]]])
>>> print sess.run(tens1)[1,1,0]
5
```

This is a tensor of rank three, because in each element of the containing *matrix*, there is a vector element:

Rank	Math entity	Code definition example
0	Scalar	scalar = 1000
1	Vector	vector = [2, 8, 3]
2	Matrix	matrix = [[4, 2, 1], [5, 3, 2], [5, 5, 6]]
3	3-tensor	tensor = [[[4], [3], [2]], [[6], [100], [4]], [[5], [1], [4]]]
n	n-tensor	...

Tensor shape

The TensorFlow documentation uses three notational conventions to describe tensor dimensionality: rank, shape, and dimension number. The following table shows how these relate to one another:

Rank	Shape	Dimension number	Example
0	[]	0	4
1	[D0]	1	[2]
2	[D0, D1]	2	[6, 2]
3	[D0, D1, D2]	3	[7, 3, 2]
n	[D0, D1, ... Dn-1]	n-D	A tensor with shape *[D0, D1, ... Dn-1]*.

In the following example, we create a sample rank three tensor, and print the shape of it:

```
>>> import tensorflow as tf
>>> tens1 = tf.constant([[[1,2],[2,3]],[[3,4],[5,6]]])
>>> tens1
<tf.Tensor 'Const:0' shape=(2, 2, 2) dtype=int32>
>>>
```

Tensor data types

In addition to dimensionality, tensors have a fixed data type. You can assign any one of the following data types to a tensor:

Data type	Python type	Description
DT_FLOAT	tf.float32	**32 bits floating point.**
DT_DOUBLE	tf.float64	64 bits floating point.
DT_INT8	tf.int8	8 bits signed integer.
DT_INT16	tf.int16	16 bits signed integer.
DT_INT32	tf.int32	32 bits signed integer.
DT_INT64	tf.int64	64 bits signed integer.
DT_UINT8	tf.uint8	8 bits unsigned integer.
DT_STRING	tf.string	Variable length byte arrays. Each element of a tensor is a byte array.
DT_BOOL	tf.bool	Boolean.

Creating new tensors

We can either create our own tensors, or derivate them from the well-known **numpy** library. In the following example, we create some numpy arrays, and do some basic math with them:

```
import tensorflow as tf
import numpy as np
x = tf.constant(np.random.rand(32).astype(np.float32))
y=  tf.constant ([1,2,3])
```

From numpy to tensors and vice versa

TensorFlow is interoperable with numpy, and normally the `eval()` function calls will return a numpy object, ready to be worked with the standard numerical tools.

> We must note that the tensor object is a symbolic handle for the result of an operation, so it doesn't hold the resulting values of the structures it contains. For this reason, we must run the `eval()` method to get the actual values, which is the equivalent to `Session.run(tensor_to_eval)`.

In this example, we build two numpy arrays, and convert them to tensors:

```
import tensorflow as tf #we import tensorflow
import numpy as np   #we import numpy
sess = tf.Session() #start a new Session Object
x_data = np.array([[1.,2.,3.],
[3.,2.,6.]]) # 2x3 matrix
x = tf.convert_to_tensor(x_data, dtype=tf.float32) #Finally, we create the
tensor, starting from the fload 3x matrix
```

Useful method

`tf.convert_to_tensor`: This function converts Python objects of various types to tensor objects. It accepts tensorobjects, numpy arrays, Python lists, and Python scalars.

Getting things done – interacting with TensorFlow

As with the majority of Python's modules, TensorFlow allows the use of Python's interactive console:

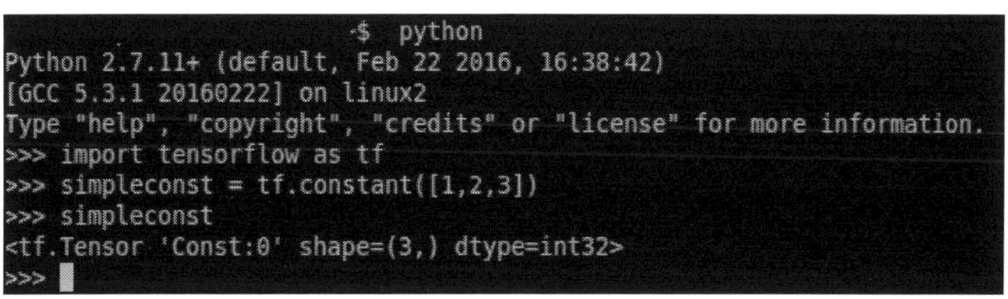

Simple interaction with Python's interpreter and TensorFlow libraries

In the previous figure, we call the Python interpreter (by simply calling Python) and create a tensor of constant type. Then we invoke it again, and the Python interpreter shows the shape and type of the tensor.

We can also use the IPython interpreter, which will allow us to employ a format more compatible with notebook-style tools, such as Jupyter:

```
:~$ ipython
Python 2.7.11+ (default, Feb 22 2016, 16:38:42)
Type "copyright", "credits" or "license" for more information.

IPython 2.4.1 -- An enhanced Interactive Python.
?         -> Introduction and overview of IPython's features.
%quickref -> Quick reference.
help      -> Python's own help system.
object?   -> Details about 'object', use 'object??' for extra details.

In [1]: 
```

IPython prompt

When talking about running TensorFlow **Sessions** in an interactive manner, it's better to employ the `InteractiveSession` object.

Unlike the normal `tf.Session` class, the `tf.InteractiveSession` class installs itself as the default session on construction. So when you try to eval a tensor, or run an operation, it will not be necessary to pass a `Session` object to indicate which session it refers to.

Handling the computing workflow – TensorFlow's data flow graph

TensorFlow's data flow graph is a symbolic representation of how the computation of the models will work:

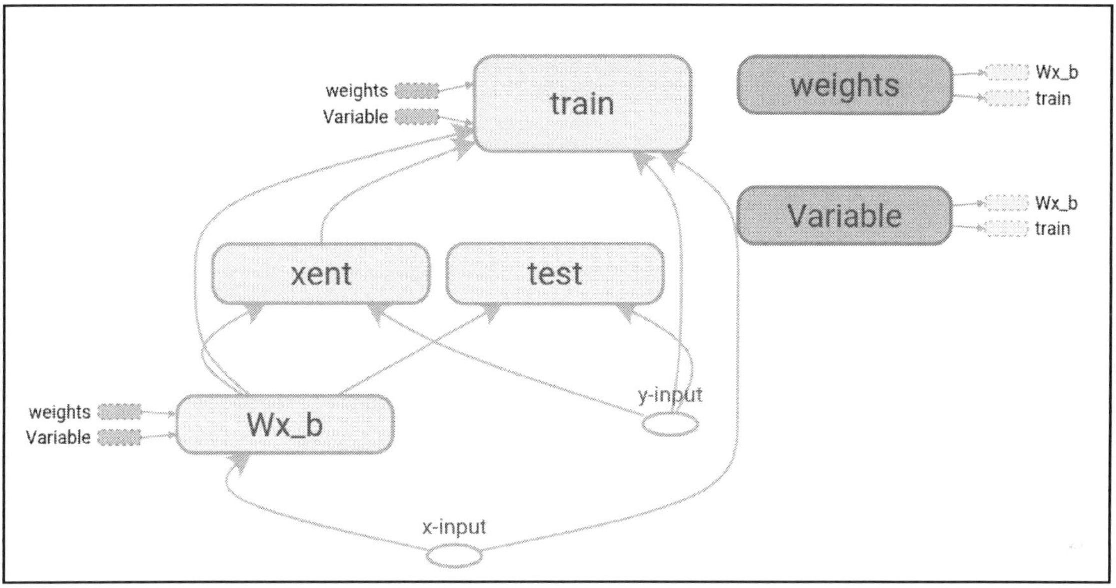

A simple data flow graph representation, as drawn on TensorBoard

A data flow graph is, succinctly, a complete TensorFlow computation, represented as a graph where nodes are operations and edges are data flowing between operations.

Normally, nodes implement mathematical operations, but also represent a connection to feed in data or a variable, or push out results.

Edges describe the input/output relationships between nodes. These data edges exclusively transport tensors. Nodes are assigned to computational devices and execute asynchronously and in parallel once all the tensors on their incoming edges become available.

All operations have a name and represent an abstract computation (for example, *matrix inverse* or *product*).

Computation graph building

The computation graph is normally built while the library user creates the tensors and operations the model will support, so there is no need to build a `Graph()` object directly. The Python tensor constructors, such as `tf.constant()`, will add the necessary element to the default graph. The same occurs for TensorFlow operations.

For example, `c = tf.matmul(a, b)` creates an operation of `MatMul` type that takes tensors `a` and `b` as input and produces `c` as output.

Useful operation object methods

- `tf.Operation.type`: Returns the type of the operation (for example, `MatMul`)
- `tf.Operation.inputs`: Returns the list of tensor objects representing the operation's inputs
- `tf.Graph.get_operations()`: Returns the list of operations in the graph
- `tf.Graph.version`: Returns the graph's autonumeric version

Feeding

TensorFlow also provides a feed mechanism for patching a tensor directly into any operation in the graph.

A feed temporarily replaces the output of an operation with a tensor value. You supply feed data as an argument to a `run()` call. The feed is only used for the run call to which it is passed. The most common use case involves designating specific operations to be `feed` operations by using `tf.placeholder()` to create them.

Variables

In most computations, a graph is executed multiple times. Most tensors do not survive past a single execution of the graph. However, a variable is a special kind of operation that returns a handle to a persistent, mutable tensor that survives across executions of a graph. For machine learning applications of TensorFlow, the parameters of the model are typically stored in tensors held in variables, and are updated when running the training graph for the model.

Variable initialization

To initialize a variable, simply call the `Variable` object constructor, with a tensor as a parameter.

In this example, we initialize some variables with an array of `1000` zeros:

```
b = tf.Variable(tf.zeros([1000]))
```

Saving data flow graphs

Data flow graphs are written using Google's protocol buffers, so they can be read afterwards in a good variety of languages.

Graph serialization language – protocol buffers

Protocol buffers are a language-neutral, platform-neutral, extensible mechanism for serializing structured data. You define the data structure first, and then you can use specialized generated code to read and write it with a variety of languages.

Useful methods

`tf.Graph.as_graph_def(from_version=None, add_shapes=False)`: returns a serialized `GraphDef` representation of this graph.

Parameters:

- `from_version`: If this is set, it returns a `GraphDef` with nodes that were added from this version
- `add_shapes`: If `true`, adds a shape attribute to each node

Example graph building

In this example we will build a very simple data flow graph, and observe an overview of the generated protobuffer file:

```
import tensorflow as tf
g = tf.Graph()
with g.as_default():
import tensorflow as tf
sess = tf.Session()
W_m = tf.Variable(tf.zeros([10, 5]))
x_v = tf.placeholder(tf.float32, [None, 10])
result = tf.matmul(x_v, W_m)
print g.as_graph_def()
```

The generated protobuffer (summarized) reads:

```
node {
  name: "zeros"
  op: "Const"
  attr {
    key: "dtype"
    value {
      type: DT_FLOAT
    }
  }
  attr {
    key: "value"
    value {
      tensor {
        dtype: DT_FLOAT
        tensor_shape {
          dim {
            size: 10
          }
          dim {
            size: 5
          }
        }
        float_val: 0.0
      }
    }
  }
}
...
node {
  name: "MatMul"
  op: "MatMul"
  input: "Placeholder"
  input: "Variable/read"
  attr {
    key: "T"
    value {
      type: DT_FLOAT
    }
  }
...
}
versions {
  producer: 8
}
```

Running our programs – Sessions

Client programs interact with the TensorFlow system by creating a Session. The Session object is a representation of the environment in which the computation will run. The Session object starts empty, and when the programmer creates the different operations and tensors, they will be added automatically to the Session, which will do no computation until the `Run()` method is called.

The `Run()` method takes a set of output names that need to be computed, as well as an optional set of tensors to be fed into the graph in place of certain outputs of nodes.

If we call this method, and there are operations on which the named operation depends, the Session object will execute all of them, and then proceed to execute the named one.

This simple line is the only one needed to create a Session:

```
s = tf.Session()
Sample command line output:
tensorflow/core/common_runtime/local_session.cc:45]Localsessioninteropparal
lelism threads:6
```

Basic tensor methods

In this section we will be exploring some basic methods supported by TensorFlow. They are useful for initial data exploration and for preparing the data for better parallel computation.

Simple matrix operations

TensorFlow supports many of the more common matrix operations, such as transpose, multiplication, getting the determinant, and inverse.

Here is a little example of those functions applied to sample data:

```
In [1]: import tensorflow as tf
In [2]: sess = tf.InteractiveSession()
In [3]: x = tf.constant([[2, 5, 3, -5],
...:                  [0, 3,-2,  5],
...:                  [4, 3, 5,  3],
...:                  [6, 1, 4,  0]])

In [4]: y = tf.constant([[4, -7, 4, -3, 4],
...:                  [6, 4,-7,  4, 7],
```

```
...:                  [2, 3, 2,  1, 4],
...:                  [1, 5, 5,  5, 2]])
In [5]: floatx = tf.constant([[2., 5., 3., -5.],
...:                        [0., 3.,-2.,  5.],
...:                        [4., 3., 5.,  3.],
...:                        [6., 1., 4.,  0.]])
In [6]: tf.transpose(x).eval() # Transpose matrix
Out[6]:
array([[ 2,  0,  4,  6],
[ 5,  3,  3,  1],
[ 3, -2,  5,  4],
[-5,  5,  3,  0]], dtype=int32)

In [7]: tf.matmul(x, y).eval() # Matrix multiplication
Out[7]:
array([[ 39, -10, -46,  -8,  45],
[ 19,  31,   0,  35,  23],
[ 47,  14,  20,  20,  63],
[ 38, -26,  25, -10,  47]], dtype=int32)

In [8]: tf.matrix_determinant(floatx).eval() # Matrix determinant
Out[8]: 818.0

In [9]: tf.matrix_inverse(floatx).eval() # Matrix inverse
Out[9]:
array([[-0.00855745,  0.10513446, -0.18948655,  0.29584351],
[ 0.12958434,  0.12224938,  0.01222495, -0.05134474],
[-0.01955992, -0.18826403,  0.28117359, -0.18092911],
[-0.08557458,  0.05134474,  0.10513448, -0.0415648 ]], dtype=float32)

In [10]: tf.matrix_solve(floatx, [[1],[1],[1],[1]]).eval() # Solve Matrix
system
Out[10]:
array([[ 0.20293398],
[ 0.21271393],
[-0.10757945],
[ 0.02933985]], dtype=float32)
```

Reduction

Reduction is an operation that applies an operation across one of the tensor's dimensions, leaving it with one less dimension.

The supported operations include (with the same parameters) product, minimum, maximum, mean, all, any, and accumulate_n).

```
In [1]: import tensorflow as tf

In [2]: sess = tf.InteractiveSession()
In [3]: x = tf.constant([[1,  2, 3],
...:                  [3,  2, 1],
...:                  [-1,-2,-3]])
In [4]:

In [4]: boolean_tensor = tf.constant([[True,  False, True],
...:                  [False, False, True],
...:                  [True, False, False]])

In [5]: tf.reduce_prod(x, reduction_indices=1).eval() # reduce prod
Out[5]: array([ 6,  6, -6], dtype=int32)

In [6]: tf.reduce_min(x, reduction_indices=1).eval() # reduce min
Out[6]: array([ 1,  1, -3], dtype=int32)

In [7]: tf.reduce_max(x, reduction_indices=1).eval() # reduce max
Out[7]: array([ 3,  3, -1], dtype=int32)

In [8]: tf.reduce_mean(x, reduction_indices=1).eval() # reduce mean
Out[8]: array([ 2,  2, -2], dtype=int32)

In [9]: tf.reduce_all(boolean_tensor, reduction_indices=1).eval() # reduce
all
Out[9]: array([False, False, False], dtype=bool)

In [10]: tf.reduce_any(boolean_tensor, reduction_indices=1).eval() # reduce
any
Out[10]: array([ True,  True,  True], dtype=bool)
```

Tensor segmentation

Tensor segmentation is a process in which one of the dimensions is reduced, and the resulting elements are determined by an index row. If some elements in the row are repeated, the corresponding index goes to the value in it, and the operation is applied between the indexes with repeated indexes.

The index array size should be the same as the size of dimension 0 of the index array, and they must increase by one.

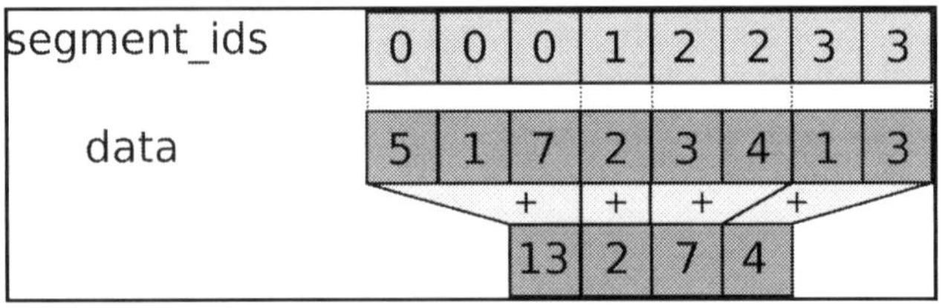

Segmentation explanation (redo)

```
In [1]: import tensorflow as tf
In [2]: sess = tf.InteractiveSession()
In [3]: seg_ids = tf.constant([0,1,1,2,2]); # Group indexes : 0|1,2|3,4
In [4]: tens1 = tf.constant([[2, 5, 3, -5],
...:                     [0, 3,-2,  5],
...:                     [4, 3, 5,  3],
...:                     [6, 1, 4,  0],
...:                     [6, 1, 4,  0]])  # A sample constant matrix

In [5]: tf.segment_sum(tens1, seg_ids).eval()   # Sum segmentation
Out[5]:
array([[ 2,  5,  3, -5],
[ 4,  6,  3,  8],
[12,  2,  8,  0]], dtype=int32)

In [6]: tf.segment_prod(tens1, seg_ids).eval() # Product segmentation
Out[6]:
array([[  2,   5,   3,  -5],
[  0,   9, -10,  15],
[ 36,   1,  16,   0]], dtype=int32)

In [7]: tf.segment_min(tens1, seg_ids).eval() # minimun value goes to group
Out[7]:
array([[ 2,  5,  3, -5],
[ 0,  3, -2,  3],
[ 6,  1,  4,  0]], dtype=int32)

In [8]: tf.segment_max(tens1, seg_ids).eval() # maximum value goes to group
Out[8]:
array([[ 2,  5,  3, -5],
[ 4,  3,  5,  5],
[ 6,  1,  4,  0]], dtype=int32)

In [9]: tf.segment_mean(tens1, seg_ids).eval() # mean value goes to group
```

```
Out[9]:
array([[ 2,  5,  3, -5],
[ 2,  3,  1,  4],
[ 6,  1,  4,  0]], dtype=int32)
```

Sequences

Sequence utilities include methods such as `argmin` and `argmax` (showing the minimum and maximum value of a dimension), `listdiff` (showing the complement of the intersection between lists), `where` (showing the index of the true values on a tensor), and `unique` (showing unique values on a list).

```
In [1]: import tensorflow as tf
In [2]: sess = tf.InteractiveSession()
In [3]: x = tf.constant([[2, 5, 3, -5],
...:                  [0, 3,-2,  5],
...:                  [4, 3, 5,  3],
...:                  [6, 1, 4,  0]])
In [4]: listx = tf.constant([1,2,3,4,5,6,7,8])
In [5]: listy = tf.constant([4,5,8,9])

In [6]:

In [6]: boolx = tf.constant([[True,False], [False,True]])

In [7]: tf.argmin(x, 1).eval() # Position of the maximum value of columns
Out[7]: array([3, 2, 1, 3])

In [8]: tf.argmax(x, 1).eval() # Position of the minimum value of rows
Out[8]: array([1, 3, 2, 0])

In [9]: tf.listdiff(listx, listy)[0].eval() # List differences
Out[9]: array([1, 2, 3, 6, 7], dtype=int32)

In [10]: tf.where(boolx).eval() # Show true values
Out[10]:
array([[0, 0],
[1, 1]])

In [11]: tf.unique(listx)[0].eval() # Unique values in list
Out[11]: array([1, 2, 3, 4, 5, 6, 7, 8], dtype=int32)
```

Tensor shape transformations

These kinds of functions are related to a matrix shape.They are used to adjust unmatched data structures and to retrieve quick information about the measures of data. This can be useful when deciding a processing strategy at runtime.

In the following examples, we will start with a rank two tensor and will print some information about it.

Then we'll explore the operations that modify the matrix dimensionally, be it adding or removing dimensions, such as `squeeze` and `expand_dims`:

```
In [1]: import tensorflow as tf
In [2]: sess = tf.InteractiveSession()
In [3]: x = tf.constant([[2, 5, 3, -5],
...:                  [0, 3,-2,  5],
...:                  [4, 3, 5,  3],
...:                  [6, 1, 4,  0]])

In [4]: tf.shape(x).eval() # Shape of the tensor
Out[4]: array([4, 4], dtype=int32)

In [5]: tf.size(x).eval() # size of the tensor
Out[5]: 16

In [6]: tf.rank(x).eval() # rank of the tensor
Out[6]: 2

In [7]: tf.reshape(x, [8, 2]).eval() # converting to a 10x2 matrix
Out[7]:
array([[ 2,  5],
[ 3, -5],
[ 0,  3],
[-2,  5],
[ 4,  3],
[ 5,  3],
[ 6,  1],
[ 4,  0]], dtype=int32)

In [8]: tf.squeeze(x).eval() #  squeezing
Out[8]:
array([[ 2,  5,  3, -5],
[ 0,  3, -2,  5],
[ 4,  3,  5,  3],
[ 6,  1,  4,  0]], dtype=int32)

In [9]: tf.expand_dims(x,1).eval() #Expanding dims
```

```
Out[9]:
array([[[ 2,  5,  3, -5]],
[[ 0,  3, -2,  5]],
[[ 4,  3,  5,  3]],
[[ 6,  1,  4,  0]]], dtype=int32)
```

Tensor slicing and joining

In order to extract and merge useful information from big datasets, the slicing and joining methods allow you to consolidate the required column information without having to occupy memory space with nonspecific information.

In the following examples, we'll extract matrix slices, split them, add padding, and pack and unpack rows:

```
In [1]: import tensorflow as tf
In [2]: sess = tf.InteractiveSession()
In [3]: t_matrix = tf.constant([[1,2,3],
...:                           [4,5,6],
...:                           [7,8,9]])
In [4]: t_array = tf.constant([1,2,3,4,9,8,6,5])
In [5]: t_array2= tf.constant([2,3,4,5,6,7,8,9])

In [6]: tf.slice(t_matrix, [1, 1], [2,2]).eval() # cutting an slice
Out[6]:
array([[5, 6],
[8, 9]], dtype=int32)

In [7]: tf.split(0, 2, t_array) # splitting the array in two
Out[7]:
[<tf.Tensor 'split:0' shape=(4,) dtype=int32>,
<tf.Tensor 'split:1' shape=(4,) dtype=int32>]

In [8]: tf.tile([1,2],[3]).eval() # tiling this little tensor 3 times
Out[8]: array([1, 2, 1, 2, 1, 2], dtype=int32)

In [9]: tf.pad(t_matrix, [[0,1],[2,1]]).eval() # padding
Out[9]:
array([[0, 0, 1, 2, 3, 0],
[0, 0, 4, 5, 6, 0],
[0, 0, 7, 8, 9, 0],
[0, 0, 0, 0, 0, 0]], dtype=int32)

In [10]: tf.concat(0, [t_array, t_array2]).eval() #concatenating list
Out[10]: array([1, 2, 3, 4, 9, 8, 6, 5, 2, 3, 4, 5, 6, 7, 8, 9],
dtype=int32)
```

```
In [11]: tf.pack([t_array, t_array2]).eval() # packing
Out[11]:
array([[1, 2, 3, 4, 9, 8, 6, 5],
[2, 3, 4, 5, 6, 7, 8, 9]], dtype=int32)

In [12]: sess.run(tf.unpack(t_matrix)) # Unpacking, we need the run method
to view the tensors
Out[12]:
[array([1, 2, 3], dtype=int32),
array([4, 5, 6], dtype=int32),
array([7, 8, 9], dtype=int32)]

In [13]: tf.reverse(t_matrix, [False,True]).eval() # Reverse matrix
Out[13]:
array([[3, 2, 1],
[6, 5, 4],
[9, 8, 7]], dtype=int32)
```

Dataflow structure and results visualization – TensorBoard

Visualizing summarized information is a vital part of any data scientist's toolbox.

TensorBoard is a software utility that allows the graphical representation of the data flow graph and a dashboard used for the interpretation of results, normally coming from the logging utilities:

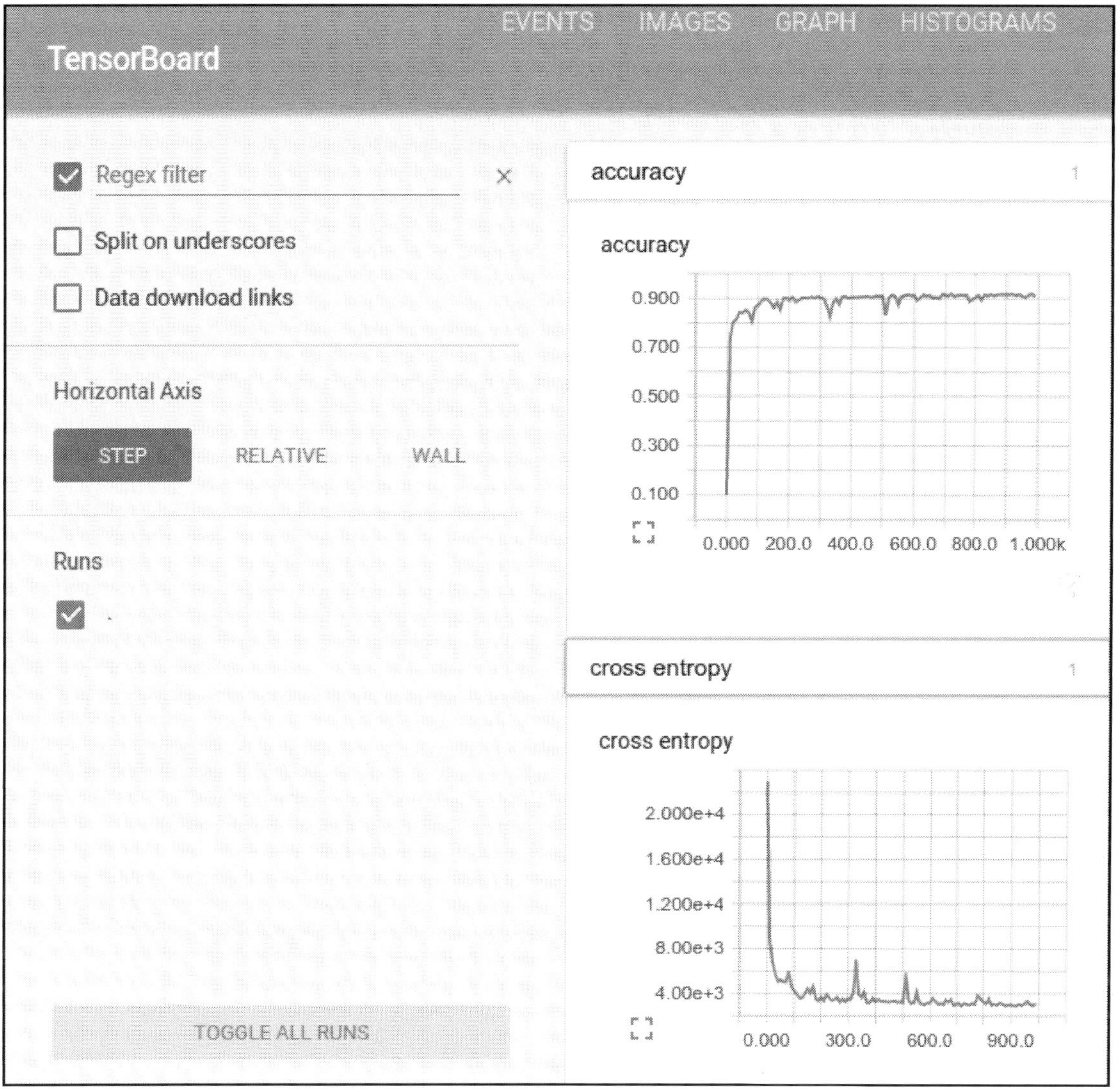

TensorBoard GUI

All the tensors and operations of a graph can be set to write information to logs. TensorBoard analyzes that information, written normally, while the Session is running, and presents the user with many graphical items, one for each graph item.

Command line use

To invoke TensorBoard, the command line is:

```
~$
~$ tensorboard -h
usage: tensorboard [-h] [--logdir LOGDIR] [--debug [DEBUG]] [--nodebug]
                   [--host HOST] [--port PORT]
```

How TensorBoard works

Every computation graph we build, TensorFlow has a real-time logging mechanism for, in order to save almost all the information that a model possesses.

However, the model builder has to take into account which of the possible hundred information dimensions it should save, to later serve as an analysis tool.

To save all the required information, TensorFlow API uses data output objects, called **Summaries**.

These Summaries write results into TensorFlow event files, which gather all the required data generated during a Session's run.

In the following example, we'll running TensorBoard directly on a generated event log directory:

```
:/tmp/mnist_logs$ tensorboard --logdir=. --port=8000
Starting TensorBoard  on port 8000
(You can navigate to http://0.0.0.0:8000)
```

Adding Summary nodes

All Summaries in a TensorFlow Session are written by a `SummaryWriter` object. The main method to call is:

```
tf.train.SummaryWriter.__init__(logdir, graph_def=None)
```

This command will create a `SummaryWriter` and an event file, in the path of the parameter.

The constructor of the the `SummaryWriter` will create a new event file in `logdir`. This event file will contain `Event` type protocol buffers constructed when you call one of the following functions: `add_summary()`, `add_session_log()`, `add_event()`, or `add_graph()`.

If you pass a `graph_def` protocol buffer to the constructor, it is added to the event file. (This is equivalent to calling `add_graph()` later).

When you run TensorBoard, it will read the graph definition from the file and display it graphically so you can interact with it.

First, create the TensorFlow graph that you'd like to collect summary data from and decide which nodes you would like to annotate with summary operations.

Operations in TensorFlow don't do anything until you run them, or an operation that depends on their output. And the summary nodes that we've just created are peripheral to your graph: none of the ops you are currently running depend on them. So, to generate summaries, we need to run all of these summary nodes. Managing them manually would be tedious, so use `tf.merge_all_summaries` to combine them into a single op that generates all the summary data.

Then, you can just run the merged summary op, which will generate a serialized Summary `protobuf` object with all of your summary data at a given step. Finally, to write this summary data to disk, pass the Summary `protobuf` to a `tf.train.SummaryWriter`.

The `SummaryWriter` takes a `logdir` in its constructor, this `logdir` is quite important, it's the directory where all of the events will be written out. Also, the `SummaryWriter` can optionally take a `GraphDef` in its constructor. If it receives one, then TensorBoard will visualize your graph as well.

Now that you've modified your graph and have a `SummaryWriter`, you're ready to start running your network! If you want, you could run the merged summary op every single step, and record a ton of training data. That's likely to be more data than you need, though. Instead, consider running the merged summary op every *n* steps.

Common Summary operations

This is a list of the different Summary types, and the parameters employed on its construction:

- `tf.scalar_summary` (tag, values, collections=None, name=None)
- `tf.image_summary` (tag, tensor, max_images=3, collections=None, name=None)
- `tf.histogram_summary` (tag, values, collections=None, name=None)

Special Summary functions

These are special functions, that are used to merge the values of different operations, be it a collection of summaries, or all summaries in a graph:

- `tf.merge_summary` (inputs, collections=None, name=None)
- `tf.merge_all_summaries` (key='summaries')

Finally, as one last aid to legibility, the visualization uses special icons for constants and summary nodes. To summarize, here's a table of node symbols:

Symbol	Meaning
	High-level node representing a name scope. Double-click to expand a high-level node.
	Sequence of numbered nodes that are not connected to each other.
	Sequence of numbered nodes that are connected to each other.
	An individual operation node.
	A constant.

	A summary node.
	Edge showing the data flow between operations.
	Edge showing the control dependency between operations.
	A reference edge showing that the outgoing operation node can mutate the incoming tensor.

Interacting with TensorBoard's GUI

Navigate the graph by panning and zooming. Click and drag to pan, and use a scroll gesture to zoom. Double-click on a node, or click on its + button, to expand a name scope that represents a group of operations. To easily keep track of the current viewpoint when zooming and panning, there is a minimap in the bottom-right corner:

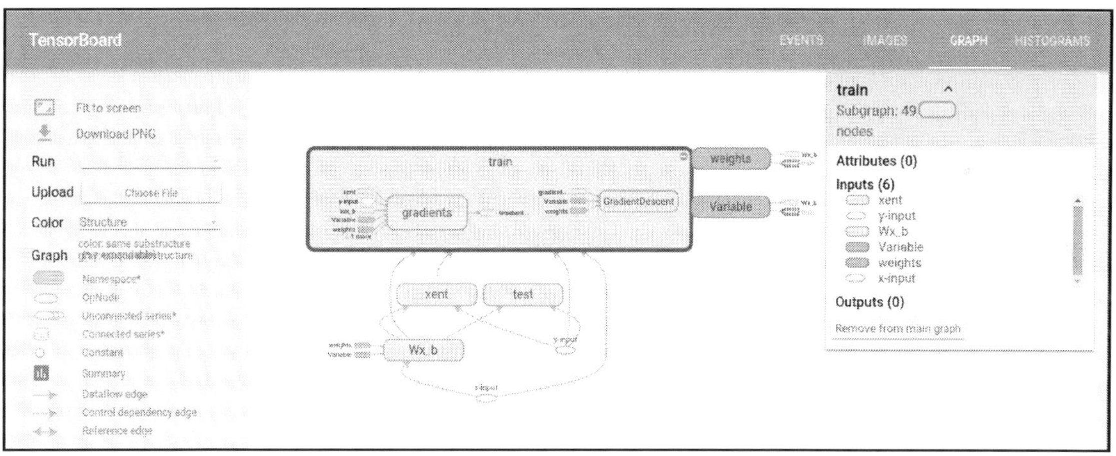

Openflow with one expanded operations group and legends

To close an open node, double-click it again or click its – button. You can also click once to select a node. It will turn a darker color, and details about it and the nodes it connects to will appear in the info card in the upper-right corner of the visualization.

Selection can also be helpful in understanding high-degree nodes. Select any high-degree node, and the corresponding node icons for its other connections will be selected as well. This makes it easy, for example, to see which nodes are being saved and which aren't.

Clicking on a node name in the info card will select it. If necessary, the viewpoint will automatically pan so that the node is visible.

Finally, you can choose two color schemes for your graph, using the color menu above the legend. The default *Structure View* shows the structure: when two high-level nodes have the same structure, they appear in the same color of the rainbow. Uniquely structured nodes are gray. There's a second view, which shows what device the different operations run on. Name scopes are colored proportionally, to the fraction of devices for the operations inside them.

Reading information from disk

TensorFlow reads a number of the most standard formats, including the well-known CSV, image files (JPG and PNG decoders), and the standard TensorFlow format.

Tabulated formats – CSV

For reading the well-known CSV format, TensorFlow has its own methods. In comparison with other libraries, such as **pandas**, the process to read a simple CSV file is somewhat more complicated.

The reading of a CSV file requires a couple of the previous steps. First, we must create a filename queue object with the list of files we'll be using, and then create a `TextLineReader`. With this line reader, the remaining operation will be to decode the CSV columns, and save it on tensors. If we want to mix homogeneous data together, the pack method will work.

The Iris dataset

The Iris flower dataset or Fisher's Iris dataset is a well know benchmark for classification problems. It's a multivariate data set introduced by Ronald Fisher in his 1936 paper *The use of multiple measurements in taxonomic problems* as an example of linear discriminant analysis.

The data set consists of 50 samples from each of three species of Iris (Iris setosa, Iris virginica, and Iris versicolor). Four features were measured in each sample: the length and the width of the sepals and petals, in centimeters. Based on the combination of these four features, Fisher developed a linear discriminant model to distinguish the species from each other. (You'll be able to get the `.csv` file for this dataset in the code bundle of the book.)

In order to read the CSV file, you will have to download it and put it in the same directory as where the Python executable is running.

In the following code sample, we'll be reading and printing the first five records from the well-known Iris database:

```
import tensorflow as tf
sess = tf.Session()
filename_queue = tf.train.string_input_producer(
tf.train.match_filenames_once("./*.csv"),
shuffle=True)
reader = tf.TextLineReader(skip_header_lines=1)
key, value = reader.read(filename_queue)
record_defaults = [[0.], [0.], [0.], [0.], [""]]
col1, col2, col3, col4, col5 = tf.decode_csv(value,
record_defaults=record_defaults)  # Convert CSV records to tensors. Each
column maps to one tensor.
features = tf.pack([col1, col2, col3, col4])

tf.initialize_all_variables().run(session=sess)
coord = tf.train.Coordinator()
threads = tf.train.start_queue_runners(coord=coord, sess=sess)

for iteration in range(0, 5):
 example = sess.run([features])
 print(example)
 coord.request_stop()
 coord.join(threads)
```

And this is how the output would look:

```
[array([ 5.0999999 ,  3.5       ,  1.39999998,  0.2       ], dtype=float32)]
[array([ 4.9000001 ,  3.        ,  1.39999998,  0.2       ], dtype=float32)]
[array([ 4.69999981,  3.20000005,  1.29999995,  0.2       ], dtype=float32)]
[array([ 4.5999999,  3.0999999,  1.5       ,  0.2       ], dtype=float32)]
[array([ 5.        ,  3.5999999 ,  1.39999998,  0.2       ], dtype=float32)]
```

Reading image data

TensorFlow allows importing data from image formats, it will really be useful for importing custom image inputs for image oriented models.The accepted image formats will be JPG and PNG, and the internal representation will be `uint8` tensors, one rank two tensor for each image channel:

Sample image to be read

Loading and processing the images

In this example, we will load a sample image and apply some additional processing to it, saving the resulting images in separate files:

```
import tensorflow as tf
sess = tf.Session()
filename_queue =
tf.train.string_input_producer(tf.train.match_filenames_once("./blue_jay.jp
g"))
reader = tf.WholeFileReader()
key, value = reader.read(filename_queue)
image=tf.image.decode_jpeg(value)
flipImageUpDown=tf.image.encode_jpeg(tf.image.flip_up_down(image))
flipImageLeftRight=tf.image.encode_jpeg(tf.image.flip_left_right(image))
tf.initialize_all_variables().run(session=sess)
coord = tf.train.Coordinator()
threads = tf.train.start_queue_runners(coord=coord, sess=sess)
example = sess.run(flipImageLeftRight)
print example
file=open ("flippedUpDown.jpg", "wb+")
file.write (flipImageUpDown.eval(session=sess))
file.close()
file=open ("flippedLeftRight.jpg", "wb+")
file.write (flipImageLeftRight.eval(session=sess))
file.close()
```

The `print example` line will show a line-by-line summary of the RGB values in the image:

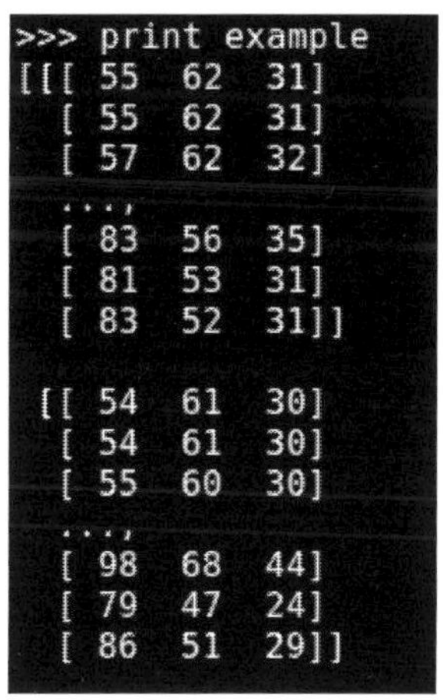

```
>>> print example
[[[ 55  62  31]
  [ 55  62  31]
  [ 57  62  32]
  ...,
  [ 83  56  35]
  [ 81  53  31]
  [ 83  52  31]]

 [[ 54  61  30]
  [ 54  61  30]
  [ 55  60  30]
  ...,
  [ 98  68  44]
  [ 79  47  24]
  [ 86  51  29]]
```

The final images will look like:

Original and altered images compared (flipUpDown and flipLeftRight)

Reading from the standard TensorFlow format

Another approach is to convert the arbitrary data you have, into the official format. This approach makes it easier to mix and match data sets and network architectures.

You can write a little program that gets your data, stuffs it in an example protocol buffer, serializes the protocol buffer to a string, and then writes the string to a `TFRecords` file using the `tf.python_io.TFRecordWriter` class.

To read a file of `TFRecords`, use `tf.TFRecordReader` with the `tf.parse_single_example` decoder. The `parse_single_example` `op` decodes the example protocol buffers into tensors.

Summary

In this chapter we have learned the main data structures and simple operations we can apply to data, and a succinct summary of the parts of a computational graph.

These kinds of operations will be the foundation for the forthcoming techniques. They allow the data scientist to decide on simpler models if the separation of classes or the adjusting functions look sufficiently clear, or to advance directly to much more sophisticated tools, having looked at the overall characteristics of the current data.

In the next chapter, we will begin building and running graphs, and will solve problems using some of the methods found in this chapter.

2
Clustering

In this chapter, we will start applying the data transforming operations that we learned in the previous chapter, and will begin finding interesting patterns in some given information, discovering groups of data, or clusters, using clustering techniques.

In this process we will also gain two new tools: the ability to generate synthetic sample sets from a collection of representative data structures via the scikit-learn library, and the ability to graphically plot our data and model results, this time via the matplotlib library.

The topics we will cover in this chapter are as follows:

- Getting an idea of how clustering works, and comparing it to alternative, existing classification techniques
- Using scikit-learn and matplotlib to enrich the possibilities of dataset choices, and to get a professional-looking graphical representation of the data
- Implementing the **k-means** clustering algorithm
- Implementing the nearest neighbor method, and comparing the results with that of the k-means

Learning from data - unsupervised learning

In this chapter we will be reviewing two cases of unsupervised learning.

Unsupervised learning basically consists of finding patterns on a previous dataset. Normally, little or no information is given for this technique and the procedure should be able to automatically determine how the information is organized, and recognize the different structures in the data organization.

Clustering

One of the simplest operations that can be initially to unlabeled dataset is to try to understand the possible groups of the dataset members' common features.

To do so, the dataset can be split into an arbitrary number of segments, where each can be represented as a central mass (centroid) point that represents the points belonging to a determined group or cluster.

In order to define the criteria that assigns the same group to different group members, we need to define a concept that represents the distance between data elements, so we can simply say that all class members are closer to their own centroids than to any other centroid.

In the following graphic, we can see the results of a typical clustering algorithm and the representation of the cluster centers:

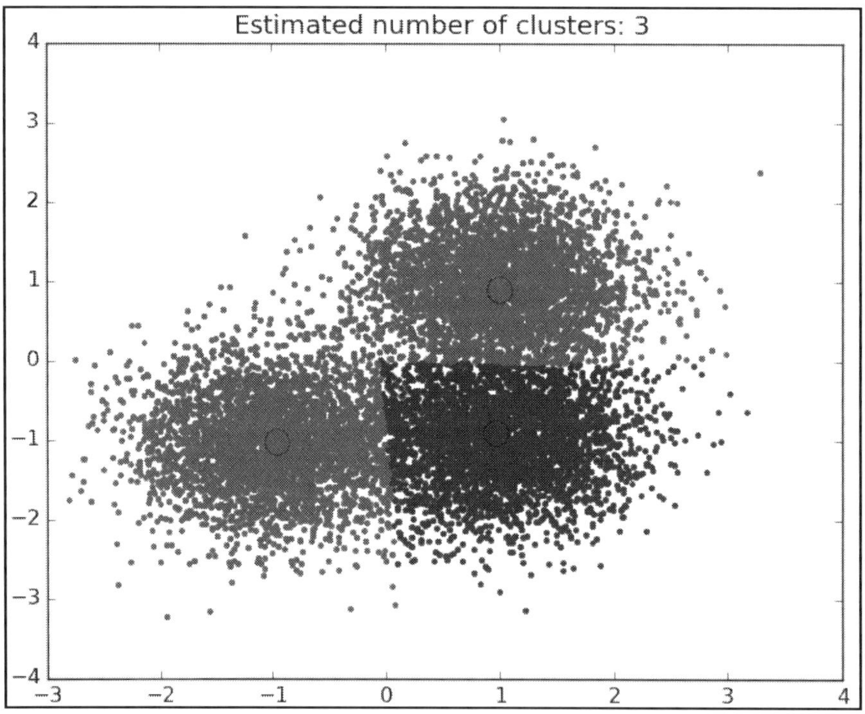

Sample clustering algorithm output

k-means

k-means is a very popular clustering algorithm and it can be easily implemented. It is very straight forward, and applying it as a first procedure to datasets with good class separation can provide a good a priori understanding of the data.

Mechanics of k-means

k-means tries to divide a set of samples in *k* disjoint groups or clusters using the mean value of the members as the main indicator. This point is normally called a **Centroid**, referring to the arithmetical entity with the same name, and is represented as a vector in a space of arbitrary dimensions.

k-means is a naive method because it works by looking for the appropriate centroids but doesn't know a priori what the number of clusters is.

In order to get an evaluation of how many clusters give a good representation of the provided data, one of the more popular methods is the **Elbow method**.

Algorithm iteration criterion

The criterion and goal of this method is to minimize the sum of squared distances from the cluster's member to the actual centroid of all cluster-contained samples. This is also known as **Minimization of Inertia**.

$$\sum_{i=0}^{n}\lim_{\mu_j \epsilon C}(\left\| x_{j} - \mu_i \right\|^{2})$$

Error Minimization criteria for k-means

Latex: *\sum_{i=0}^{n}\lim_{\mu_j\epsilon C}(\left \| x_{j} – \mu_i \right \|^{2}).*

k-means algorithm breakdown

The mechanism of the k-means algorithm can be summarized by the following flowchart:

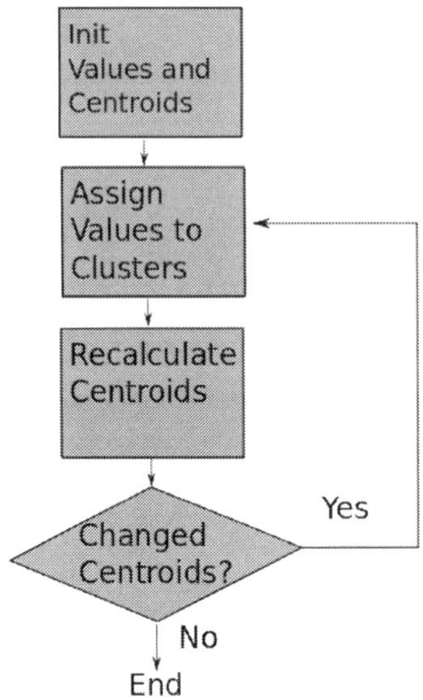

Simplified flowchart of the k-means process

The algorithm can be simplified as follows:

1. We start with the unclassified samples and take k elements as the starting centroids. There are also possible simplifications of this algorithm that take the first elements in the element list for the sake of brevity.
2. We then calculate the distances between the samples and the first chosen samples and get the first, calculated centroids (or other representative values). You can see the centroids in the illustration move toward a more common-sense centroid.
3. After the centroids change, their displacement will provoke the individual distances to change, and so the cluster membership can change.
4. This is the time when we recalculate the centroids and repeat the first steps in case the *stop* condition isn't met.

The stopping conditions could be of various types:

- After *N* iterations it could be that either we chose a very large number and we'll have unnecessary rounds of computing, or it could converge slowly and we will have very unconvincing results if the centroid doesn't have a very stable means. This *stop* condition could also be used as a last resort, in case we have a very long iterative process.
- Referring to the previous mean result, a possible better criterion for the convergence of the iterations is to take a look at the changes of the centroids, be it in total displacement or total cluster element switches. The last one is employed normally, so we will stop the process once there are no more elements changing from its current cluster to another one.

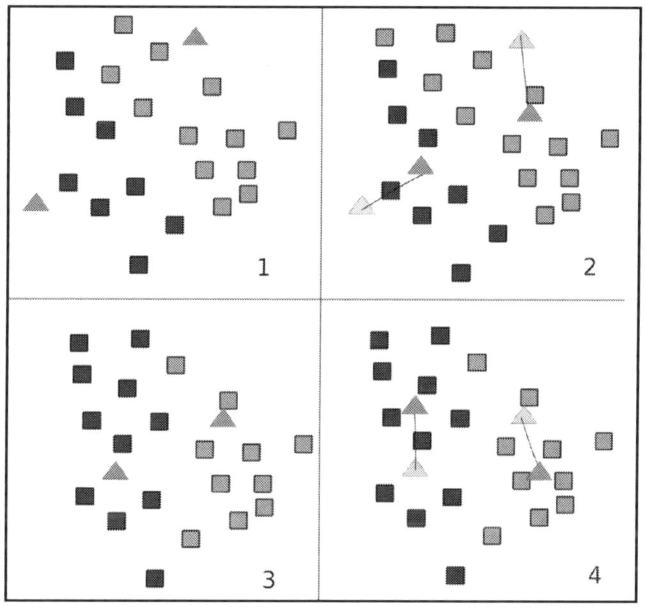

k-means simplified graphic

Pros and cons of k-means

The advantages of this method are:

- It scales very well (most of the calculations can be run in parallel)
- It has been used in a very large range of applications

But simplicity also comes with a cost (no silver bullet rule applies):

- It requires a-priori knowledge (the number of possible clusters should be known beforehand)
- The outlier values can *Push* the values of the centroids, as they have the same value as any other sample
- As we assume that the figure is convex and isotropic, it doesn't work very well with non-circle-like delimited clusters

k-nearest neighbors

k-nearest neighbors (**k-nn**) is a simple, classical method for clustering that will serve as a good introduction to this class of techniques, looking at the vicinity of each sample, and supposing that each new sample should pertain to the class of the already known data points.

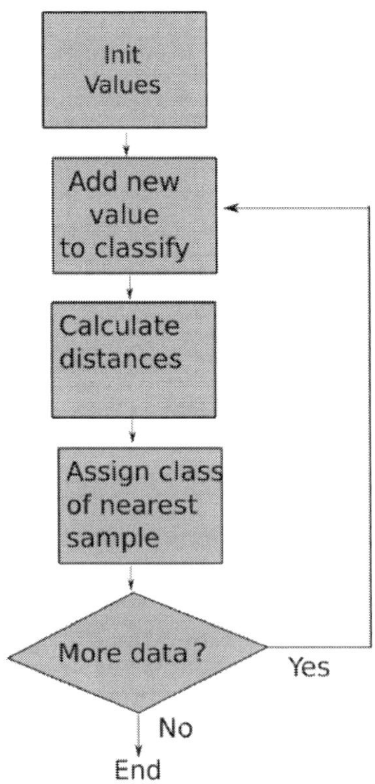

Mechanics of k-nearest neighbors

k-nn can be implemented in more than one of our configurations, but in this chapter we will use the **Semi Supervised** approach. We will start from a certain number of already assigned samples, and we will later guess the cluster membership based on the characteristics of the train set.

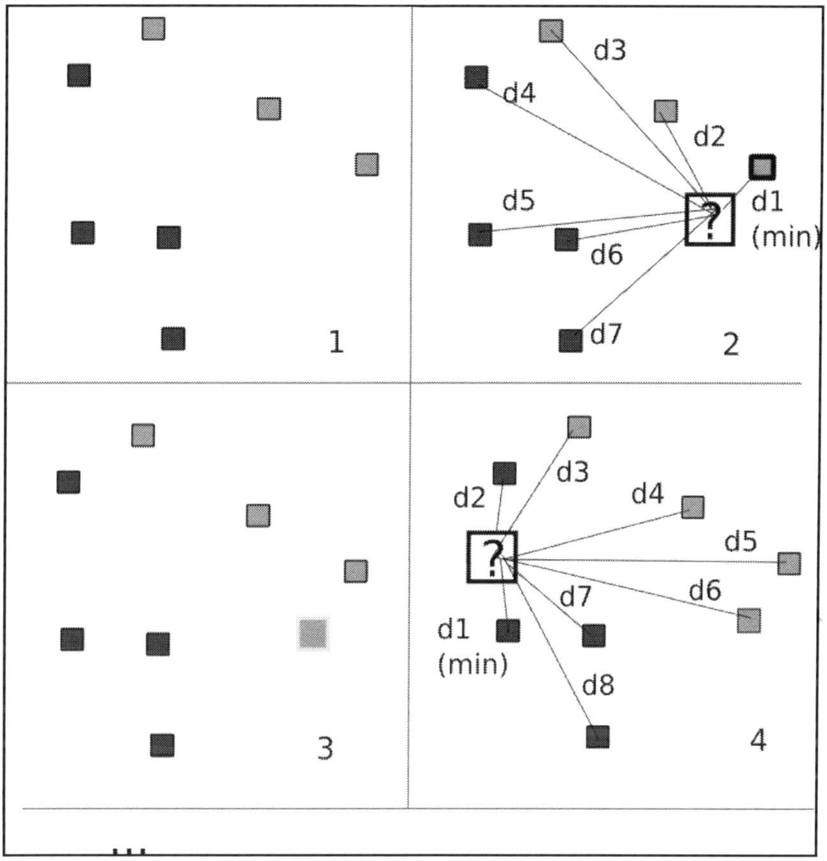

Nearest neighbor algorithm

In the previous figure, we can see a breakdown of the algorithm. It can be summarized by the following steps:

1. We place the previously known samples on the data structures.
2. We then read the next sample to be classified and calculate the Euclidean distance from the new sample to every sample of the training set.
3. We decide the class of the new element by selecting the class of the nearest sample by Euclidean distance. The k-nn method requires the vote of the *k* closest samples.
4. We repeat the procedure until there are no more remaining samples.

Pros and cons of k-nn

The advantages of this method are:

- Simplicity; no need for tuning parameters
- No formal training; we just need more training examples to improve the model

The disadvantages:

- Computationally expensive (All distances between points and every new sample have to be calculated)

Practical examples for Useful libraries

We will discuss some useful libraries in the following sections.

matplotlib plotting library

Data plotting is an integral part of data science discipline. For this reason, we need a very powerful framework to be able to plot our results. For this task, we do not have a general solution implemented in TensorFlow, we will use the matplotlib library.

From the matplotlib site (`http://matplotlib.org/`), the definition is:

> *"matplotlib is a Python 2D plotting library which produces publication quality figures in a variety of hardcopy formats and interactive environments across platforms."*

Sample synthetic data plotting

In this example, we will generate a list of 100 random numbers, generate a plot of the samples, and save the results in a graphics file:

```
import tensorflow as tf
import numpy as np
import matplotlib.pyplot as plt
with tf.Session() as sess:
    fig, ax = plt.subplots()
    ax.plot(tf.random_normal([100]).eval(), tf.random_normal([100]
).eval(),'o')
    ax.set_title('Sample random plot for TensorFlow')
    plt.savefig("result.png")
```

This is the resulting image:

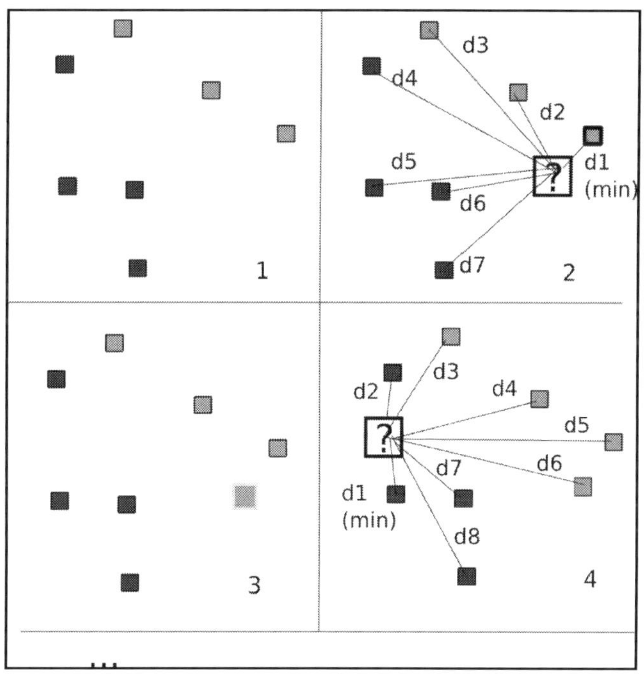

Sample plot generated with TensorFlow and matplotlib

> TIP: In order to see a more general explanation of the scikit dataset module, please refer to: `http://matplotlib.org/`.

scikit-learn dataset module

TensorFlow is not currently implementing methods for the easy generation of synthetic datasets. For this reason, we'll be using the `sklearn` library as a helper.

About the scikit-learn library

From its website (`http://scikit-learn.org/stable/`):

> *"scikit-learn (formerly scikits.learn) is an open source machine learning library for the Python programming language. It features various classification, regression and clustering, and is designed to interoperate with the Python numerical and scientific libraries NumPy and SciPy."*

In this example, we will use the dataset module, which deals with the generation and loading of many well-known synthetic, and field extracted, datasets.

> TIP: In order to see a more general explanation of the scikit dataset module, please refer to `http://scikit-learn.org/stable/datasets/`.

Synthetic dataset types

Some of the generated dataset types we'll be using are:

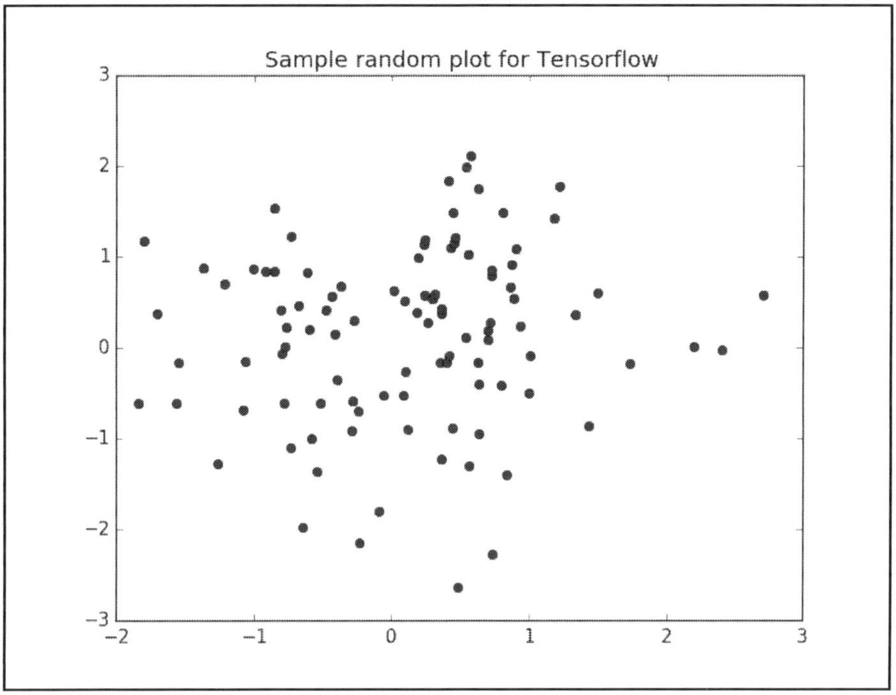

Blob, circle, and moon dataset types

Blobs dataset

This dataset is ideal for testing simple clustering algorithms. It doesn't present problems because the data is grouped coherently and the separation of classes is clear.

Employed method

The following method is used for employed method:

```
sklearn.datasets.make_blobs(n_samples=100, n_features=2,  centers=3,
cluster_std=1.0, center_box=(-10.0, 10.0),  shuffle=True,
random_state=None)
```

Here, `n_samples` is the total data numbers, `n_features` is the quantity of columns or features our data has, `centers` is a list of centers or a number of random centers, `cluster_std` is the standard deviation, `center_box` is the bounding box for each cluster center when centers are generated at random, `shuffle` indicates if we have to shuffle the samples, and `random_state` is the random seed.

Circle dataset

This is a dataset that has circles within other circles. It is a nonlinear, separable problem, so it needs to be solved by a nonlinear model. This rules out the simple algorithms such as k-means. In this chapter we'll try to use it anyway, to make a point.

Employed method

The following method is used for employed method:

```
sklearn.datasets.make_circles(n_samples=100,shuffle=True,noise=None,
random_state=None,factor=0.8)
```

Here, `n_samples` is the total data numbers, `shuffle` indicates whether we have to shuffle the samples, `noise` is the number of random amounts to be applied to the circular data, `random_state` is the random seed, and `factor` is the scale factor between circles.

Moon dataset

This is another nonlinear problem but with another type of class separation, because there is no closure such as in the circle's ring.

Project 1 – k-means clustering on synthetic datasets

Dataset description and loading

During this chapter, we'll be using generated datasets that are specially crafted to have special properties. Two of the target properties are the possibility of linear separation of classes and the existence of clearly separated clusters (or not).

Generating the dataset

With these lines, we create the data structures that will contain all the elements for working on the solutions, that is:

```
centers = [(-2, -2), (-2, 1.5), (1.5, -2), (2, 1.5)]
data, features = make_blobs (n_samples=200, centers=centers, n_features =
2, cluster_std=0.8, shuffle=False, random_state=42)
```

Graphing the dataset via matplotlib:

```
    ax.scatter(np.asarray(centers).transpose()[0],
np.asarray(centers).transpose()[1], marker = 'o', s = 250)
    plt.plot()
```

Model architecture

The points variable contains the 2D coordinates of the dataset points, the centroids variable will contain the coordinates of the center points of the groups, and the `cluster_assignments` variable contains the centroid index for each data element.

For example, `cluster_assignments[2] = 1` indicates that the `data[2]` data point pertains to the cluster with the center, centroid `1`. The location of centroid `1` is located in `centroids[1]`.

```
points=tf.Variable(data)
cluster_assignments = tf.Variable(tf.zeros([N], dtype=tf.int64))
centroids = tf.Variable(tf.slice(points.initialized_value(), [0,0], [K,2]))
```

Then we can draw the position of these centroids using matplotlib:

```
fig, ax = plt.subplots()
ax.scatter(np.asarray(centers).transpose()[0],
np.asarray(centers).transpose()[1], marker = 'o', s = 250)
plt.show()
```

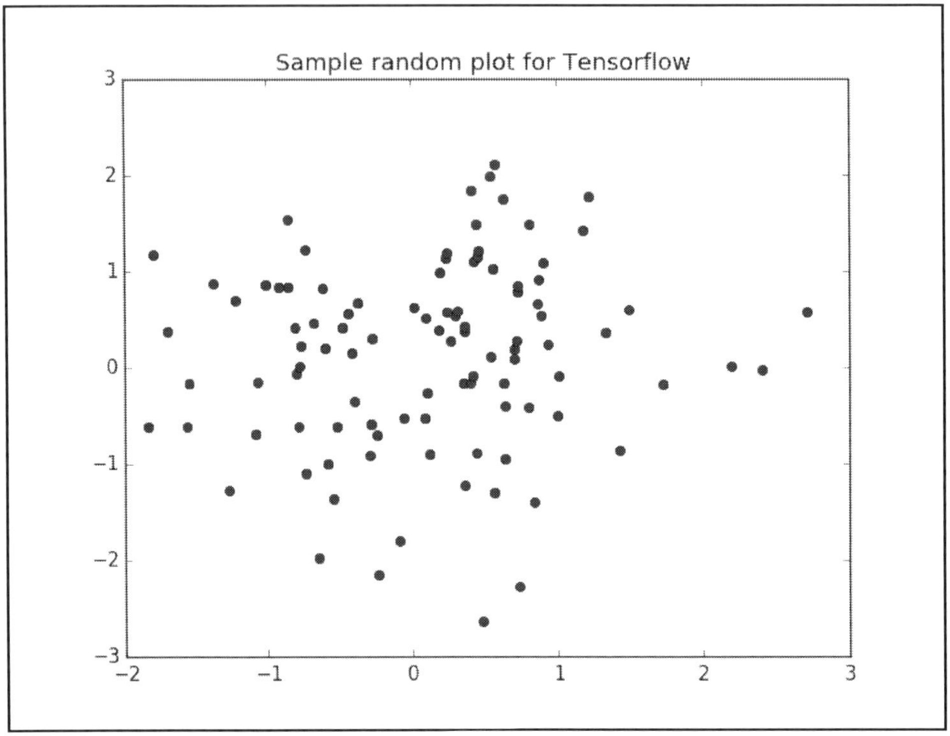

Initial center seeding

Loss function description and optimizer loop

Then we will do *N* copies of all centroids, *K* copies of each point, and *N x K* copies of every point so we can calculate the distances between each point and every centroid, for each dimension:

```
rep_centroids = tf.reshape(tf.tile(centroids, [N, 1]), [N, K, 2])
rep_points = tf.reshape(tf.tile(points, [1, K]), [N, K, 2])
sum_squares = tf.reduce_sum(tf.square(rep_points - rep_centroids),
reduction_indices=2)
```

Then we perform the sum for all dimensions and get the index of the lowest sum (this will be the index of the centroid or cluster assigned for each point):

```
best_centroids = tf.argmin(sum_squares, 1)
```

Centroids will also be updated with a `bucket:mean` function, defined in the full source code.

Stop condition

This is the stop condition that the new centroids and assignments don't change:

```
did_assignments_change = tf.reduce_any(tf.not_equal(best_centroids,
cluster_assignments))
```

Here, we use `control_dependencies` to calculate whether we need to update the centroids:

```
with tf.control_dependencies([did_assignments_change]):
    do_updates = tf.group(
    centroids.assign(means),
    cluster_assignments.assign(best_centroids))
```

Results description

We get the following output when the program is executed:

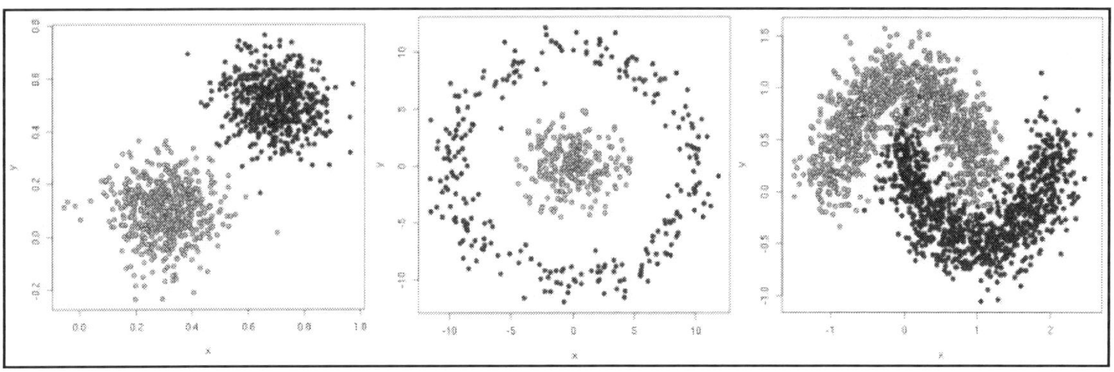

This is a summarizing graphic of the centroid changes after a round of iterations with the original clusters drawn as they were generated from the algorithm.

In the following image, we represent the different stages in the application of the k-means algorithm for this clearly separated case:

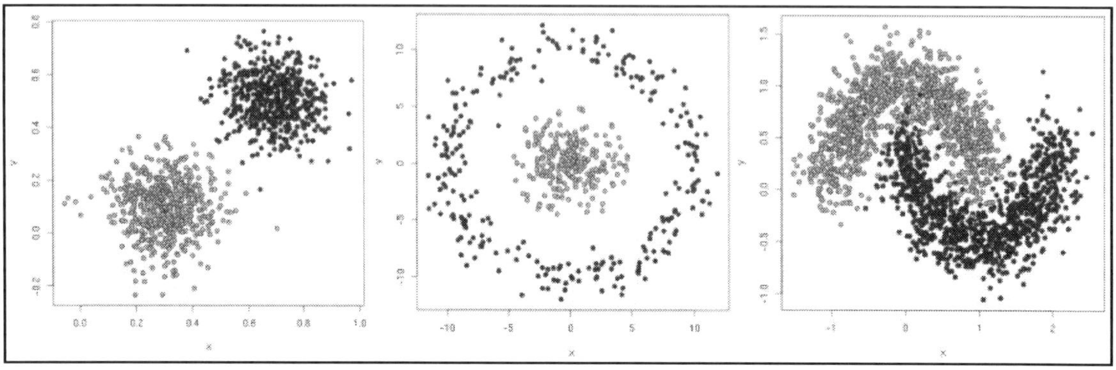

Centroid changes per iteration

Full source code

Following is the complete source code:

```
import tensorflow as tf
import numpy as np
import time

import matplotlib
import matplotlib.pyplot as plt

from sklearn.datasets.samples_generator import make_blobs
from sklearn.datasets.samples_generator import make_circles

DATA_TYPE = 'blobs'

# Number of clusters, if we choose circles, only 2 will be enough
if (DATA_TYPE == 'circle'):
    K=2
else:
    K=4

# Maximum number of iterations, if the conditions are not met
MAX_ITERS = 1000
```

```
start = time.time()

centers = [(-2, -2), (-2, 1.5), (1.5, -2), (2, 1.5)]
if (DATA_TYPE == 'circle'):
    data, features = make_circles(n_samples=200, shuffle=True, noise= 0.01,
factor=0.4)
else:
    data, features = make_blobs (n_samples=200, centers=centers, n_features
= 2, cluster_std=0.8, shuffle=False, random_state=42)

fig, ax = plt.subplots()
ax.scatter(np.asarray(centers).transpose()[0],
np.asarray(centers).transpose()[1], marker = 'o', s = 250)
plt.show()

fig, ax = plt.subplots()
if (DATA_TYPE == 'blobs'):
ax.scatter(np.asarray(centers).transpose()[0],
np.asarray(centers).transpose()[1], marker = 'o', s = 250)
ax.scatter(data.transpose()[0], data.transpose()[1], marker = 'o', s = 100,
c = features, cmap=plt.cm.coolwarm )
plt.plot()

points=tf.Variable(data)
cluster_assignments = tf.Variable(tf.zeros([N], dtype=tf.int64))
centroids = tf.Variable(tf.slice(points.initialized_value(), [0,0], [K,2]))

sess = tf.Session()
sess.run(tf.initialize_all_variables())

rep_centroids = tf.reshape(tf.tile(centroids, [N, 1]), [N, K, 2])
rep_points = tf.reshape(tf.tile(points, [1, K]), [N, K, 2])
sum_squares = tf.reduce_sum(tf.square(rep_points - rep_centroids),
reduction_indices=2)
best_centroids = tf.argmin(sum_squares, 1)

did_assignments_change = tf.reduce_any(tf.not_equal(best_centroids,
cluster_assignments))

def bucket_mean(data, bucket_ids, num_buckets):
total = tf.unsorted_segment_sum(data, bucket_ids, num_buckets)
count = tf.unsorted_segment_sum(tf.ones_like(data), bucket_ids,
num_buckets)
return total / count

means = bucket_mean(points, best_centroids, K)

with tf.control_dependencies([did_assignments_change]):
```

```
do_updates = tf.group(
centroids.assign(means),
cluster_assignments.assign(best_centroids))

changed = True
iters = 0

fig, ax = plt.subplots()
if (DATA_TYPE == 'blobs'):
    colourindexes=[2,1,4,3]
else:
    colourindexes=[2,1]
while changed and iters < MAX_ITERS:
fig, ax = plt.subplots()
iters += 1
[changed, _] = sess.run([did_assignments_change, do_updates])
[centers, assignments] = sess.run([centroids, cluster_assignments])
ax.scatter(sess.run(points).transpose()[0],
sess.run(points).transpose()[1], marker = 'o', s = 200, c = assignments,
cmap=plt.cm.coolwarm )
ax.scatter(centers[:,0],centers[:,1], marker = '^', s = 550, c =
colourindexes, cmap=plt.cm.plasma)
ax.set_title('Iteration ' + str(iters))
plt.savefig("kmeans" + str(iters) +".png")

ax.scatter(sess.run(points).transpose()[0],
sess.run(points).transpose()[1], marker = 'o', s = 200, c = assignments,
cmap=plt.cm.coolwarm )
plt.show()

end = time.time()
print ("Found in %.2f seconds" % (end-start)), iters, "iterations"
print "Centroids:"
print centers
print "Cluster assignments:", assignments
```

This is the simplest case for observing the algorithm mechanics. When the data comes from the real world, the classes are normally not so clearly separated and it is more difficult to label the data samples.

k-means on circle synthetic data

For the circular plot, we observe that this data characterization is not simple to represent by a simple set of means. As the image clearly shows, the two circles either share a Centroid position, or are really close and so we cannot predict a clear outcome:

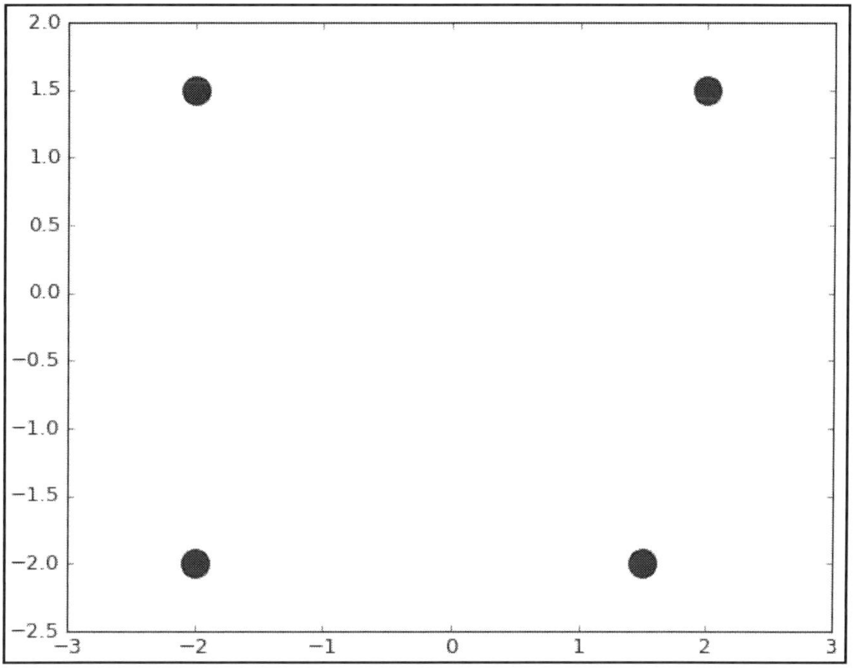

Circle type dataset

For this dataset, we are only using two classes to be sure the main drawbacks of this algorithm are understood:

```
Found in 407.12 seconds 8 iterations
Centroids:
[[ 1.65289262 -2.04643427]
 [-2.0763623   1.61204964]
 [-2.08862822 -2.07255306]
 [ 2.09831502  1.55936014]]
Cluster assignments: [2 2 2 2 2 2 2 2 2 2 2 2 2 2 2 2 2 2 2 2 2 2 2 2 2 2 2 2 2 2 2 2 2 2 2 2 2
 2 2 2 2 2 2 2 2 2 2 2 2 2 1 1 1 1 1 1 1 1 1 1 1 1 1 1 1 1 1 1 1 1 1 1 1 1
 1 1 1 1 1 1 1 1 1 1 1 1 1 1 1 1 1 1 1 1 1 1 1 1 1 1 0 0 0 0 3 0 0 0 0 0 0
 0 0 0 0 0 0 0 0 0 0 0 0 0 0 0 0 0 0 0 0 2 0 0 0 0 0 0 0 0 0 0 0 0 0 0 0 0
 0 0 3 3 3 3 3 3 3 3 3 3 3 3 3 3 3 3 3 3 3 3 3 3 3 3 3 3 3 3 3 3 3 3 3 3 3
 3 3 3 3 3 3 3 3 3 3 3 3 3 3 3]
```

k-means applied to a circular synthetic dataset

As we can see, the initial centers drifted toward the areas that had the most concentrated sample numbers, and so divided the data linearly. This is one of the limitations of the simple models we are employing at this stage. To cope with nonlinear separability samples, we can try other statistical approaches outside the scope of this chapter, such as **density-based spatial clustering of applications with noise** (DBSCAN).

Project 2 – nearest neighbor on synthetic datasets

In this project, we will be loading a dataset with which the previous algorithm (k-means) has problems separating classes.

Dataset generation

The dataset is the same circular classes dataset from the first example with two classes, but this time we will increase the error probability by adding a bit more noise (from `0.01` to `0.12`):

```
    data, features = make_circles(n_samples=N, shuffle=True,
noise=0.12,factor=0.4)
```

This is the resulting training data plot:

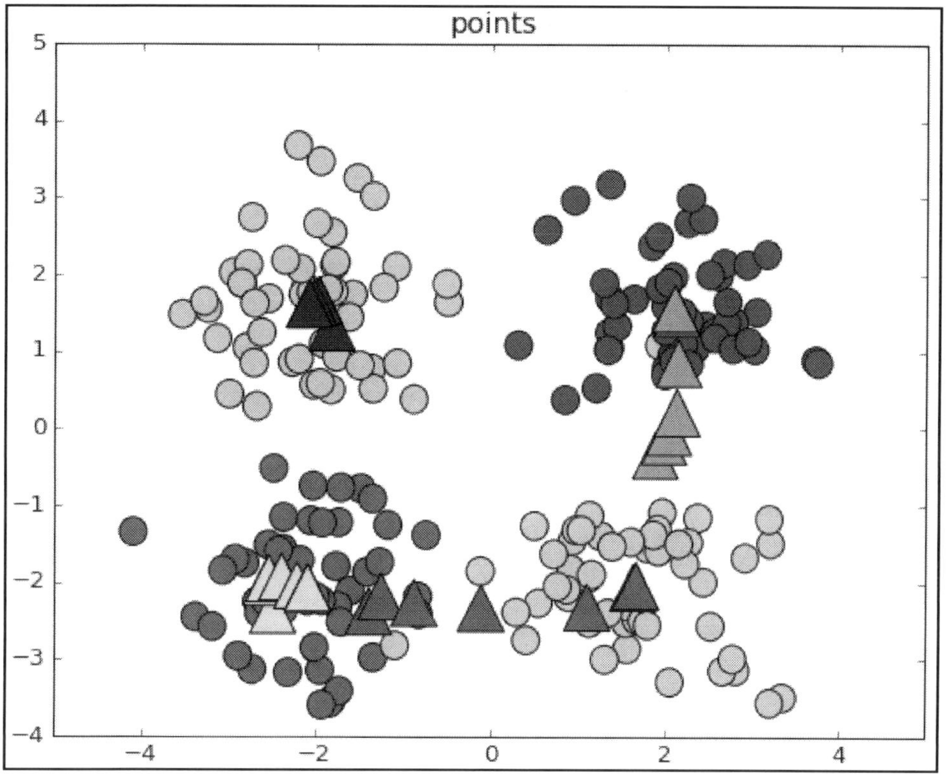

Model architecture

The variables that will sustain data are simply the original data and a test list, which will hold the calculated classes for the test data:

```
    data, features = make_circles(n_samples=N, shuffle=True, noise= 0.12,
factor=0.4)
    tr_data, tr_features= data[:cut], features[:cut]
    te_data,te_features=data[cut:], features[cut:]
    test=[]
```

Loss function description

In clustering, we will use the function to optimize as the Euclidean distance, the same as `Chapter 1`, *Exploring and Transforming Data*. It is calculated on the cluster assignment loop, getting the distance from the new point to the existing training points, asking for the index of the minimum, and then using that index to search the class of the nearest neighbor:

```
    distances = tf.reduce_sum(tf.square(tf.sub(i ,
tr_data)),reduction_indices=1)
    neighbor = tf.arg_min(distances,0)
```

Stop condition

In this simple example, we will finish once all the elements of the test partition have been visited.

Results description

Here is a graphic of the test data class assignation where we can see the clearly separated classes. We can observe that, at least with this limited dataset scope, this method works better than the non-overlapping, blob-optimizing, k-means method.

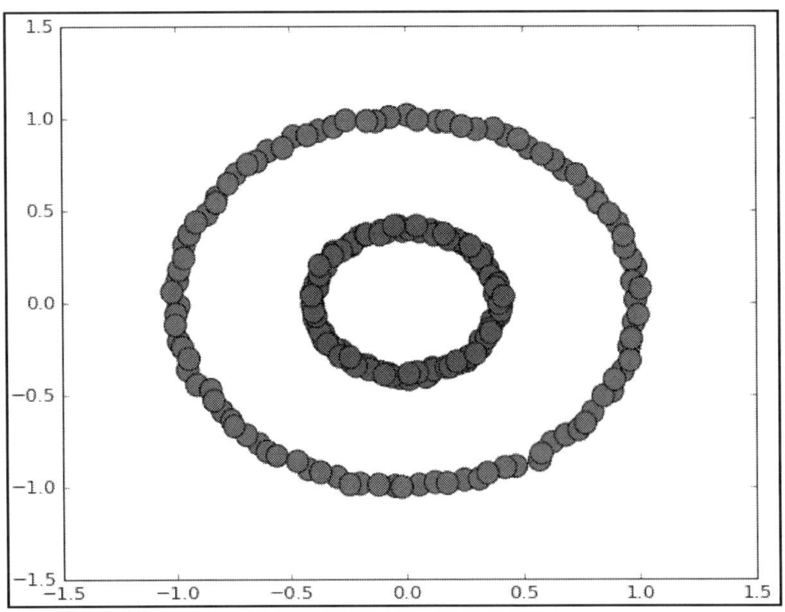

Full source code

Following is the complete source code:

```
import tensorflow as tf
import numpy as np
import time

import matplotlib
import matplotlib.pyplot as plt

from sklearn.datasets.samples_generator import make_circles

N=210
K=2
# Maximum number of iterations, if the conditions are not met
MAX_ITERS = 1000
cut=int(N*0.7)

start = time.time()

data, features = make_circles(n_samples=N, shuffle=True, noise= 0.12,
factor=0.4)
tr_data, tr_features= data[:cut], features[:cut]
te_data,te_features=data[cut:], features[cut:]
test=[]

fig, ax = plt.subplots()
ax.scatter(tr_data.transpose()[0], tr_data.transpose()[1], marker = 'o', s
= 100, c = tr_features, cmap=plt.cm.coolwarm )
plt.plot()

sess = tf.Session()
sess.run(tf.initialize_all_variables())

for i, j in zip(te_data, te_features):
    distances = tf.reduce_sum(tf.square(tf.sub(i ,
tr_data)),reduction_indices=1)
    neighbor = tf.arg_min(distances,0)

    test.append(tr_features[sess.run(neighbor)])
print test
fig, ax = plt.subplots()
ax.scatter(te_data.transpose()[0], te_data.transpose()[1], marker = 'o', s
= 100, c = test, cmap=plt.cm.coolwarm )
plt.plot()

end = time.time()
```

```
print ("Found in %.2f seconds" % (end-start))

print "Cluster assignments:", test
```

Summary

In this chapter, we've seen a simple overview of some of the most basic models we can implement, but tried to be as detailed in the explanation as possible.

From now on, we will be able to generate synthetic datasets, allowing us to rapidly test the adequacy of a model for different data configurations and so evaluate the advantages and shortcomings of them, without having to load models with a greater number of unknown characteristics.

Additionally, we have implemented the first iterative methods and tested convergence, a task that will continue in the following chapters in a similar way, but with finer and much more exact methods.

In the next chapter, we will solve classification problems using linear functions, and for the first time, use previous data from training sets to learn from its characteristics. This is the objective of supervised learning techniques and is more useful in general for a lot of real-life problem-solving.

3 Linear Regression

In this chapter, we will begin applying all the standard steps employed in a machine learning project in order to fit previously given data with a line that minimizes error and loss functions.

In the previous chapter, we saw problems with both a limited scope and a number of possible solutions. These types of models are also related with a qualitative assessment type, that is, assigning a label to a sample, based on previous labeling. This result is normally found in problems pertaining to the social domain.

We could also be interested in predicting the exact numeric output value of a (previously modeled) function. This approach is akin to the physical domain and can be used to predict the temperature or humidity or the value of a certain good, knowing a series of its historical values before hand, and it is called **regression analysis**.

In the case of linear regression, we look for a determinate relationship between the input and the output variables, represented by a linear equation.

Univariate linear modelling function

As previously stated, in linear regression, we try to find a linear equation that minimizes the distance between data points and the modeled line.

This relationship can be represented by this canonical linear function:

$$y = \beta_0 + \beta_1 x$$

The model function takes the form:

Here, `ss0` or `bias` is the intercept, the function value for *x* is zero, and `ss1` is the slope of the modeled line. The variable *x* is normally called the **independent variable**, and *y* the dependent one, but they can also be called the regressor and response variables respectively.

Sample data generation

In the following example, we will generate an approximate sample random distribution based on a line with `ss0` = `2.0`, summed with a vertical noise of maximum amplitude `0.4`.

```
In[]:
#Indicate the matplotlib to show the graphics inline
%matplotlib inline
import matplotlib.pyplot as plt # import matplotlib
import numpy as np # import numpy
trX = np.linspace(-1, 1, 101) # Linear space of 101 and [-1,1]
#Create The y function based on the x axis
trY = 2 * trX + np.random.randn(*trX.shape) * 0.4 + 0.2
plt.figure() # Create a new figure
plt.scatter(trX,trY) #Plot a scatter draw of the random datapoints
# Draw one line with the line function
plt.plot (trX, .2 + 2 * trX)
```

And the resulting graph will look like this:

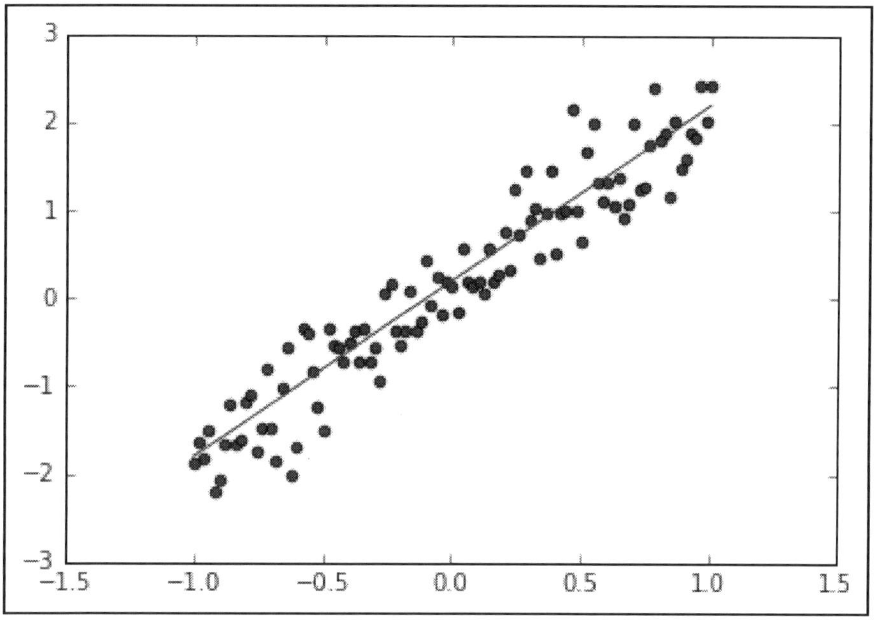

Noise added linear sampling and linear function

Determination of the cost function

As with all machine learning techniques, we have to determine an error function, which we need to minimize, that indicates the appropriateness of the solution to the problem.

The most generally used `cost` function for linear regression is called **least squares**.

Least squares

In order to calculate the least squares error for a function, we look for a measure of how close the points are to the modeling line, in a general sense. So we define a function that measures for each tuple x_n, y_n how far it is from the modeled line's corresponding value.

For 2D regression, we have a list of number tuples $(X_0,Y_0),(X_1,Y_1)...(X_n,Y_n)$, and the values to find are of β_0 and β_1, by minimizing the following function:

$$J(\beta_0,\beta_1)=\sum_{i=0}^{n}(y_i-\beta_0-\beta_1 x_i)^2$$

In simple terms, the summation represents the sum of Euclidean distances between predicted and actual values.

The reason for the operations is that the summation of the squared errors gives us a unique and simple global number, the difference between expected and real number gives us the proper distance, and the square power gives us a positive number, which penalizes distances in a more-than-linear fashion.

Minimizing the cost function

The next step is to set a method to minimize the `cost` function. In linear calculus, one of the fundamental elements of the task of locating minima is reduced to calculating the derivatives of the function and to seek its zeroes. For this, the function has to have a derivative and preferably be convex; it can be proved that the least squares function complies with these two conditions. This is very useful for avoiding the known problems of local minima.

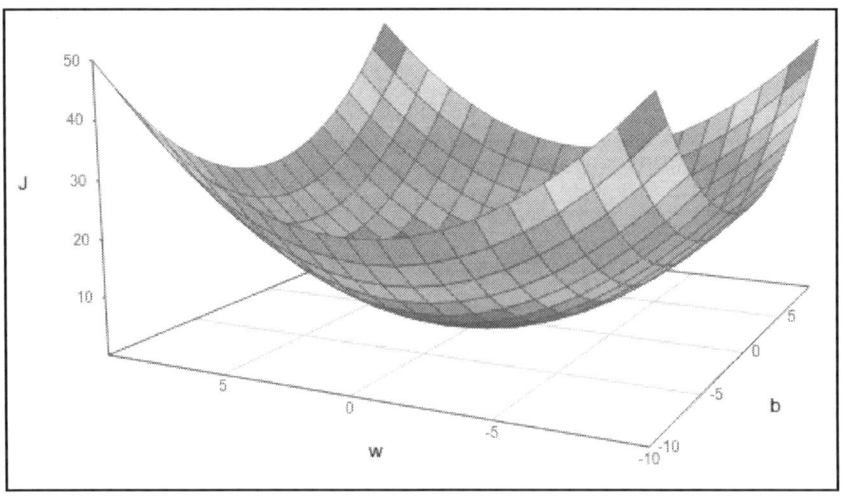

Loss function representation

General minima for least squares

The kind of problem we are trying to solve (least squares) can be presented in matrix form:

$$J(\theta)=\frac{1}{2m}(X\theta-y)^T(X\theta-y)$$

Here, *J* is the cost function and has the following solution:

$$\theta=\left(X^TX\right)^{-1}X^Ty$$

In this chapter, we will use an iterative method gradient descent, which will be useful in the following chapters in a more generalized fashion.

Iterative methods - gradient descent

The **gradient descent** is by its own nature an iterative method and the most generally used optimization algorithm in the machine learning field. It combines a simple approach with a good convergence rate, considering the complexity of parameter combinations that it can be optimized with it.

A 2D linear regression starts with a function with randomly defined weights or multipliers for the linear coefficient. After the first values are defined, the second step is to apply a recurrent function in the following form:

$$\theta_j:=\theta_j-\alpha\frac{\partial}{\partial\theta_j}J(\theta)$$

In this equation, we can easily derive the mechanism of the method. We start with the initial set of coefficients and then move in the opposite direction of maximum change in the function. The α variable is named the step and will affect how far we will move in the direction of the gradient searching for minimal.

The final step is to optionally test the changes between iteration and see whether the changes are greater than an epsilon or to check whether the iteration number is reached.

If the function is not convex, it is suggested to run gradient descent multiple times with random values and then select coefficients for which the cost value is the lowest. In the case of non-convex functions, the gradient descent ends up in a minimum, which can be local. Therefore, as for non-convex functions, the result depends on initial values, it is suggested to randomly set them multiple times and among all the solutions, pick the one with lowest cost.

Example section

Let's now discuss useful libraries and modules.

Optimizer methods in TensorFlow – the train module

The training or parameter optimization stage is a vital part of the machine learning workflow.

For this matter, TensorFlow has a `tf.train` module, which is a helper set of objects dedicated to implementing a range of different optimizing strategies that the data scientist will need. The main object provided by this module is called **Optimizer**.

The tf.train.Optimizer class

The `Optimizer` class allows you to calculate gradients for a `loss` function and apply them to different variables of a model. Among the most well-known algorithm subclasses, we find *gradient descent, Adam*, and *Adagrad*.

One major tip regarding this class is that the `Optimizer` class itself cannot be instantiated; one of the subclasses should be.

As discussed previously, TensorFlow allows you to define the functions in a symbolic way, so the gradients will be applied in a symbolic fashion, too, improving the accuracy of the results and the versatility of the operations to be applied to the data.

In order to use the `Optimizer` class, we need to perform the following steps:

1. Create an `Optimizer` with the desired parameters (in this case, gradient descent).

   ```
   opt = GradientDescentOptimizer(learning_rate= [learning rate])
   ```

2. Create an operation calling the `minimize` method for the `cost` functions.

   ```
   optimization_op = opt.minimize(cost, var_list=[variables list])
   ```

The `minimize` method has the following form:

```
tf.train.Optimizer.minimize(loss, global_step=None, var_list=None,
gate_gradients=1, aggregation_method=None,
colocate_gradients_with_ops=False, name=None)
```

The main parameters are as follows:

- `loss`: This is a tensor that contains the values to be minimized.
- `global_step`: This variable will increment by one after the `Optimizer` works.
- `var_list`: This contains variables to optimize.

> TIP: In practice, the `optimize` method combines calls to `compute_gradients()` and `apply_gradients()`. If you want to process the gradient before applying them, call `compute_gradients()` and `apply_gradients()` explicitly instead of using this function. If we want to perform only one step of training, we must execute the `run` method in the form of `opt_op.run()`.

Other Optimizer instance types

Following are the other `Optimizer` instance types:

- `tf.train.AdagradOptimizer`: This is an adaptive method based on the frequency of parameters, with a monotonically descending learning rate.
- `tf.train.AdadeltaOptimizer`: This is an improvement on *Adagrad*, that doesn't carry a descending learning rate.
- `tf.train.MomentumOptimizer`: This is an adaptive method that accounts for different change rates between dimensions.
- And there are other more specific ones, such as `tf.train.AdamOptimizer`, `tf.train.FtrlOptimizer`, `tf.train.RMSPropOptimizer`.

Example 1 – univariate linear regression

We will now work on a project in which we will apply all the concepts we succinctly covered in the preceding pages. In this example, we will create one approximately linear distribution; afterwards, we will create a regression model that tries to fit a linear function that minimizes the error function (defined by least squares).

This model will allow us to predict an outcome for an input value, given one new sample.

Dataset description

For this example, we will be generating a synthetic dataset consisting of a linear function with added noise:

```
import TensorFlow as tf
import numpy as np
trX = np.linspace(-1, 1, 101)
trY = 2 * trX + np.random.randn(*trX.shape) * 0.4 + 0.2 # create a y value
which is approximately linear but with some random noise
```

With these lines, we can represent the lines as a scatter plot and the ideal line function.

```
import matplotlib.pyplot as plt
plt.scatter(trX,trY)
plt.plot (trX, .2 + 2 * trX)
```

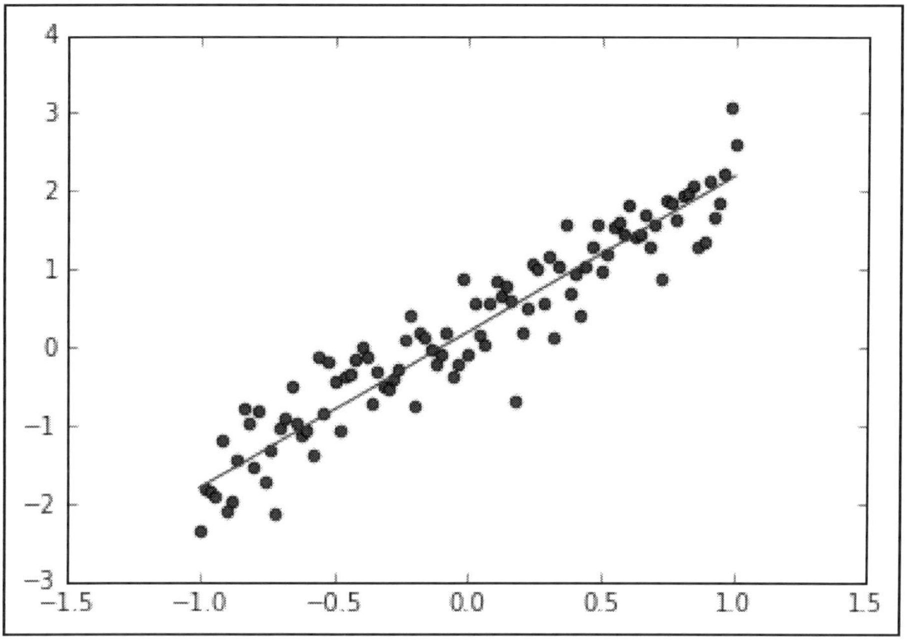

Generated samples and original linear function without noise

Model architecture

1. Now we create a variable to hold the values in the x and y axes. Then we symbolically define the model as the multiplication of X and the weights w.
2. Then we generate some variables, to which we assign initial values in order to launch the model:

```
In[]:
X = tf.placeholder("float", name="X") # create symbolic variables
Y = tf.placeholder("float", name = "Y")
```

3. We now define our model by declaring `name_scope` as `Model`. This scope groups all the variables it contains in order to form a unique entity with homogeneous entities. In this scope, we first define a function that receives the variables of the `x` axis coordinates, the weight (slope), and the bias. Then we create a new variable, `objects`, to hold the changing parameters and instantiate the model with the `y_model` variable:

```
with tf.name_scope("Model"):

  def model(X, w, b):
    return tf.mul(X, w) + b # just define the line as X*w + b0

  w = tf.Variable(-1.0, name="b0") # create a shared variable
  b = tf.Variable(-2.0, name="b1") # create a shared variable
  y_model = model(X, w, b)
```

In the dashboard, you can see the image of the loss function we have been recollecting. In the graph section, when you zoom into the **Model**, you can see the sum and multiplication operation, the parameter variables **b0** and **b1**, and the **gradient** operation applied over the **Model**, as shown next:

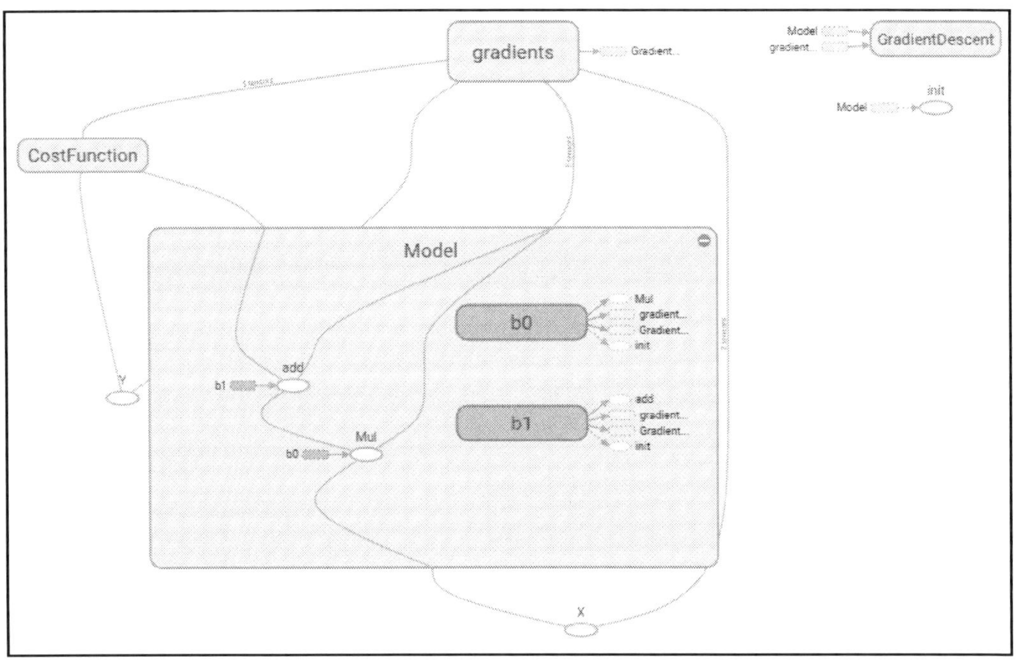

Cost function description and Optimizer loop

1. In the `Cost Function`, we create a new scope to include all the operations of this group and use the previously created `y_model` to account for the calculated `y` axis values that we use to calculate the loss.

```
with tf.name_scope("CostFunction"):
cost = (tf.pow(Y-y_model, 2)) # use sqr error for cost
```

2. To define the chosen `optimizer`, we initialize a `GradientDescentOptimizer`, and the step will be of `0.01`, which seems like a reasonable start for convergence.

```
train_op = tf.train.GradientDescentOptimizer(0.05).minimize(cost)
```

3. It's time to create the session and to initialize the variables we want to save for reviewing in TensorBoard. In this example, we will be saving one scalar variable with the error result of the last sample for each iteration. We will also save the graph structure in a file for reviewing.

```
sess = tf.Session()
init = tf.initialize_all_variables()
tf.train.write_graph(sess.graph,
  '/home/ubuntu/linear','graph.pbtxt')
cost_op = tf.scalar_summary("loss", cost)
merged = tf.merge_all_summaries()
sess.run(init)
writer = tf.train.SummaryWriter('/home/ubuntu/linear',
  sess.graph)
```

4. For model training, we set an objective of 100 iterations, where we send each of the samples to the `train` operation of the gradient descent. After each iteration, we plot the modeling line and add the value of the last error to the `summary`.

```
In[]:
for i in range(100):
 for (x, y) in zip(trX, trY):
   sess.run(train_op, feed_dict={X: x, Y: y})
   summary_str = sess.run(cost_op, feed_dict={X: x, Y: y})
   writer.add_summary(summary_str, i)
 b0temp=b.eval(session=sess)
 b1temp=w.eval(session=sess)
 plt.plot (trX, b0temp + b1temp * trX )
```

The resulting plot is as follows; we can see how the initial line rapidly converges into a more plausible result:

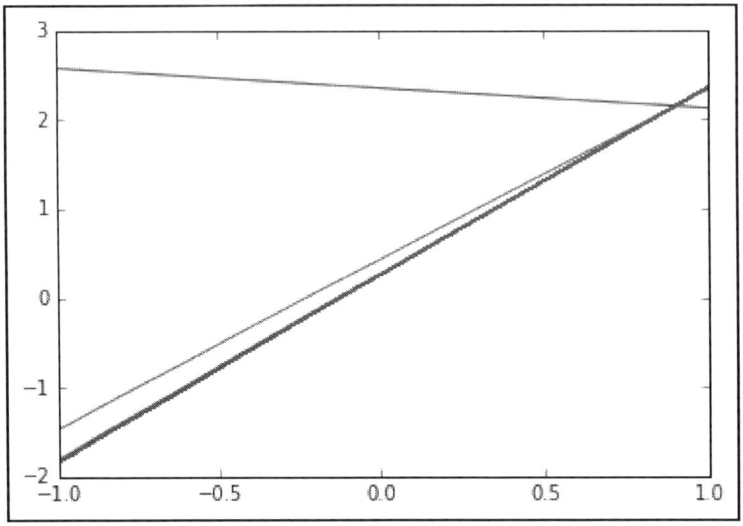

With the **CostFunction** scope zoomed in, we can see the power and subtraction operations and also the written summary, as shown in the following figure:

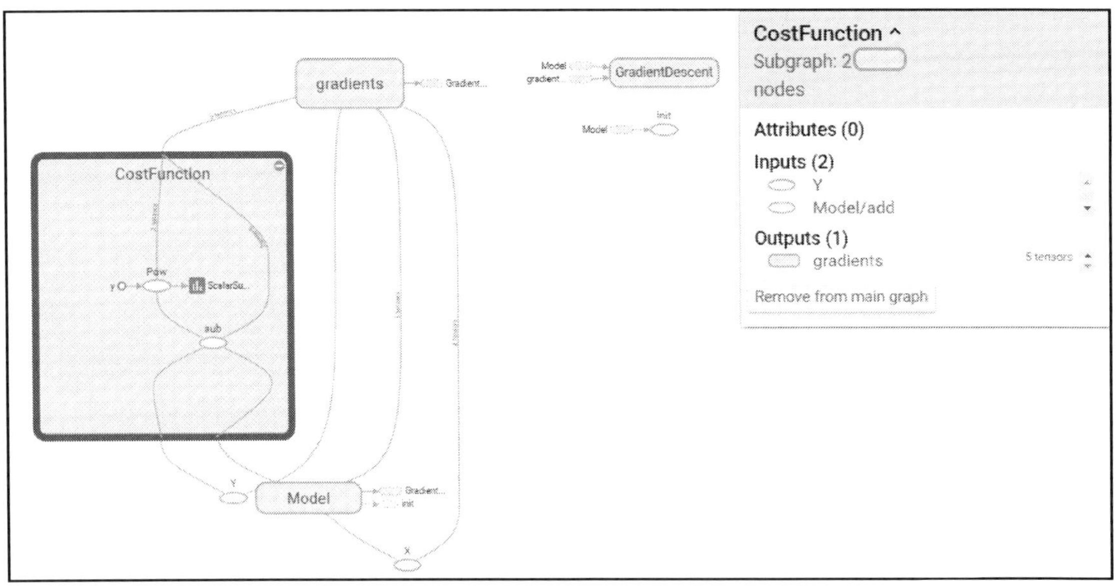

Stop condition

Results description

Now let's check the parameter results, printing the `run` output of the `w` and `b` variables:

```
printsess.run(w) # Should be around 2
printsess.run(b) #Should be around 0.2
2.09422
0.256044
```

It's time to graphically review the data again and the suggested final line.

```
plt.scatter(trX,trY)
plt.plot (trX, testb + trX * testw)
```

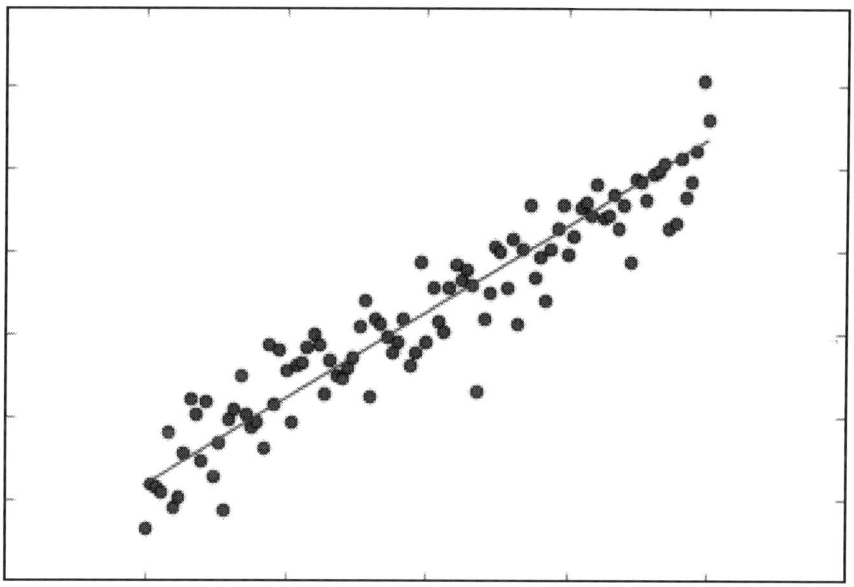

Reviewing results with TensorBoard

Now let's review the data we saved in TensorBoard.

In order to start TensorBoard, you can go to the logs directory and execute the following line:

```
$ tensorboard --logdir=.
```

TensorBoard will load the event and graph files and will be listening on the `6006` port. You can then go from your browser to `localhost:6000` and see the TensorBoard dashboard as shown in the following figure:

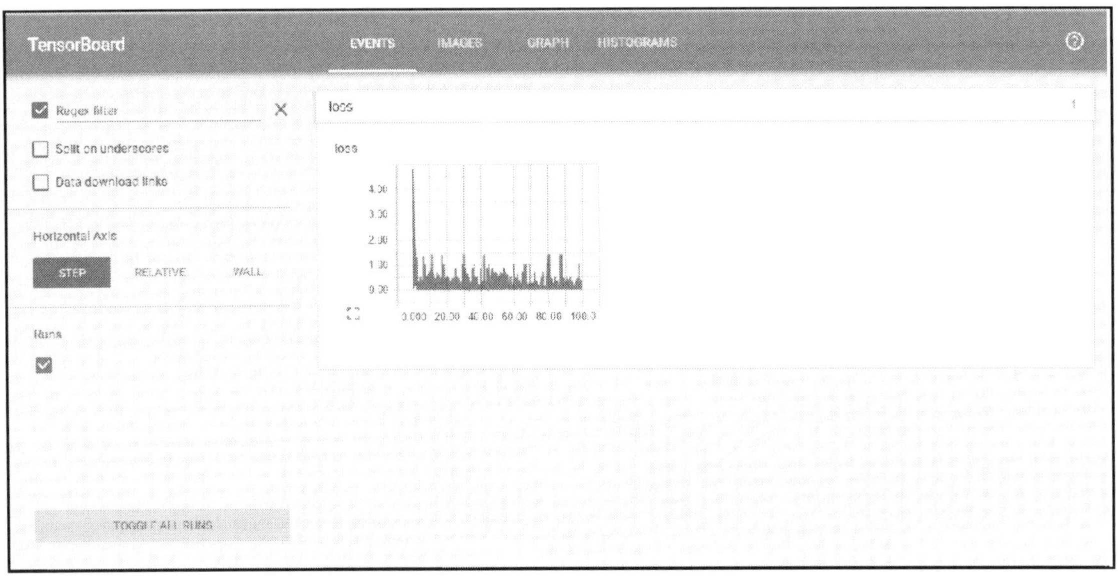

Full source code

The following is the complete source code:

```
import matplotlib.pyplot as plt # import matplotlib
import numpy as np # import numpy
import tensorflow as tf
import numpy as np

trX = np.linspace(-1, 1, 101) #Create a linear space of 101 points between
1 and 1
```

```
trY = 2 * trX + np.random.randn(*trX.shape) * 0.4 + 0.2 #Create The y
function based on the x axis
plt.figure() # Create a new figure
plt.scatter(trX,trY) #Plot a scatter draw of the random datapoints
plt.plot (trX, .2 + 2 * trX) # Draw one line with the line function

get_ipython().magic(u'matplotlib inline')

import matplotlib.pyplot as plt
import tensorflow as tf
import numpy as np

trX = np.linspace(-1, 1, 101)
trY = 2 * trX + np.random.randn(*trX.shape) * 0.4 + 0.2 # create a y value
which is approximately linear but with some random noise

plt.scatter(trX,trY)
plt.plot (trX, .2 + 2 * trX)

X = tf.placeholder("float", name="X") # create symbolic variables
Y = tf.placeholder("float", name = "Y")

withtf.name_scope("Model"):

    def model(X, w, b):
        returntf.mul(X, w) + b # We just define the line as X*w + b0

    w = tf.Variable(-1.0, name="b0") # create a shared variable
    b = tf.Variable(-2.0, name="b1") # create a shared variable
    y_model = model(X, w, b)


withtf.name_scope("CostFunction"):
    cost = (tf.pow(Y-y_model, 2)) # use sqr error for cost function

train_op = tf.train.GradientDescentOptimizer(0.05).minimize(cost)


sess = tf.Session()
init = tf.initialize_all_variables()
tf.train.write_graph(sess.graph, '/home/ubuntu/linear','graph.pbtxt')
cost_op = tf.scalar_summary("loss", cost)
merged = tf.merge_all_summaries()
sess.run(init)
writer = tf.train.SummaryWriter('/home/ubuntu/linear', sess.graph)

fori in range(100):
for (x, y) in zip(trX, trY):
```

```
sess.run(train_op, feed_dict={X: x, Y: y})
summary_str = sess.run(cost_op, feed_dict={X: x, Y: y})
writer.add_summary(summary_str, i)
    b0temp=b.eval(session=sess)
    b1temp=w.eval(session=sess)
plt.plot (trX, b0temp + b1temp * trX )


printsess.run(w) # Should be around 2
printsess.run(b) #Should be around 0.2


plt.scatter(trX,trY)
plt.plot (trX, sess.run(b) + trX * sess.run(w))
```

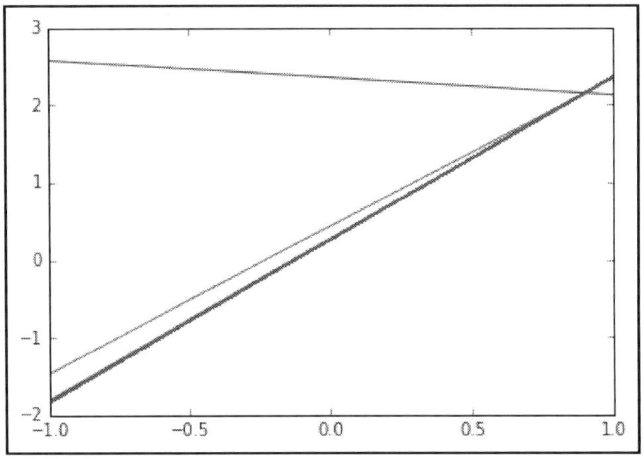

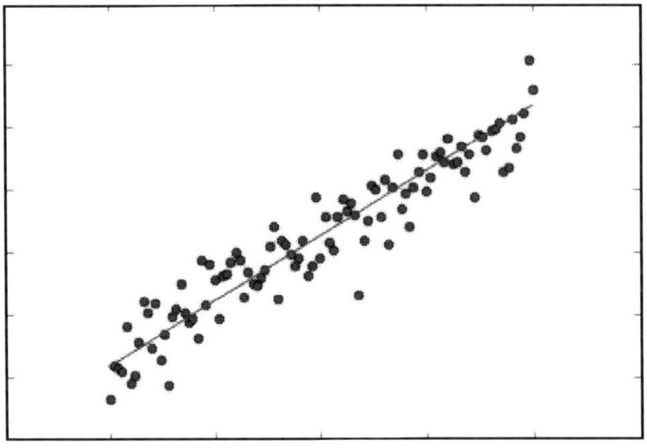

Example – multivariate linear regression

In this example, we will work on a regression problem involving more than one variable.

This will be based on a 1993 dataset of a study of different prices among some suburbs of Boston. It originally contained 13 variables and the mean price of the properties there.

The only change in the file from the original one is the removal of one variable `(b)`, which racially profiled the different suburbs.

Apart from that, we will choose a handful of variables that we consider have good conditions to be modeled by a linear function.

Useful libraries and methods

This section contains a list of useful libraries that we will be using in this example and in some parts of the rest of the book, outside TensorFlow, to assist the solving of different problems we will be working on.

Pandas library

When we want to rapidly read and get hints about normally sized data files, the creation of read buffers and other additional mechanisms can vea overhead. This is one of the current real-life use cases for **Pandas**.

This is an excerpt from the Pandas site (`pandas.pydata.org`):

> *"Pandas is an open source, BSD-licensed library providing high-performance, easy-to-use data structures and data analysis tools for Python."*

Pandas main features are as follows:

- It has read write file capabilities from CSV and text files, MS Excel, SQL databases, and even the scientifically oriented HDF5 format
- The CSV file-loading routines automatically recognize column headings and support a more direct addressing of columns
- The data structures are automatically translated into NumPy multidimensional arrays

Dataset description

The dataset is represented in a CSV file, and we will open it using the Pandas library.

The dataset includes the following variables:

- CRIM: Per capita crime rate by town
- ZN: Proportion of residential land zoned for lots over 25,000 sq.ft.
- INDUS: Proportion of non-retail business acres per town
- CHAS: Charles River dummy variable (= 1 if tract bounds river; 0 otherwise)
- NOX: Nitric oxides concentration (parts per 10 million)
- RM: Average number of rooms per dwelling
- AGE: Proportion of owner-occupied units built prior to 1940
- DIS: Weighted distances to five Boston employment centers
- RAD: Index of accessibility to radial highways
- TAX: Full-value property-tax rate per $10,000
- PTRATIO: Pupil-teacher ratio by town
- LSTAT: % lower status of the population
- MEDV: Median value of owner-occupied homes in $1000's

Here, we have a simple program that will read the dataset and create a detailed account of the data:

```
import tensorflow.contrib.learn as skflow
fromsklearn import datasets, metrics, preprocessing
import numpy as np
import pandas as pd

df = pd.read_csv("data/boston.csv", header=0)
printdf.describe()
```

This will output a statistical summary of the dataset's variable. The first six results are as follows:

```
CRIM            ZN        INDUS         CHAS         NOX           RM  \
count  506.000000 506.000000  506.000000  506.000000  506.000000
506.000000
mean     3.613524  11.363636   11.136779    0.069170    0.554695
6.284634
std      8.601545  23.322453    6.860353    0.253994    0.115878
0.702617
```

```
min       0.006320    0.000000    0.460000    0.000000    0.385000
3.561000
25%       0.082045    0.000000    5.190000    0.000000    0.449000
5.885500
50%       0.256510    0.000000    9.690000    0.000000    0.538000
6.208500
75%       3.677082   12.500000   18.100000    0.000000    0.624000
6.623500
max      88.976200  100.000000   27.740000    1.000000    0.871000
8.780000
```

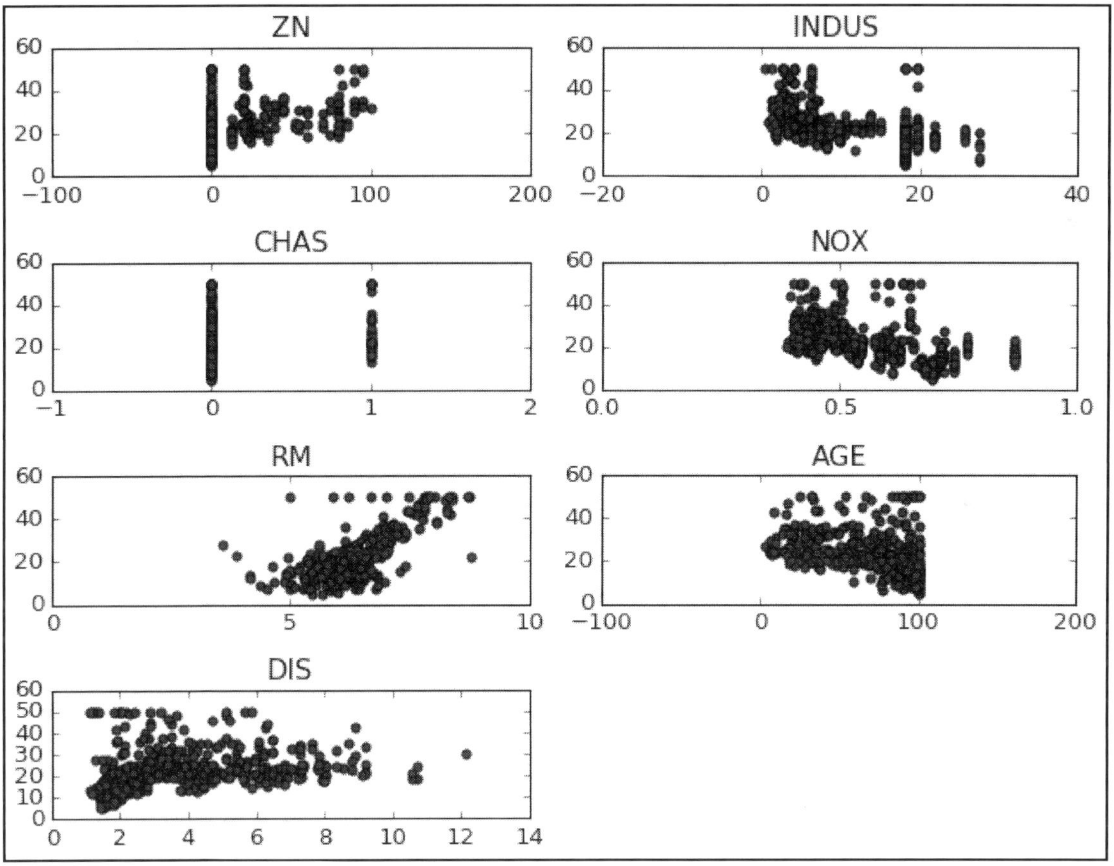

Model architecture

The model we will employ in this example is simple but has almost all the elements that we will need to tackle a more complex one.

In the following diagram, we see the different actors of the whole setup: a model, the **CostFunction**, and the **gradients**. A really useful feature of TensorFlow is the ability to automatically differentiate between the **Model** and functions.

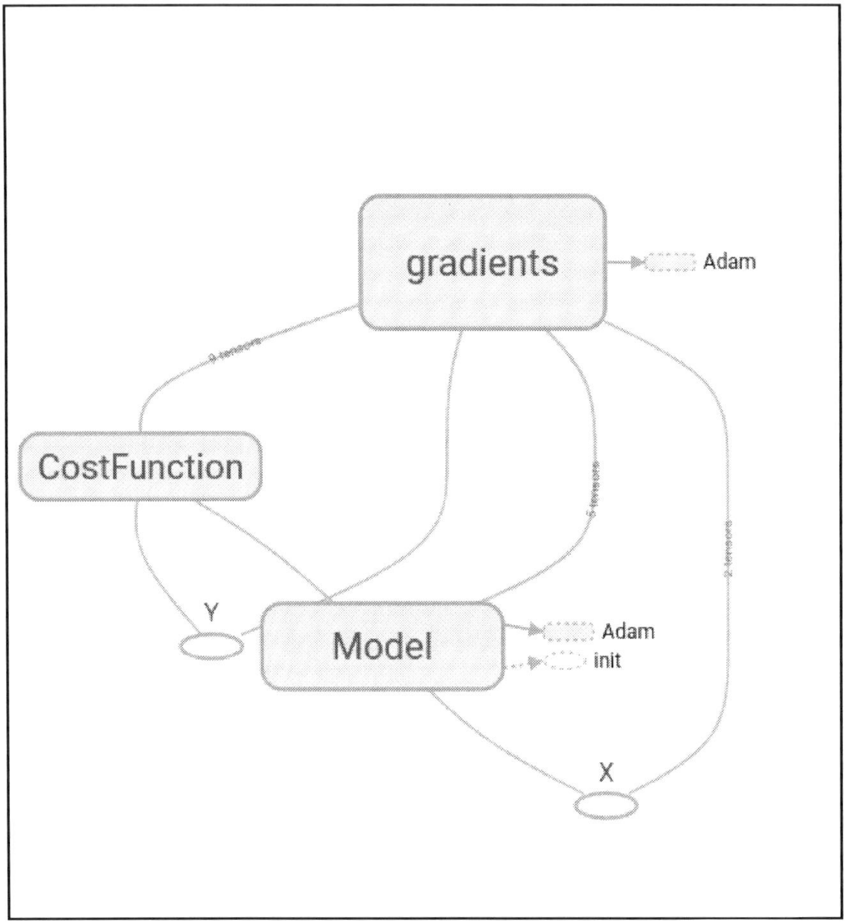

Here, we can find the definition of the variables represented in the preceding section: w, b, and the model linear equation.

```
X = tf.placeholder("float", name="X") # create symbolic variables
Y = tf.placeholder("float", name = "Y")

withtf.name_scope("Model"):
    w = tf.Variable(tf.random_normal([2], stddev=0.01), name="b0") # create
a shared variable
    b = tf.Variable(tf.random_normal([2], stddev=0.01), name="b1") # create
a shared variable
def model(X, w, b):
returntf.mul(X, w) + b # We just define the line as X*w + b0
y_model = model(X, w, b)
```

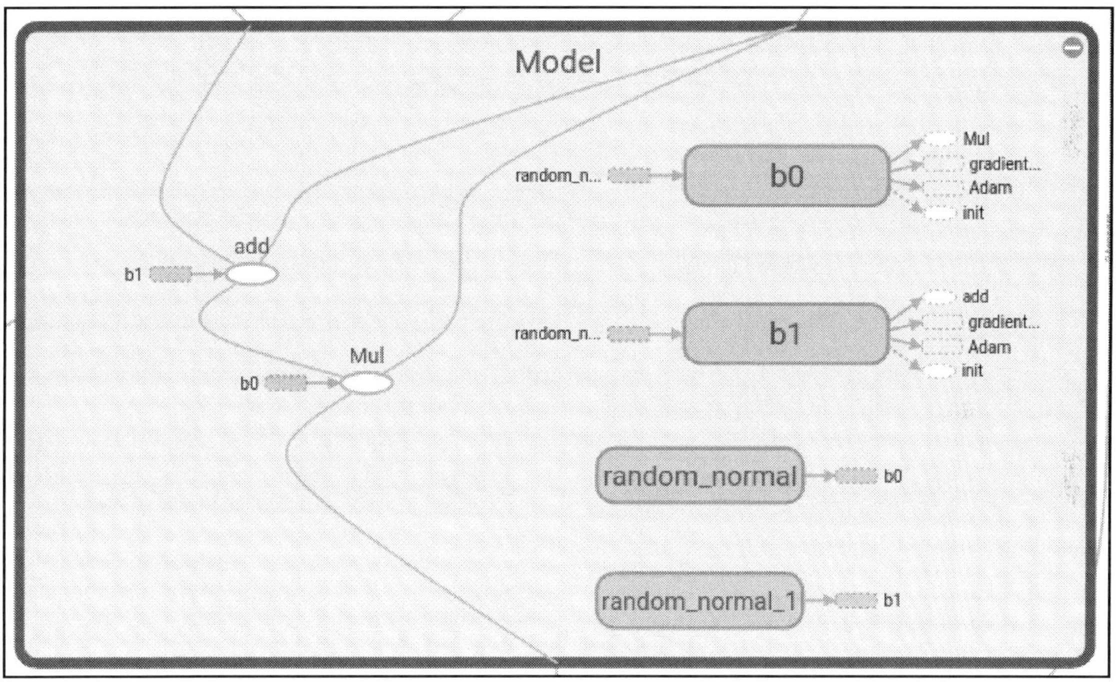

Loss function description and Optimizer loop

In this example, we will use the commonly employed mean squared error, but this time with a multivariable; so we apply reduce_mean to collect error values across the different dimensions:

```
withtf.name_scope("CostFunction"):
    cost = tf.reduce_mean(tf.pow(Y-y_model, 2)) # use sqr error for cost
function
train_op = tf.train.AdamOptimizer(0.1).minimize(cost)
```

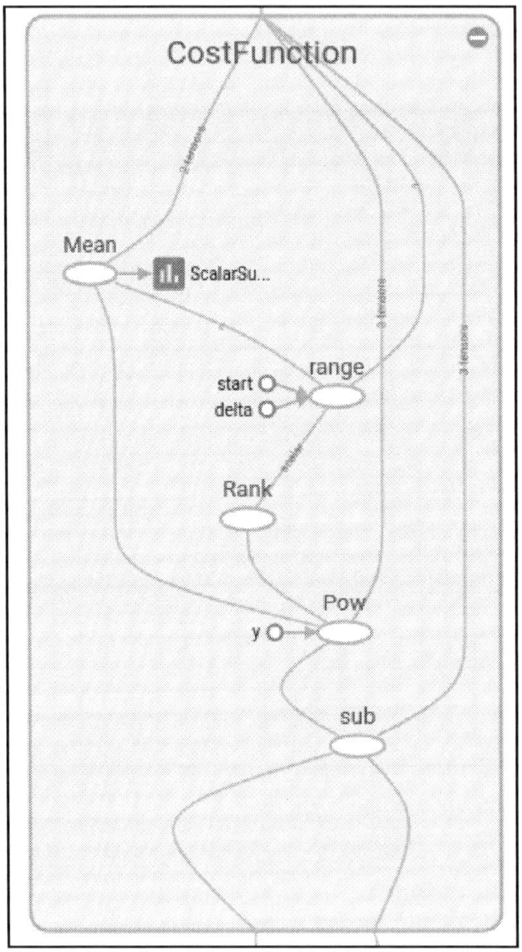

```
 for a in range (1,10):
    cost1=0.0
fori, j in zip(xvalues, yvalues):
sess.run(train_op, feed_dict={X: i, Y: j})
        cost1+=sess.run(cost, feed_dict={X: i, Y: i})/506.00
        #writer.add_summary(summary_str, i)
xvalues, yvalues = shuffle (xvalues, yvalues)
```

Stop condition

The stop condition will simply consist of training the parameters with all data samples for the number of epochs determined in the outer loop.

Results description

The following is the result:

```
1580.53295174
[ 2.25225258  1.30112672]
[ 0.80297691  0.22137061]
1512.3965525
[ 4.62365675  2.90244412]
[ 1.16225874  0.28009811]
1495.47174799
[ 6.52791834  4.29297304]
[ 0.824792270.17988272]
...
1684.6247849
[ 29.71323776  29.96078873]
[-0.68271929 -0.13493828]
1688.25864746
[ 29.78564262  30.09841156]
[-0.58272243 -0.08323665]
1684.27538102
[ 29.75390816  30.13044167]
[-0.59861398 -0.11895057]
```

From the results, we see that in the final stage of the training, the modeling lines settle on the following coefficients simultaneously:

price = 0.6 x Industry + 29.75

price = 0.1 x Age + 30.13

Full source code

The following is the complete source code:

```
import matplotlib.pyplot as plt
import tensorflow as tf
import tensorflow.contrib.learn as skflow
from sklearn.utils import shuffle
import numpy as np
import pandas as pd

df = pd.read_csv("data/boston.csv", header=0)
printdf.describe()

f, ax1 = plt.subplots()
plt.figure() # Create a new figure

y = df['MEDV']

for i in range (1,8):
    number = 420 + i
    ax1.locator_params(nbins=3)
    ax1 = plt.subplot(number)
    plt.title(list(df)[i])
    ax1.scatter(df[df.columns[i]],y) #Plot a scatter draw of the datapoints
plt.tight_layout(pad=0.4, w_pad=0.5, h_pad=1.0)


X = tf.placeholder("float", name="X") # create symbolic variables
Y = tf.placeholder("float", name = "Y")


with tf.name_scope("Model"):

    w = tf.Variable(tf.random_normal([2], stddev=0.01), name="b0") # create
a shared variable
    b = tf.Variable(tf.random_normal([2], stddev=0.01), name="b1") # create
a shared variable
```

```
    def model(X, w, b):
        return tf.mul(X, w) + b # We just define the line as X*w + b0

    y_model = model(X, w, b)

with tf.name_scope("CostFunction"):
    cost = tf.reduce_mean(tf.pow(Y-y_model, 2)) # use sqr error for cost
function

train_op = tf.train.AdamOptimizer(0.001).minimize(cost)


sess = tf.Session()
init = tf.initialize_all_variables()
tf.train.write_graph(sess.graph, '/home/bonnin/linear2','graph.pbtxt')
cost_op = tf.scalar_summary("loss", cost)
merged = tf.merge_all_summaries()
sess.run(init)
writer = tf.train.SummaryWriter('/home/bonnin/linear2', sess.graph)

xvalues = df[[df.columns[2], df.columns[4]]].values.astype(float)
yvalues = df[df.columns[12]].values.astype(float)
b0temp=b.eval(session=sess)
b1temp=w.eval(session=sess)


for a in range (1,10):
    cost1=0.0
for i, j in zip(xvalues, yvalues):
sess.run(train_op, feed_dict={X: i, Y: j})
        cost1+=sess.run(cost, feed_dict={X: i, Y: i})/506.00
        #writer.add_summary(summary_str, i)
xvalues, yvalues = shuffle (xvalues, yvalues)
print (cost1)
b0temp=b.eval(session=sess)
b1temp=w.eval(session=sess)
print (b0temp)
print (b1temp)
#plt.plot (trX, b0temp + b1temp * trX )
```

Summary

In this chapter, we built our first complete model with a standard loss function using TensorFlow's training utilities. We also built a multivariate model to account for more than one dimension to calculate regression. Apart from that, we used TensorBoard to observe the variable's behavior during the training phase.

In the next chapter, we will begin working with non-linear models, through which we will get closer to the domain of neural networks, which is the main supported field of TensorFlow and the area where its utilities provide great value.

4
Logistic Regression

In the previous chapter, we have seen an approach to model a part of reality as a linear function, which has independent variables and bias minimized an error function.

This particular analysis is not enough except for some very clearly defined problems, with expected results being continuous variables and function.

But what would happen if we are faced with data with qualitative dependent variables? For example, the presence or absence of a determinate feature; has a subject got blond hair? Has the patient had a previous illness?

These are the kinds of problem that we will be working on in this chapter.

Problem description

The kind of problem that linear regression aims to solve is not the prediction of a value based on a continuous function, this time we want to know the **probability** for a sample of pertaining to a determined class.

In this chapter, we will rely on a generalization of the linear model solving a regression, but with the final objective of solving classification problems where we have to apply tags or assign all the elements from an observation set to predefined groups.

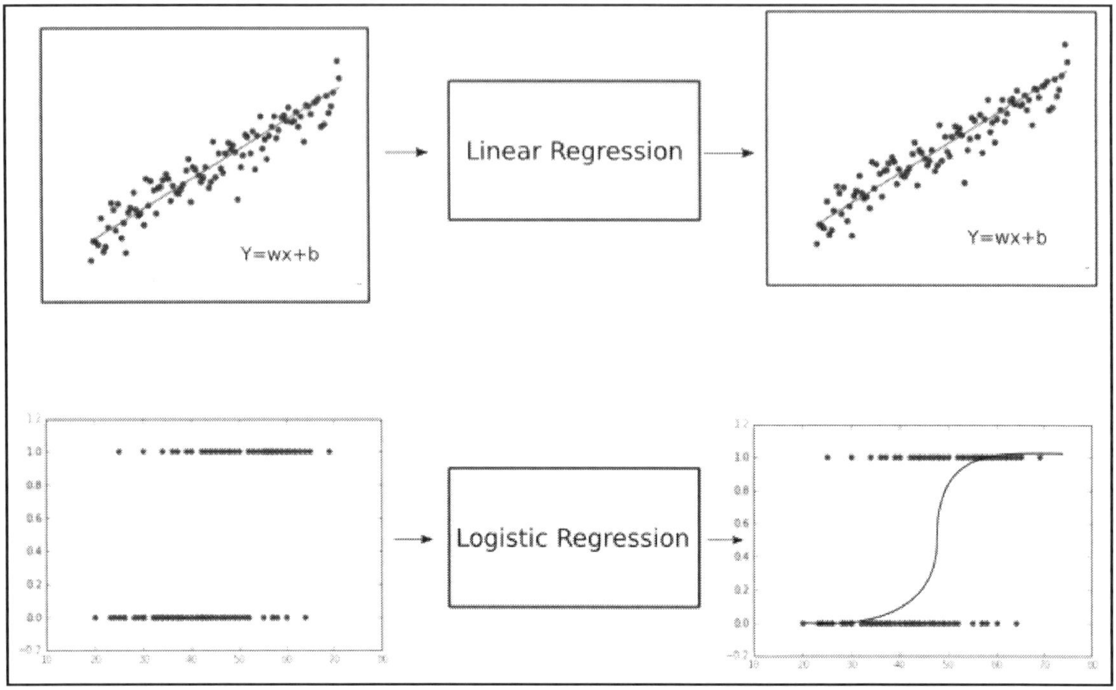

In the preceding figure, we can see how the old and new problems can be classified. The first one (linear regression) can be imagined as a continuum of increasingly growing values.

The other is a domain where the output can have just two different values, based on the x value. In the particular case of the second graphic, we can see a particular bias to one of the options, toward the extremes: on the left there is a bias towards the 0 y value, and to the right the bias is towards a value of 1.

This terminology can be bit tricky given that even when we are doing a regression, thus looking for a continuous value, in reality, the final objective is building a prediction for a classification problem, with discrete variables.

The key here is to understand that we will obtain probabilities of an item pertaining to a class, and not a totally discrete value.

Logistic function predecessor – the logit functions

Before we study the logistic function, we will review the original function on which it is based, and which gives it some of its more general properties.

Essentially, when we talk about the `logit` function, we are working with the function of a random variable *p*, more specifically, one corresponding with a **Bernoulli distribution**.

Bernoulli distribution

Before explaining theoretical details it is worthwhile noting that a Bernoulli distribution is a random variable that:

- Takes a value of 0 with a failure probability of $q = 1 - p$
- Takes a value of 1 with a success probability of p

It can be expressed as follows (for a random variable X with Bernoulli distribution):

$$\Pr(X = 1) = 1 - \Pr(X = 0) = 1 - q = p$$

This is the kind of probability distribution that will represent the probability of occurrence of the events as binary options, just as we want to represent our variables (existence of features, event occurrence, causality of phenomena, and so on).

Link function

As we are trying to build a generalized linear model, we want to start from a linear function, and from the dependent variable, obtain a mapping to a probability distribution.

Since the options are of a binary nature, the normally chosen distribution is the recently mentioned Bernoulli distribution, and the link function, leaning toward the logistic function, is the `logit` function.

Logit function

One of the possible variables that we could utilize, is the natural logarithm of the odds that *p* equals one. This function is called the `logit` function:

$$\text{logit}(p) = \log\left(\frac{p}{1-p}\right)$$

We can also call the `logit` function a log-odd function, because we are calculating the log of the odds *(p/1-p)* for a given probability *p*:

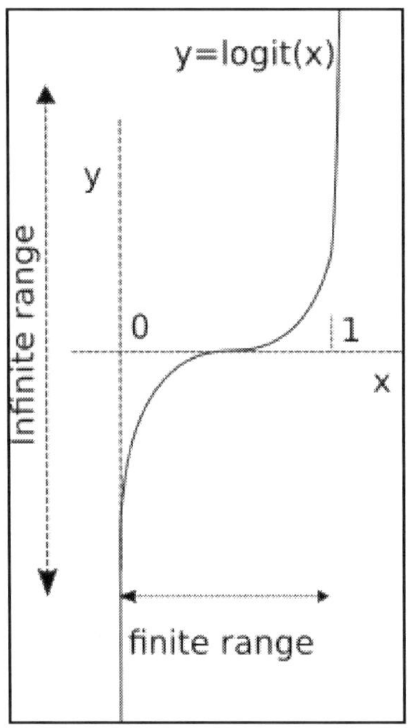

So, as we can visually infer, replacing *X* with the combination of the independent variables, no matter the value of them, replacing *X* with any occurrence from minus infinity to infinity, we are scaling the response to be within *0* and *1*.

The importance of the logit inverse

Suppose that we calculate the inverse of the `logit` function. This will let us write the following function:

$$\text{logit}^{-1}(\alpha) = \text{logistic}(\alpha) = \frac{1}{1+\exp(-\alpha)} = \frac{\exp(\alpha)}{\exp(\alpha)+1}$$

This function is a `sigmoid` function.

The logistic function

The logistic function will serve us to represent the binary options in our new regression tasks.

In the following figure, you will find the graphical representation of the `sigmoid` function:

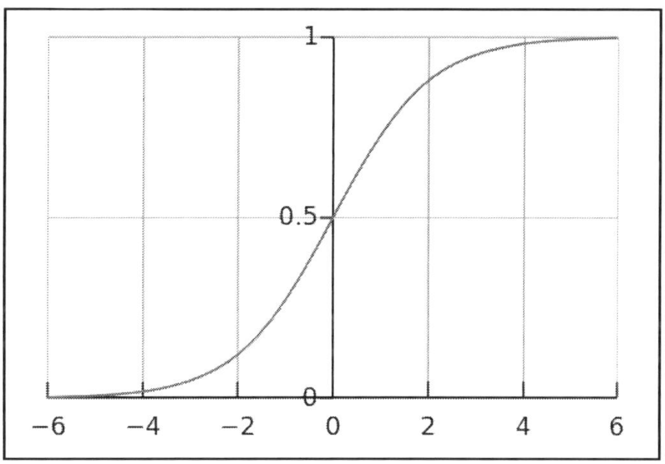

Graphical representation of the logistic function or Sigmoid

Logistic function as a linear modeling generalization

The logistic function *δ(t)* is defined as follows:

$$\sigma(t) = \frac{e^t}{e^t + 1} = \frac{1}{1 + e^{-t}}$$

The normal interpretation of this equation is that *t* represents a simple independent variable. But we will improve this model, and will assume that *t* is a linear function of a single explanatory variable *x* (the case where t is a linear combination of multiple explanatory variables is treated similarly).

We will then express *t* as the following:

$$t = wx + b$$

Final estimated regression equation

So we start from the following equation:

$$\text{login}(p) = \text{In}\left(\frac{p}{1-p}\right) = wx + b$$

With all these elements, we can calculate the regression equation, which will give us the regressed probability:

$$\hat{p} = \frac{e^{\beta_0 + \beta_1 x_1}}{1 + e^{\beta_0 + \beta_1 x_1}}$$

The following graphic will show how the mapping from arbitrary range will be finally transformed to *range [0, 1]*, which can be interpreted as probability p of the occurrence of the event being represented:

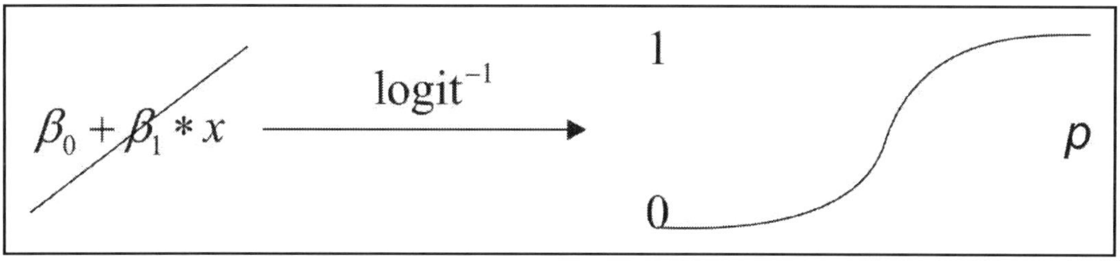

What effects will make changes to the parameters of the linear function? They are the values that will change the central slope and the displacement from zero of the `sigmoid` function, allowing it to more exactly reduce the error between the regressed values and the real data points.

Properties of the logistic function

Every curve in the function space can be described by the possible objectives it could be applied to. In the case of the logistic function, they are:

- Model the probability of an event *p* depending on one or more independent variables. For example, the probability of being awarded a prize, given previous qualifications.
- Estimate (this is the regression part) *p* for a determined observation, related to the possibility of the event not occurring.
- Predict the effect of the change of independent variables on a binary response.
- Classify observations by calculating the probability of an item being of a determined class.

Loss function

In the previous section we saw our approximated function, which will model the probability of a sample being of a particular class. In order to measure how well we are approximating to the solution, we will look for a carefully chosen *loss* function.

This *loss* function is expressed as:

$$loss = -\sum_i y_i . \log(ypred_i) + (1 - y_i) . \log(1 - ypred_i)$$

The main property of this *loss* function is that it doesn't penalize the error in a similar manner, the error penalization factor grows asymptotically when the error increases far beyond 0.5.

Multiclass application – softmax regression

Up until now, we have been classifying for the case of only two classes, or in probabilistic language, event occurrence probabilities, *p*.

In the case of having more than two classes to decide from, there are two main approaches; one versus one, and one versus all.

- The first technique consists of calculating many models that represent the probability of every class against all the other ones.
- The second one consists of one set of probabilities, in which we represent the probability of one class against all the others.
- This second approach is the output format of the `softmax` regression, a generalization of the logistic regression for n classes.

So we will be changing, for training samples, from binary labels ($y(i)\varepsilon\{0,1\}$), to vector labels, using the handle $y(i)\varepsilon\{1,...,K\}$, where *K* is the number of classes, and the label Y can take on *K* different values, rather than only two.

So for this particular technique, given a test input *X*, we want to estimate the probability that $P(y=k|x)$ for each value of $k=1,...,K$. The `softmax` regression will output a *K*-dimensional vector (whose elements sum to 1), giving us our *K* estimated probabilities.

In the following diagram, we represent the mapping that occurs on the probability mappings of the uniclass and multiclass logistic regression:

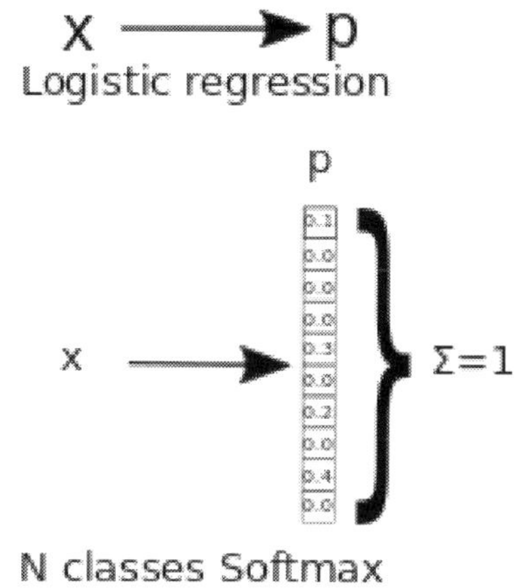

Cost function

The cost function of the `softmax` function is an adapted cross entropy function, which is not linear, and thus penalizes the big order function differences much more than the very small ones.

$$loss = \sum_{i} \sum_{c} y_c . \log(ypred_c)$$

Here, *c* is the class number and *I* the individual train sample index, and *yc* is 1 for the expected class and 0 for the rest.

Expanding this equation, we get the following:

$$loss = \sum_{i} \sum_{c} y_c \cdot \frac{e^{-x_c}}{\sum_{j=0}^{C-1} \log\left(e^{-x_j}\right)}$$

Data normalization for iterative methods

As we will see in the following sections, for logistic regression we will be using the `gradient descent` method for minimizing a cost function.

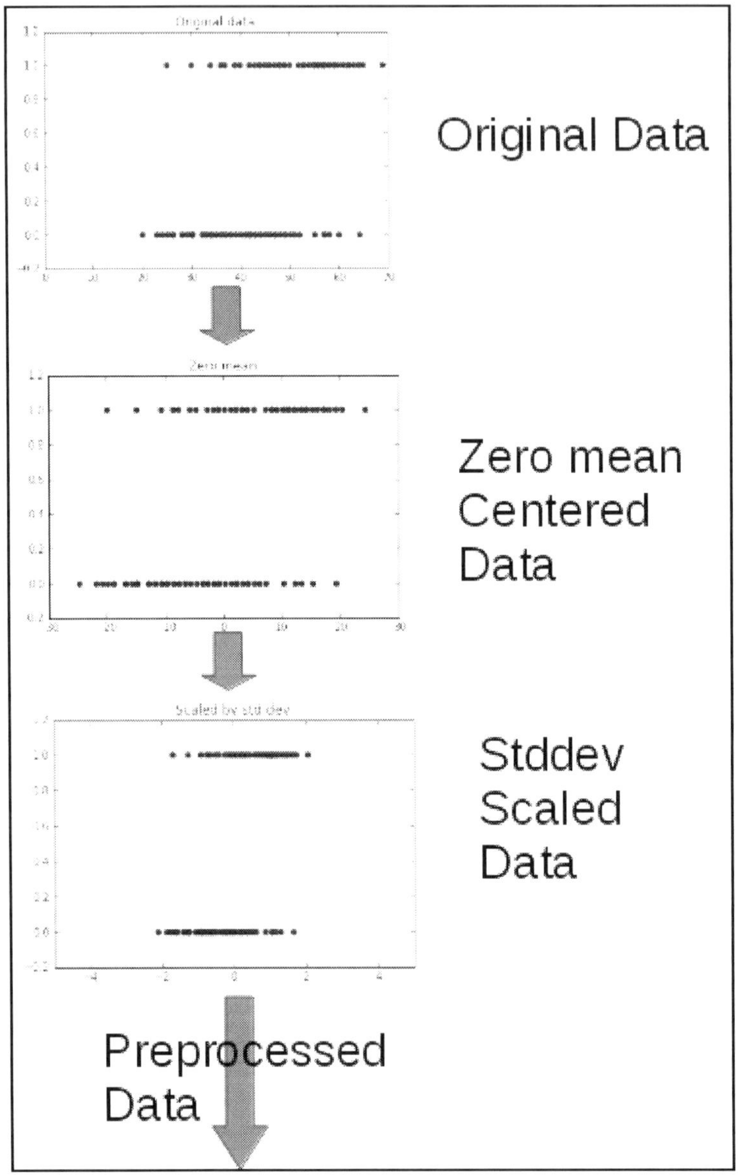

This method is very sensitive to the form and the distribution of the feature data.

For this reason, we will be doing some preprocessing in order to get better and faster converging results.

We will leave the theoretical reasons for this method to other books, but we will summarize the reason saying that with normalization, we are smoothing the error surface, allowing the iterative `gradient descent` to reach the minimum error faster.

One hot representation of outputs

In order to use the `softmax` function as the regression function, we must use a type of encoding known as one hot. This form of encoding simply transforms the numerical integer value of a variable into an array, where a list of values is transformed into a list of arrays, each with a length of as many elements as the maximum value of the list, and the value of each elements is represented by adding a one on the index of the value, and leaving the others at zero.

For example, this will be the representation of the list [1, 3, 2, 4] in one hot encoding:

```
[[0 1 0 0 0]
[0 0 0 1 0]
[0 0 1 0 0]
[0 0 0 0 1]]
```

Example 1 – univariate logistic regression

In this first example, we will work approximating the probability of the presence of heart disease, using an univariate logistic regression, being this variable, the patients age.

Useful libraries and methods

Since version 0.8, TensorFlow has provided a means of generating one hot. The function used for this generation is `tf.one_hot`, which has this form:

```
    tf.one_hot(indices, depth, on_value=1, off_value=0, axis=None,
dtype=tf.float32, name=None)
```

This functions generates a generalized one hot encoding data structure, which can specify the values, axis of generation, data type, and so on.

In the resulting tensors, the indicated values of the indexes will take the `on_value`, default `1`, and the others will have `off_value`, default `0`.

`Dtype` is the data type of the generated tensor; the default is `float32`.

The depth variable defines how many columns each element will have. We suppose it logically should be `max(indices) + 1`, but it could be also cut.

TensorFlow's softmax implementation

The included method for applying`softmax` regression in TensorFlow is `tf.nn.log_softmax, with the following form:`

```
tf.nn.log_softmax(logits, name=None)
```

Here, the arguments are:

- `logits`: A tensor must be one of the following types: `float32`, `float64` 2D with shape `[batch_size, num_classes]`
- `name`: A name for the operation (optional)

This function returns a tensor with the same type and shape as `logits`.

Dataset description and loading

The first case we will cover is where we want to fit a logistic regression, measuring only one variable and we only have a binary possible result.

The CHDAGE dataset

For the first simple example, we will use a very simple and studied dataset, first known for being published in the book; *Applied Logistic Regression-Third Edition, David W. Hosmer Jr., Stanley Lemeshow, Rodney X. Sturdivant, by Wiley.*

Lists the `age` in years (AGE), and presence or absence of evidence of significant **Coronary Heart Disease** (**CHD**) for 100 subjects in a hypothetical study of risk factors for heart disease. The table also contains an identifier variable (ID) and an age group variable (AGEGRP). The outcome variable is CHD, which is coded with a value of `0` to indicate that CHD is absent, or `1` to indicate that it is present in the individual. In general, any two values could be used, but we have found it most convenient to use zero and one. We refer to this data set as the CHDAGE data.

CHDAGE dataset format

The CHDAGE dataset is a two-column CSV file that we will download from an external repository.

In the `chapter 1`, *Exploring and Transforming Data,* we used native TensorFlow methods for the reading of the dataset. In this chapter, we will use a complementary and popular library to get the data.

The cause for this new addition is that, given that the dataset only has 100 tuples, it is practical to just have to read it in one line, and also we get simple but powerful analysis methods for free, provided by the `pandas` library.

So in the first stage of this project, we will start loading an instance of the CHDAGE dataset, then we will print vital statistics about the data, and then proceed to preprocessing.

After doing some plots of the data, we will build a model composed of the activation function, which will be a `softmax` function for special cases where it becomes a standard logistic regression; that is when there are only two classes (existence, or not, of the illness).

Dataset loading and preprocessing implementation

First, we import the required libraries, and indicate that all our `matplotlib` programs will be included inline (if we are using Jupyter):

```
>>> import pandas as pd
>>> import numpy as np
>>> %matplotlib inline
>>> import matplotlib.pyplot as plt
```

Then we read the data and ask `pandas` to check important statistical information about the dataset:

```
>>> df = pd.read_csv("data/CHD.csv", header=0)
>>> print df.describe()
```

```
age         chd
count  100.000000  100.00000
mean    44.380000    0.43000
std     11.721327    0.49757
min     20.000000    0.00000
25%     34.750000    0.00000
50%     44.000000    0.00000
75%     55.000000    1.00000
max     69.000000    1.000000
```

We then proceed with drawing the data to get an idea of the data:

```
plt.figure() # Create a new figure
plt.scatter(df['age'],df['chd']) #Plot a scatter draw of the random
datapoints
```

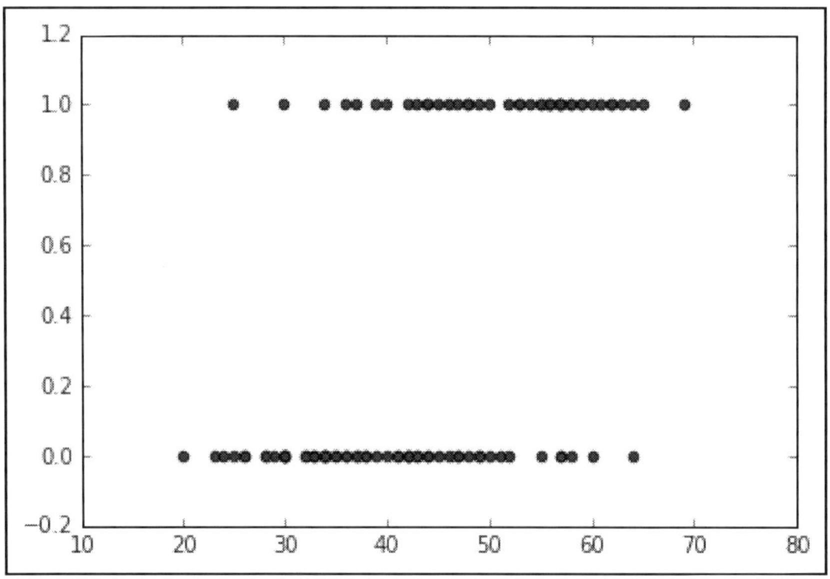

Model architecture

Here, we describe the sections of the code where we will build the elements of the model, starting from the following variables:

```
learning_rate = 0.8 #Learning speed
batch_size = 100 #number of samples for the batch
display_step = 2 #number of steps before showing progress
```

Here, we create the initial variables and placeholders for the graph, the univariate `x` and `y` float values:

```
x = tf.placeholder("float", [None, 1]) # Placeholder for the 1D data
y = tf.placeholder("float", [None, 2]) # Placeholder for the classes (2)
```

Now we will create linear model variables, which will be modified and updated as the model fitting goes on:

```
W = tf.Variable(tf.zeros([1, 2]))
b = tf.Variable(tf.zeros([2]))
```

And finally, we will build the activation function applying the `softmax` operation to the linear function:

```
activation = tf.nn.softmax(tf.matmul(x, W) + b)
```

Loss function description and optimizer loop

Here, we just define the cross correlation function as the `loss` function, and define the `optimizer` operation, which will be the `gradient descent`. This will be explained in the following chapters; for now, you can see it as a black box that will change the variables until the loss is minimized:

```
cost = tf.reduce_mean(-tf.reduce_sum(y*tf.log(activation),
reduction_indices=1))
optimizer = tf.train.GradientDescentOptimizer(learning_rate).minimize(cost)
#Iterate through all the epochs
for epoch in range(training_epochs):
        avg_cost = 0.
        total_batch = 400/batch_size
# Loop over all batches
        for i in range(total_batch):
            # Transform the array into a one hot format

        temp=tf.one_hot(indices = df['chd'].values, depth=2, on_value = 1,
```

```
off_value = 0, axis = -1 , name = "a")
        batch_xs, batch_ys =(np.transpose([df['age']])-44.38)/11.721327,
temp

        # Fit training using batch data
        sess.run(optimizer, feed_dict={x: batch_xs.astype(float), y:
batch_ys.eval()})

        # Compute average loss, suming the corrent cost divided by the
batch total number
        avg_cost += sess.run(cost, feed_dict={x: batch_xs.astype(float), y:
batch_ys.eval()})/total_batch
```

Stop condition

The process will simply stop once the data has been training according to training epochs times.

Results description

This will be the output of the program:

```
Epoch: 0001 cost= 0.638730764
[ 0.04824295 -0.04824295]
[[-0.17459483  0.17459483]]
Epoch: 0002 cost= 0.589489654
[ 0.08091066 -0.08091066]
[[-0.29231569  0.29231566]]
Epoch: 0003 cost= 0.565953553
[ 0.10427245 -0.10427245]
[[-0.37499282  0.37499279]]
Epoch: 0004 cost= 0.553756475
[ 0.12176144 -0.12176143]
[[-0.43521613  0.4352161 ]]
Epoch: 0005 cost= 0.547019333
[ 0.13527818 -0.13527818]
[[-0.48031801  0.48031798]]
```

Fitting function representations across epochs

In the following image we represent the progression of the fitting function across the different epochs:

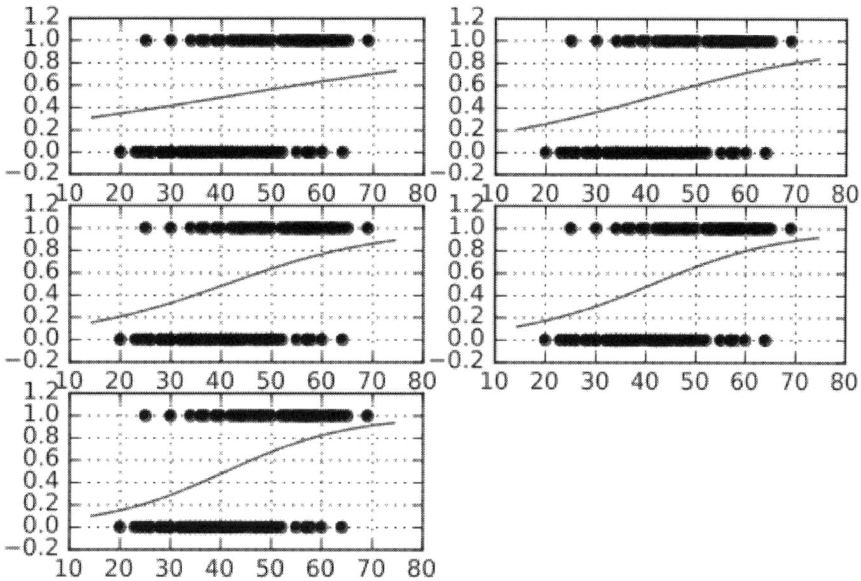

Full source code

Here is the complete source code:

```
import pandas as pd
import numpy as np
get_ipython().magic(u'matplotlib inline')
import matplotlib.pyplot as plt
import tensorflow as tf

df = pd.read_csv("data/CHD.csv", header=0)
# Parameters

learning_rate = 0.2
training_epochs = 5
```

```
batch_size = 100
display_step = 1
sess = tf.Session()
b=np.zeros((100,2))

# tf Graph Input

x = tf.placeholder("float", [None, 1])
y = tf.placeholder("float", [None, 2])

# Create model
# Set model weights
W = tf.Variable(tf.zeros([1, 2]))
b = tf.Variable(tf.zeros([2]))

# Construct model
activation = tf.nn.softmax(tf.matmul(x, W) + b)
# Minimize error using cross entropy
cost = tf.reduce_mean(-tf.reduce_sum(y*tf.log(activation),
reduction_indices=1)) # Cross entropy
optimizer = tf.train.GradientDescentOptimizer(learning_rate).minimize(cost)
# Gradient Descent

# Initializing the variables
init = tf.initialize_all_variables()

# Launch the graph

with tf.Session() as sess:
    tf.train.write_graph(sess.graph, './graphs','graph.pbtxt')
    sess.run(init)
    writer = tf.train.SummaryWriter('./graphs', sess.graph)
    #Initialize the graph structure

    graphnumber=321

    #Generate a new graph
    plt.figure(1)

    #Iterate through all the epochs
    for epoch in range(training_epochs):
        avg_cost = 0.
        total_batch = 400/batch_size
        # Loop over all batches

        for i in range(total_batch):
            # Transform the array into a one hot format
```

```
            temp=tf.one_hot(indices = df['chd'].values, depth=2, on_value =
1, off_value = 0, axis = -1 , name = "a")
            batch_xs, batch_ys =
(np.transpose([df['age']])-44.38)/11.721327, temp

            # Fit training using batch data
            sess.run(optimizer, feed_dict={x: batch_xs.astype(float), y:
batch_ys.eval()})

            # Compute average loss, suming the corrent cost divided by the
batch total number
            avg_cost += sess.run(cost, feed_dict={x:
batch_xs.astype(float), y: batch_ys.eval()})/total_batch
        # Display logs per epoch step

        if epoch % display_step == 0:
            print "Epoch:", '%05d' % (epoch+1), "cost=",
"{:.8f}".format(avg_cost)

            #Generate a new graph, and add it to the complete graph

            trX = np.linspace(-30, 30, 100)
            print (b.eval())
            print (W.eval())
            Wdos=2*W.eval()[0][0]/11.721327
            bdos=2*b.eval()[0]

            # Generate the probabiliy function
            trY = np.exp(-(Wdos*trX)+bdos)/(1+np.exp(-(Wdos*trX)+bdos) )

            # Draw the samples and the probability function, whithout the
normalization
            plt.subplot(graphnumber)
            graphnumber=graphnumber+1

            #Plot a scatter draw of the random datapoints
            plt.scatter((df['age']),df['chd'])
            plt.plot(trX+44.38,trY) #Plot a scatter draw of the random
datapoints
            plt.grid(True)

        #Plot the final graph
        plt.savefig("test.svg")
```

Graphical representation

Using the TensorBoard utility, we will see the operation chain. Note that in half of the operation graphics we define the main global operation (doftmas), and the gradient operations applied to the remaining terms, which are needed to do the `loss` function minimization. This is a theme to be talked about in the following chapters.

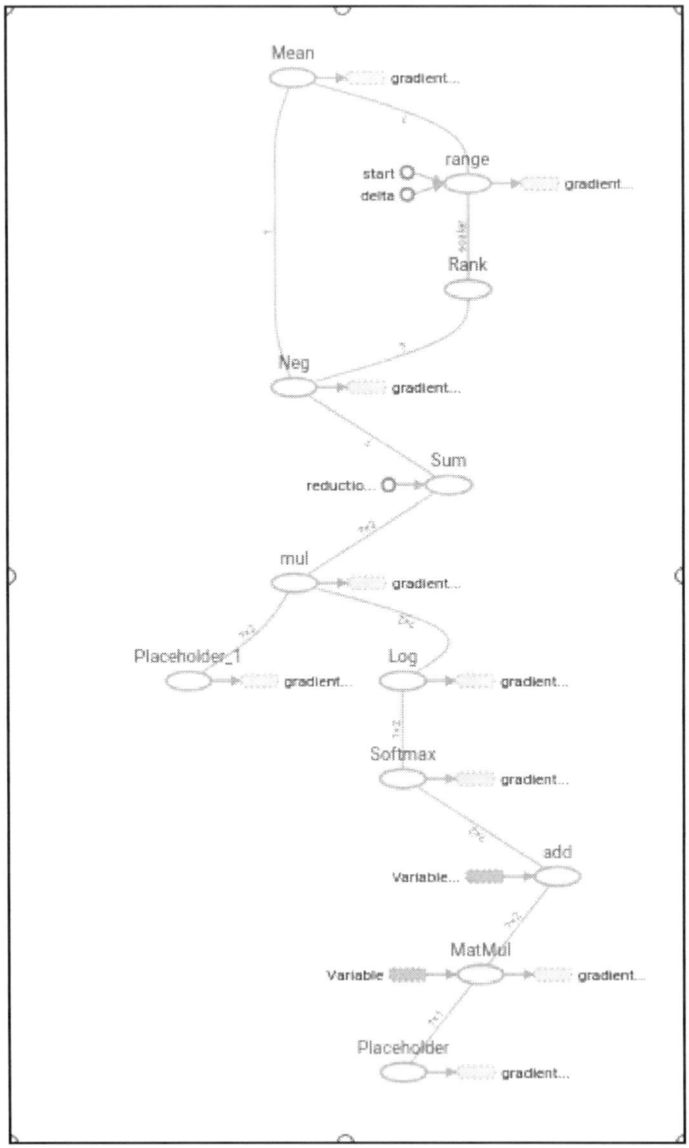

Example 2 – Univariate logistic regression with skflow

In this example, we will explore the univariate examples domain, but this time we will use help from a new library, which eases the model building for us, called `skflow`.

Useful libraries and methods

In the field of machine learning libraries, there is a great number and variety of alternatives. One of the most well-known is `sklearn`, which we talked about in `Chapter 2`, *Clustering*.

Very early after the release of TensorFlow, a new contribution library appeared, called `skflow`, with the main objective of emulating the interface and workflow of `sklearn`, which is much more succinct to work in this TensorFlow session environment.

In the following example, we will repeat the analysis of the previous regression, but using the `skflow` interface.

In the example, we will also see how skflow automatically generates a detailed and very organized graph for the regression model, just setting a log directory as a parameter.

Dataset description

The dataset loading stage is the same as the previous example, using the `pandas` library:

```
import pandas as pd

df = pd.read_csv("data/CHD.csv", header=0)
print df.describe()
```

Model architecture

Here is the code snippet for `my_model`:

```
 def my_model(X, y):
    return skflow.models.logistic_regression(X, y)

X1 =a.fit_transform(df['age'].astype(float))
y1 = df['chd'].values
classifier = skflow.TensorFlowEstimator(model_fn=my_model, n_classes=2)
```

Here we can see a detailed view of the logistic regression stage, with the `softmax` classifier:

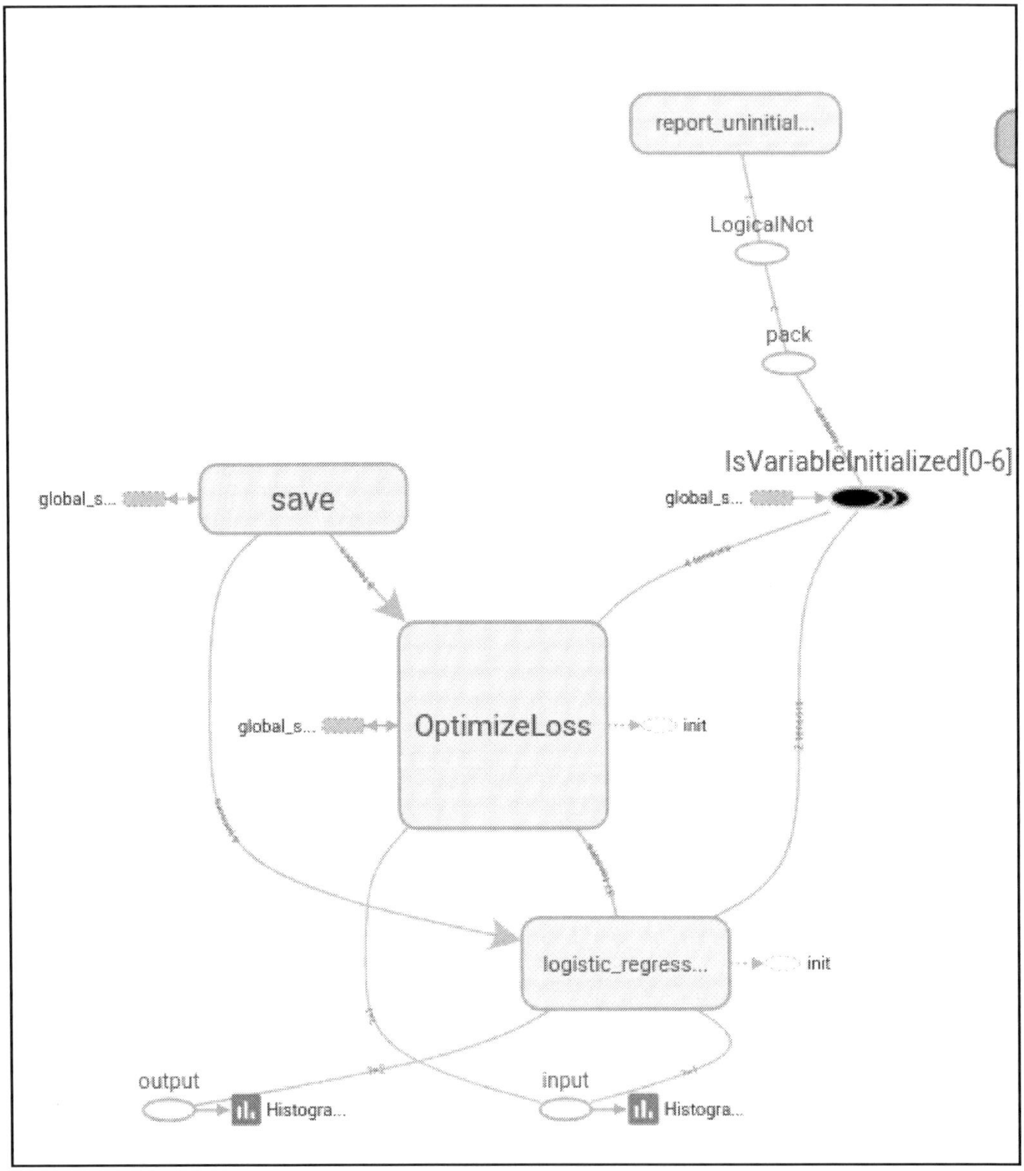

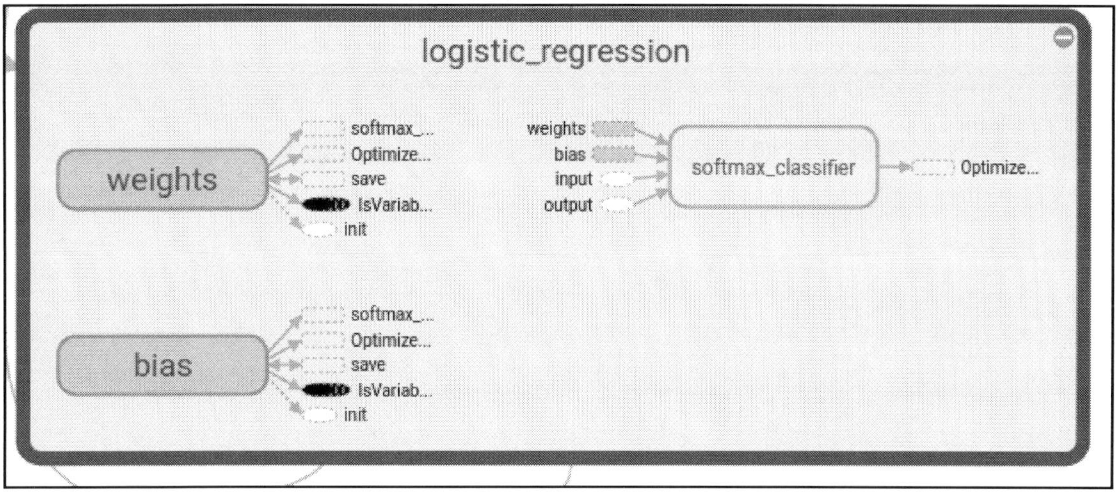

Results description

```
score = metrics.accuracy_score(df['chd'].astype(float),
classifier.predict(X))
print("Accuracy: %f" % score)
```

The output result is a respectable (for the simplicity of the model) 74% accuracy:

```
Accuracy: 0.740000
```

Full source code

Here is the complete source code:

```
import tensorflow.contrib.learn as skflow
from sklearn import datasets, metrics, preprocessing
import numpy as np
import pandas as pd

df = pd.read_csv("data/CHD.csv", header=0)
print df.describe()

def my_model(X, y):
    return skflow.models.logistic_regression(X, y)

a = preprocessing.StandardScaler()
```

```
X1 =a.fit_transform(df['age'].astype(float))

y1 = df['chd'].values


classifier = skflow.TensorFlowEstimator(model_fn=my_model, n_classes=2)
classifier.fit(X1,y1 , logdir='/tmp/logistic')



score = metrics.accuracy_score(df['chd'].astype(float),
classifier.predict(X))
print("Accuracy: %f" % score)
```

Summary

In this chapter, we have learned a new modeling technique, the logistic function, and began with a simple approach to the task of classification.

We also learned a new approach for the reading of text-based data via the `pandas` library.

Additionally, we have seen a complementary approach to the classical workflow, working with the `skflow` library.

In the next chapter, we will start working with more complex architectures, and enter the field where the TensorFlow library excels: the training, testing, and final implementation of neural networks to solve real-world problems.

5
Simple FeedForward Neural Networks

Neural Networks are really the area of Machine Learning where Tensorflow excels. Many types of architectures and algorithms can be implemented with it, along with the additional advantage of having a symbolic engine incorporated, which will really help in the training of more complex setups.

With this chapter, we are beginning to harness the power of high-performance primitives for solving increasingly complex problems with a high number of supported input variables.

In this chapter, we will cover the following topics:

- Preliminary concepts of neural networks
- Neural network projects on non-linear synthetic function regression
- Projects on predicting car fuel efficiency with nonlinear regression
- Learning to classify wines andmulticlass classification

Preliminary concepts

To build a simple framework into the neural network components and architectures, we will give a simple and straightforward build of the original concepts which paved the way to the current,complexand variedNeural Network landscape.

Artificial neurons

An **artificial neuron** is a mathematical function conceived as a model for a real biological neuron.

Its main features are that it receives one or more inputs (training data), *and sums them to produce an output*. Additionally, the sums are normally weighted (weight and bias), and the sum is passed to a **nonlinear function** (Activation function or transfer function).

Original example – the Perceptron

The **Perceptron** is one of the simplest ways of implementing an artificial neuron and it's an algorithm that dates back from the 1950s, first implemented in the 1960s.

It is basically an algorithm that learns a binary classification function, which maps a real function with a single binary one:

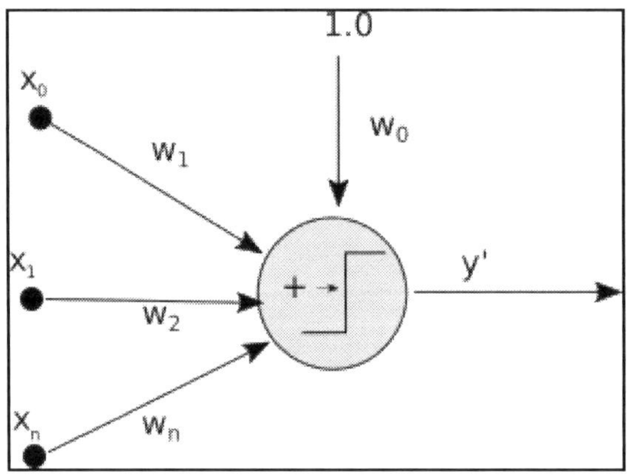

The following image shows a single layer perceptron

Perceptron algorithm

The simplified algorithm for the perceptron is:

1. Initialize the weights with a random distribution (normally low values)
2. Select an input vector and present it to the network,
3. Compute the output y' of the network for the input vector specified and the values of the weights.

4. The function for a perceptron is:

$$f(x) = \begin{cases} 1 & \text{if } w \cdot x + b > 0 \\ 0 & \text{otherwise} \end{cases}$$

5. If y' ≠ y modify all connections w_i by adding the changes $\Delta w = yx_i$
6. Return to step 2.

Neural network layers

The single layer perceptron can be generalized to many layers connected to eachother, but there is an issue remaining;the representing function is a linear combination of the inputs, and the perceptron being just a kind of linear classifier,there is no possibility of correctly fitting a nonlinear function.

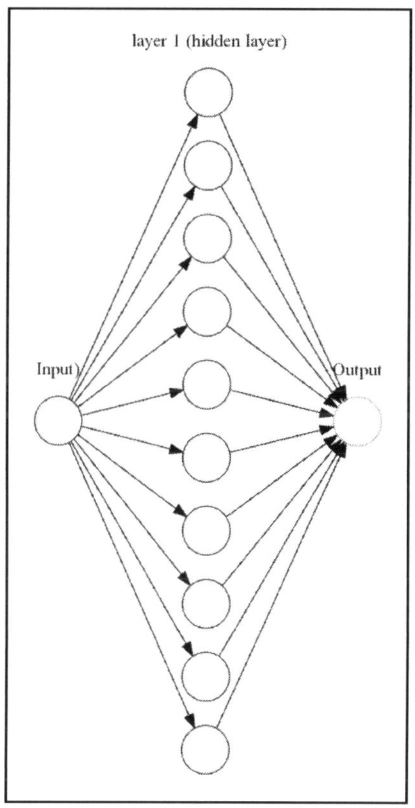

Neural Network activation functions

The learning properties of a Neural Network would not be so great with only the help of a univariate linear classifier. Even some mildly complex problemsin machine learning involve multiple nonlinear variables, so many variants were developed as replacements of the transfer functions of the perceptron.

In order to represent nonlinear models, a number of different nonlinear functions can be used in the activation function. This implies changes in the way the neurons will react to changes in the input variables. The most common activation functions used in practice are:

- **Sigmoid** : The canonical activation function, and has very good qualities for calculating probabilities in classification properties.

$$f(z) = \frac{1}{1 + \exp(-z)}.$$

- **Tanh**: Very similar to the sigmoid, but its value range is [-1,1] instead of [0,1]

$$f(z) = \tanh(z) = \frac{e^z - e^{-z}}{e^z + e^{-z}},$$

- **Relu**: This is called a rectified linear unit, and one of its main advantages is that it is not affected by the Vanishing Gradients problem, which generally exists on the first layers of a network to tend to values of 0, or a tiny epsilon:

$$f(x) = \max(0, x).$$

Gradients and the back propagation algorithm

When we described the learning phase of the perceptron, we described a stage in which the weights were adjusted proportionally according to the "responsibility" of a weight in the final error.

In this complex network of neurons, the responsibility of the error will be distributed among all the functions applied to the data in the whole architecture.

So once we have calculated the total error, and we have the whole function applied to the original data, we must now try to adjust all variables in the equation to minimize it.

What we need to know to be able to minimize this error, as the Optimization field has studied, is the gradient of the loss function.

Given that the data goes through many weights and transfer functions, the resulting compound function's gradient will have to be solved by the chain rule.

Minimizing loss function: Gradient descent

Lets have a look at the following graph to understand the loss function:

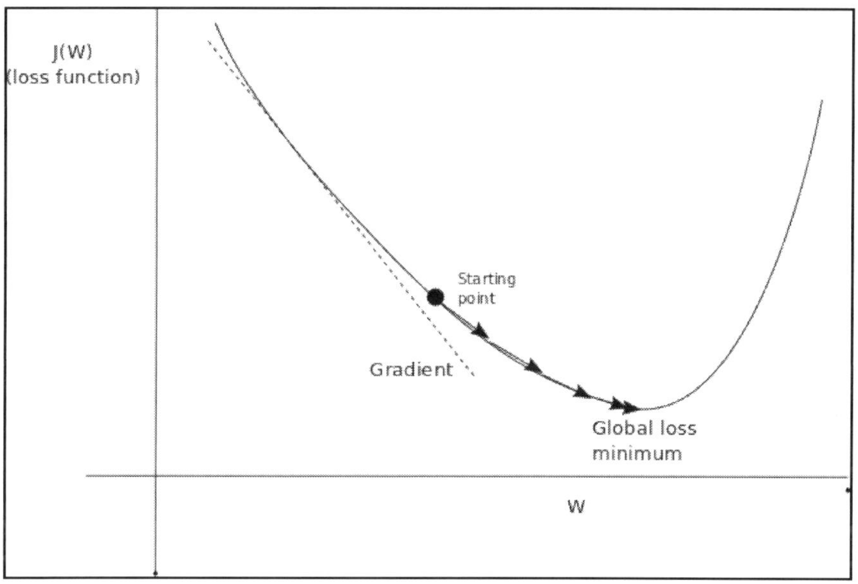

Neural networks problem choice - Classification vs Regression

Neural Networks can be used for regression problems and classification ones. The common architectural difference resides in the output layer: in order to be able to bring a real number base result, no standardization function, like sigmoid, should be applied.In this way, we won't be changing the outcomes of the variable to one of many possible class values, getting a continuum of possible outcomes.

Useful libraries and methods

In this chapter we will be using some new utilities from TensorFlow, and also from utility libraries, these would be the most important ones:

TensorFlow activation functions

Most commonly used functions for TensorFlow navigation:

- **tf.sigmoid(x)**: The standard sigmoid function
- **tf.tanh(x)**: Hyperbolic tangent
- **tf.nn.relu(features)**: Relu transfer function

Other functions for TensorFlow navigation:

- **tf.nn.elu(features)**: Computes exponential linear: exp(features) – 1 if < 0, features otherwise
- **tf.nn.softsign(features)**: Computes softsign: features / (abs(features) + 1)
- **tf.nn.bias_add(value, bias)**: Adds bias to value

TensorFlow loss optimization methods

TensorFlow Loss optimization methods are described in the following:

- **tf.train.GradientDescentOptimizer(learning_rate, use_locking, name)**: This is the original Gradient descent method, with only the learning rate parameter
- **tf.train.AdagradOptimizer(learning_rate, initial_accumulator_value, use_locking, name)**: This method adapts the learning rate, to the frequency of the parameters, improving the efficiency of the minimum search for sparse parameters
- **tf.train.AdadeltaOptimizer (learning_rate, rho, epsilon, use_locking, name)**: This is a modified AdaGrad, which will restrict the accumulation of frequent parameters to a maximum window, so it takes in account a certain number of steps, and not the whole parameter history.
- **tf.train.AdamOptimizertf.train.AdamOptimizer.__init__(learning_rate, beta1, beta2, epsilon, use_locking, name)**: This method adds a factor when calculating gradients, corresponding to the average of the past gradients, equivalent to a momentum factor. Thus the name Adam, from Adaptive Moment Estimation.

Sklearn preprocessing utilities

Lets have a look at the following Sklearn preprocessing utilities:

- **preprocessing.StandardScaler():** Normalization of datasets is a *common requirement for many machine learning estimators, so in order to make convergence more straightforward the dataset will have to be more like a* standard normally distribution that is a Gaussian curve with zero mean and unit variance. In practice, we often ignore the shape of the distribution and just transform the data to center it by removing the mean value of each feature, then scale it by dividing non-constant features by their standard deviation. For this task, we use the StandardScaler, which implements the tasks previously mentioned. It also stores the transforms, in order to be able to reapply it to the testing set.
- **StandardScaler .fit_transform()**: Simply fit the data to the required form. The StandardScaler object will save the transform variables, so you will be able to get the denormalized data back.
- **cross_validation.train_test_split**: This method splits the dataset into train and test segments, we only need to provide the percentage of the dataset assigned to each stage.

First project – Non linear synthetic function regression

Artificial neural network examples normally include a great majority of classification problems, but in fact there are a great number of applications that could be expressed as regressions.

The network architectures used for regression don't differ in great measure from the ones used for classification problems: They can take multi-variable input and can use linear and nonlinear activation functions too.

In some cases, the only necessary case is just to remove the sigmoid-like function at the end of the layers to allow the full range of options to appear.

In this first example, we will model a simple, noisy quadratic function, and will try to regress it by means of a single hidden layer network and see how close we can be topredicting values taken from a test population.

Dataset description and loading

In this case, we will be using a generated dataset, which will be very similar to the one in `Chapter 3`, *Linear Regression*.

We will generate a quadratic function using the common Numpy methods, and then we will add random noise, which will help us to see how the linear regression can generalize.

The core sample creation routines are as follows:

```
import numpy as np
trainsamples = 200
testsamples = 60
dsX = np.linspace(-1, 1, trainsamples + testsamples).transpose()
dsY = 0.4* pow(dsX,2) +2 * dsX + np.random.randn(*dsX.shape) * 0.22 + 0.8
```

Dataset preprocessing

This dataset doesn't need preprocessing as it is being generated, and has good properties such asbeing centered and having a -1, 1 x sample distribution.

Modeling architecture - Loss Function description

The loss for this setup will simply be represented by the same as the mean squares error, with the line:

```
cost = tf.pow(py_x-Y, 2)/(2)
```

Loss function optimizer

In this particular case we will be using the Gradient Descent cost optimizer, which we can invoke with the line:

```
train_op = tf.train.AdamOptimizer(0.5).minimize(cost)
```

Accuracy and Convergence test

predict_op = tf.argmax(py_x, 1)

```
cost1 += sess.run(cost, feed_dict={X: [[x1]], Y: y1}) / testsamples
```

Example code

Lets have a look at the example code shown in the following:

```
import tensorflow as tf
import numpy as np
from sklearn.utils import shuffle
%matplotlib inline
import matplotlib.pyplot as plt
trainsamples = 200
testsamples = 60
#Here we will represent the model, a simple imput, a hidden layer of
sigmoid activation
def model(X, hidden_weights1, hidden_bias1, ow):
    hidden_layer =  tf.nn.sigmoid(tf.matmul(X, hidden_weights1)+ b)
    return tf.matmul(hidden_layer, ow)
dsX = np.linspace(-1, 1, trainsamples + testsamples).transpose()
dsY = 0.4* pow(dsX,2) +2 * dsX + np.random.randn(*dsX.shape) * 0.22 + 0.8
plt.figure() # Create a new figure
plt.title('Original data')
plt.scatter(dsX,dsY) #Plot a scatter draw of the datapoints
```

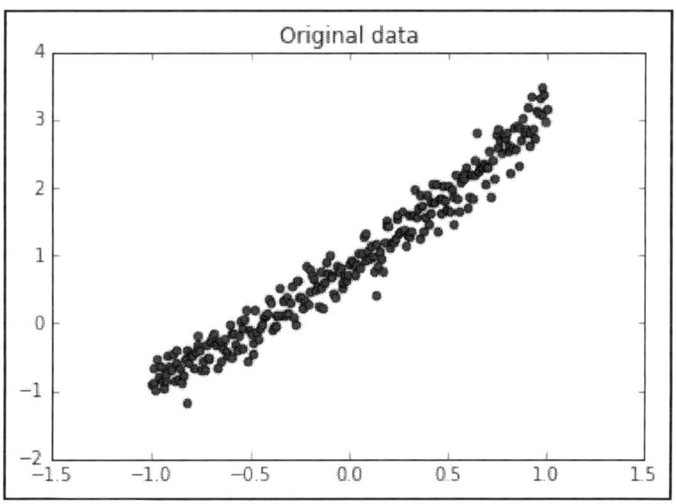

```
X = tf.placeholder("float")
Y = tf.placeholder("float")
# Create first hidden layer
hw1 = tf.Variable(tf.random_normal([1, 10], stddev=0.1))
# Create output connection
ow = tf.Variable(tf.random_normal([10, 1], stddev=0.0))
# Create bias
b = tf.Variable(tf.random_normal([10], stddev=0.1))
model_y = model(X, hw1, b, ow)
# Cost function
cost = tf.pow(model_y-Y, 2)/(2)
# construct an optimizer
train_op = tf.train.GradientDescentOptimizer(0.05).minimize(cost)
# Launch the graph in a session
with tf.Session() as sess:
    tf.initialize_all_variables().run() #Initialize all variables
    for i in range(1,100):
        dsX, dsY = shuffle (dsX.transpose(), dsY) #We randomize the samples
to mplement a better training
        trainX, trainY =dsX[0:trainsamples], dsY[0:trainsamples]
        for x1,y1 in zip (trainX, trainY):
            sess.run(train_op, feed_dict={X: [[x1]], Y: y1})
        testX, testY = dsX[trainsamples:trainsamples + testsamples],
dsY[0:trainsamples:trainsamples+testsamples]
        cost1=0.
        for x1,y1 in zip (testX, testY):
            cost1 += sess.run(cost, feed_dict={X: [[x1]], Y: y1}) /
testsamples
        if (i%10 == 0):
            print "Average cost for epoch " + str (i) + ":" + str(cost1)
```

Results description

This is a copy of the different epoch results.Note that as this is a very simple function, even the first iteration has very good results:

```
Average cost for epoch 1:[[ 0.00753353]]
Average cost for epoch 2:[[ 0.00381996]]
Average cost for epoch 3:[[ 0.00134867]]
Average cost for epoch 4:[[ 0.01020064]]
Average cost for epoch 5:[[ 0.00240157]]
Average cost for epoch 6:[[ 0.01248318]]
Average cost for epoch 7:[[ 0.05143405]]
Average cost for epoch 8:[[ 0.00621457]]
Average cost for epoch 9:[[ 0.0007379]]
```

Second project – Modeling cars fuel efficiency with non linear regression

In this example, we will enter into an area where Neural Networks provide most of their added value; solving non linear problems. To begin this journey, we will be modeling a regression model for the fuel efficiency of several car models, based on several variables, which can be better represented by non linear functions.

Dataset description and loading

For this problem, we will be analyzing a very well-known, standard,well-formeddataset, which will allow us to analyze a multi-variable problem: guessing the mpg an automobile will have based on some related variables, discrete and continuous.

This could be considered a toy and somewhat dated example, but it will pave the way to more complex problems, and has the advantage of being already analyzed by numerous bibliographies.

Attribute Information

This dataset has the following data columns:

- **mpg**: continuous
- **cylinders**: multi-valued discrete
- **displacement**: continuous
- **horsepower**: continuous
- **weight**: continuous
- **acceleration**: continuous
- **model year:** multi-valued discrete
- **origin**: multi-valued discrete
- **car name**: string (won't be used)

We won't be doing a detailed analysis of the data, but we can informally infer that all of the continuous variables have a correlation with increasing or decreasing the goal variable:

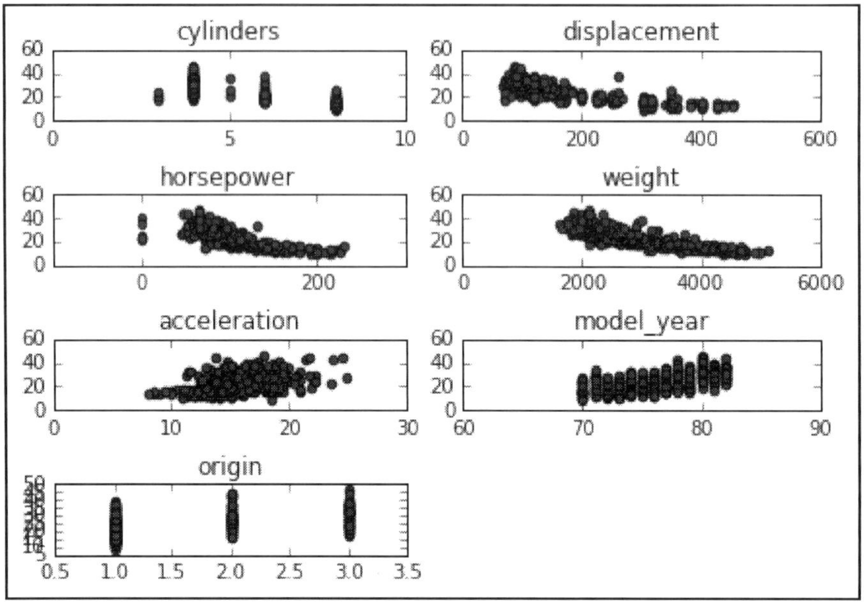

Dataset preprocessing

For this function, we will be using the previously-describedscaler objects, from sklearn:

- **scaler** = `preprocessing.StandardScaler()`
- **X_train** = `scaler.fit_transform(X_train)`

Modeling architecture

What we are about to build is a feedforward neural network, with a multivariate input, and a simple output:

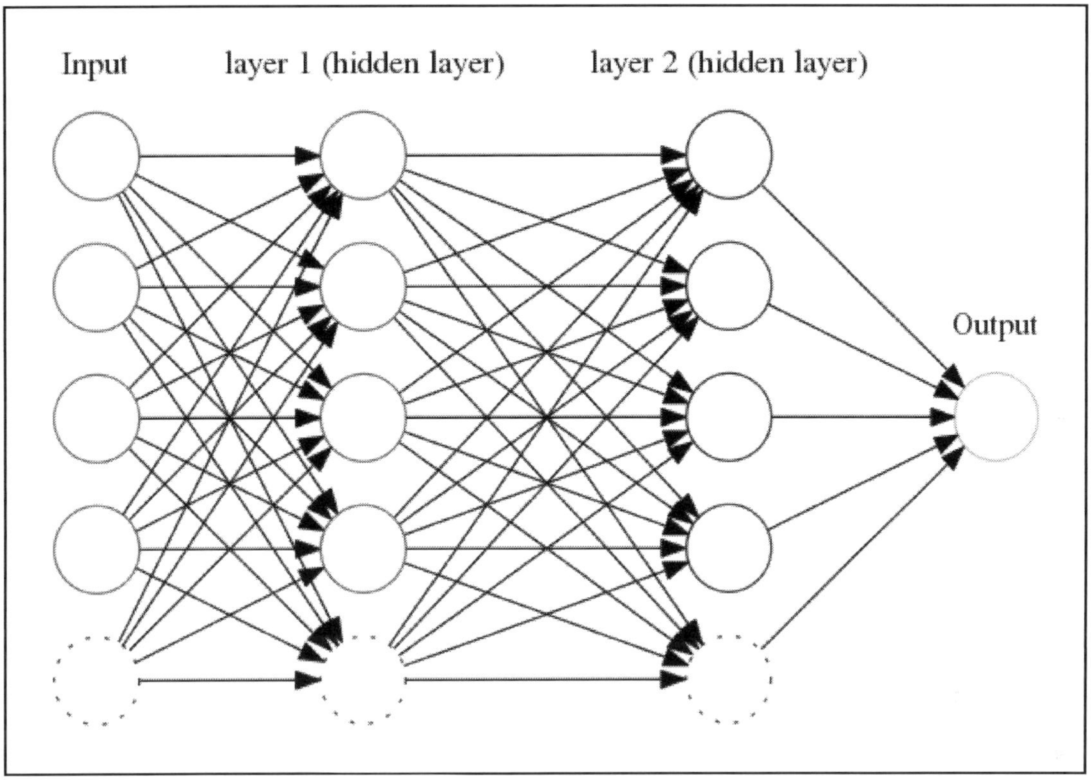

Convergency test

```
score =
metrics.mean_squared_error(regressor.predict(scaler.transform(X_test)),
y_test)
print('MSE: {0:f}'.format(score))
```

Results description

```
Step #99, avg. train loss: 182.33624
Step #199, avg. train loss: 25.09151
Step #300, epoch #1, avg. train loss: 11.92343
Step #400, epoch #1, avg. train loss: 11.20414
Step #500, epoch #1, avg. train loss: 5.14056
Total Mean Squared Error: 15.0792258911

%matplotlib inline
import matplotlib.pyplot as plt
import pandas as pd

from sklearn import datasets, cross_validation, metrics
from sklearn import preprocessing
from tensorflow.contrib import skflow

# Read the original dataset
df = pd.read_csv("data/mpg.csv", header=0)
# Convert the displacement column as float
df['displacement']=df['displacement'].astype(float)
# We get data columns from the dataset
# First and last (mpg and car names) are ignored for X
X = df[df.columns[1:8]]
y = df['mpg']

plt.figure() # Create a new figure

for i in range (1,8):
    number = 420 + i
    ax1.locator_params(nbins=3)
    ax1 = plt.subplot(number)
    plt.title(list(df)[i])
    ax1.scatter(df[df.columns[i]],y) #Plot a scatter draw of the
datapoints
plt.tight_layout(pad=0.4, w_pad=0.5, h_pad=1.0)
# Split the datasets

X_train, X_test, y_train, y_test = cross_validation.train_test_split(X, y,
```

```
test_size=0.25)

# Scale the data for convergency optimization
scaler = preprocessing.StandardScaler()

# Set the transform parameters
X_train = scaler.fit_transform(X_train)

# Build a 2 layer fully connected DNN with 10 and 5 units respectively
regressor = skflow.TensorFlowDNNRegressor(hidden_units=[10, 5],
steps=500, learning_rate=0.051, batch_size=1)

# Fit the regressor
regressor.fit(X_train, y_train)

# Get some metrics based on the X and Y test data
score =
metrics.mean_squared_error(regressor.predict(scaler.transform(X_test)),
y_test)

print(" Total Mean Squared Error: " + str(score))
```

Third project – Learning to classify wines: Multiclass classification

In this section we will work with a more complex dataset, trying to classify wines based on theirplace of origin.

Dataset description and loading

This data contains the results of a chemical analysis of wines grown in the same region in Italy but derived from three different cultivars. The analysis determined the quantities of 13 constituents found in each of the three types of wines.

Data variables:

- Alcohol
- Malic acid
- Ash
- Alcalinity of ash
- Magnesium

- Total phenols
- Flavanoids
- Nonflavanoid phenols
- Proanthocyanins
- Color intensity
- Hue
- OD280/OD315 of diluted wines
- Proline

To read the dataset, we will simply use the provided CSV file and pandas:

```
df = pd.read_csv("./wine.csv", header=0)
```

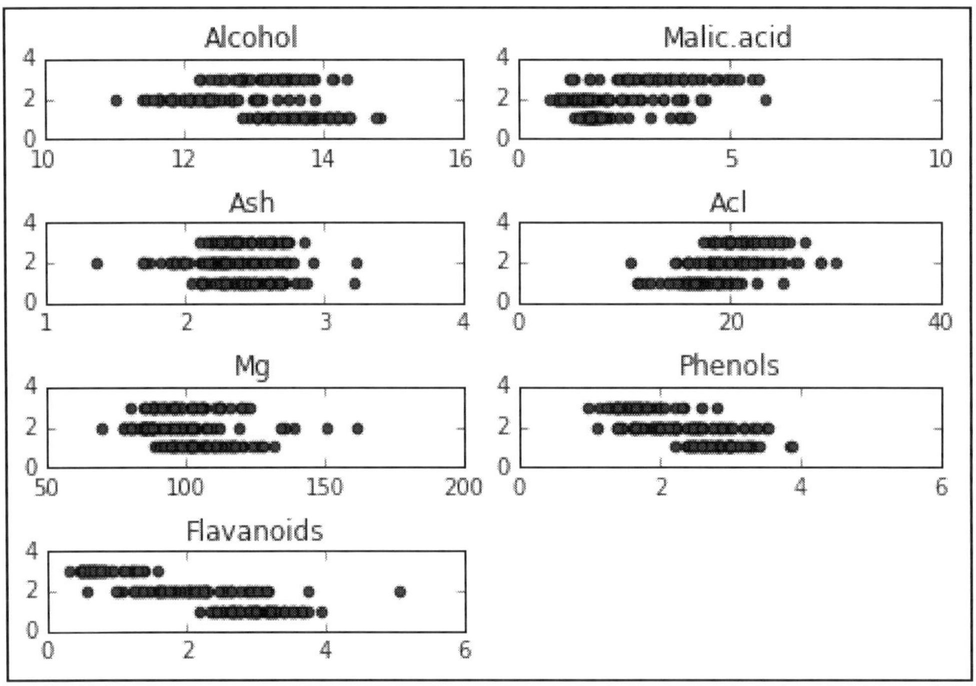

Dataset preprocessing

As the values on the csv begin at 1, we will normalize the values resting the bias:

```
y = df['Wine'].values-1
```

For the results, we will have to represent the options as a one hot list of arrays:

```
Y = tf.one_hot(indices = y, depth=3, on_value = 1., off_value = 0., axis =
1 , name = "a").eval()
```

We will also shuffle the values beforehand:

```
X, Y = shuffle (X, Y)
scaler = preprocessing.StandardScaler()
X = scaler.fit_transform(X)
```

Modeling architecture

This particular model will consist of a single layer, fully-connected, neural network:

- `x = tf.placeholder(tf.float32, [None, 12])`
- `W = tf.Variable(tf.zeros([12, 3]))`
- `b = tf.Variable(tf.zeros([3]))`
- `y = tf.nn.softmax(tf.matmul(x, W) + b)`

Loss function description

We will use the cross entropy function to measure loss:

```
y_ = tf.placeholder(tf.float32, [None, 3])
cross_entropy = tf.reduce_mean(-tf.reduce_sum(y_ * tf.log(y),
reduction_indices=[1]))
```

Loss function optimizer

Again the Gradient Descent method will be used to reduce the loss function:

```
train_step = tf.train.GradientDescentOptimizer(0.1).minimize(cross_entropy)
```

Convergence test

In the convergence test, we will cast every good regression to 1, and every false one to 0, and then get the mean of the values to measure the accuracy of the model:

```
correct_prediction = tf.equal(tf.argmax(y, 1), tf.argmax(y_, 1))
accuracy = tf.reduce_mean(tf.cast(correct_prediction, tf.float32))
print(accuracy.eval({x: Xt, y_: Yt}))
```

Results description

As we see, we have a variating accuracy as the epochs progress, but it is always superior to a 90% accuracy, with a 30% random base (if we'd generated a random number between 0 and 3 to guess the result).

```
0.973684
0.921053
0.921053
0.947368
0.921053
```

Full source code

Lets have a look at the complete source code:

```
sess = tf.InteractiveSession()
import pandas as pd
# Import data
from tensorflow.examples.tlutorials.mnist import input_data
from sklearn.utils import shuffle
import tensorflow as tf

from sklearn import preprocessing

flags = tf.app.flags
FLAGS = flags.FLAGS

df = pd.read_csv("./wine.csv", header=0)
print (df.describe())
#df['displacement']=df['displacement'].astype(float)
X = df[df.columns[1:13]].values
y = df['Wine'].values-1
Y = tf.one_hot(indices = y, depth=3, on_value = 1., off_value = 0., axis =
1 , name = "a").eval()
```

```
X, Y = shuffle (X, Y)

scaler = preprocessing.StandardScaler()
X = scaler.fit_transform(X)

# Create the model
x = tf.placeholder(tf.float32, [None, 12])
W = tf.Variable(tf.zeros([12, 3]))
b = tf.Variable(tf.zeros([3]))
y = tf.nn.softmax(tf.matmul(x, W) + b)

# Define loss and optimizer
y_ = tf.placeholder(tf.float32, [None, 3])
cross_entropy = tf.reduce_mean(-tf.reduce_sum(y_ * tf.log(y),
reduction_indices=[1]))
train_step = tf.train.GradientDescentOptimizer(0.1).minimize(cross_entropy)
# Train
tf.initialize_all_variables().run()
for i in range(100):
X,Y =shuffle (X, Y, random_state=1)

Xtr=X[0:140,:]
Ytr=Y[0:140,:]

Xt=X[140:178,:]
Yt=Y[140:178,:]
Xtr, Ytr = shuffle (Xtr, Ytr, random_state=0)
#batch_xs, batch_ys = mnist.train.next_batch(100)
batch_xs, batch_ys = Xtr , Ytr
train_step.run({x: batch_xs, y_: batch_ys})
cost = sess.run (cross_entropy, feed_dict={x: batch_xs, y_: batch_ys})
# Test trained model
correct_prediction = tf.equal(tf.argmax(y, 1), tf.argmax(y_, 1))
accuracy = tf.reduce_mean(tf.cast(correct_prediction, tf.float32))
print(accuracy.eval({x: Xt, y_: Yt}))
```

Summary

In this chapter, we have been starting the path toward implementing the real quid of TensorFlow capability: Neural Network models.

We have also seen the use of simple Neural Networks in both regression and classification tasks, with simple generated models, and experimental ones.

In the next chapter we will advance the knowledge of new architectures and ways of applying the Neural Network paradigm for other knowledge fields, such as computer vision, in the form of convolutional neural networks.

6
Convolutional Neural Networks

Convolutional neural networks are part of many of the most advanced models currently being employed. They are used in numerous fields, but the main application field is in the realm of image classification and feature detection.

The topics we will cover in this chapter are as follows:

- Getting an idea of how convolution functions and convolutional networks work and the main operation types used in building them
- Applying convolution operations to image data and learning some of the preprocessing techniques applied to images to improve the accuracy of the methods
- Classifying digits of the **MNIST** dataset using a simple setup of CNN
- Classifying real images of the **CIFAR** dataset, with a CNN model applied to color images

Origin of convolutional neural networks

The neocognitron is a predecessor to convolutional networks, introduced in a 1980 paper by *Prof. Fukushima*, and is a self-organizing neural network tolerant to shifts and deformation.

This idea appeared again in 1986 in the book version of the original back propagation paper, and it was also employed in 1988 for temporal signals in speech recognition.

The original design was later reviewed and improved in 1998 with *LeCun's* paper, gradient-based learning applied to document recognition, which presented the LeNet-5 network, which is able to classify handwritten digits. The model showed increased performance compared with other existing models, especially over several variations of SVM, one of the most performant operations in the year of publication.

Then a generalization of that paper came in 2003, with the paper *Hierarchical Neural Networks for Image Interpretation*. However, in general, we will be using a close representation of *LeCun's LeNet* paper architecture.

Getting started with convolution

In order to understand the operations being applied to the information in these kinds of operations, we will start by studying the origin of the convolution function, and then we will explain how this concept is applied to the information.

In order to begin following the historical development of the operation, we will start looking at convolution in the continuous domain.

Continuous convolution

The original use of this function comes from the eighteenth century and can be expressed, in the original application context, as an operation that blends two functions occurring on time.

Mathematically, it can be defined as follows:

$$(f * g)(\tau) = \int_{-\infty}^{\infty} f(\tau) g(t - \tau) \, d\tau$$

When we try to conceptualize this operation as an algorithm, the preceding equation can be explained in the following steps:

1. **Flip the signal**: This is the $(-\tau)$ part of the variable.
2. **Shift it**: This is given by the t summing factor for $g(\tau)$.
3. **Multiply it**: This is the product of f and g.
4. **Integrate the resulting curve**: This is the less intuitive part because each instantaneous value is the result of an integral.

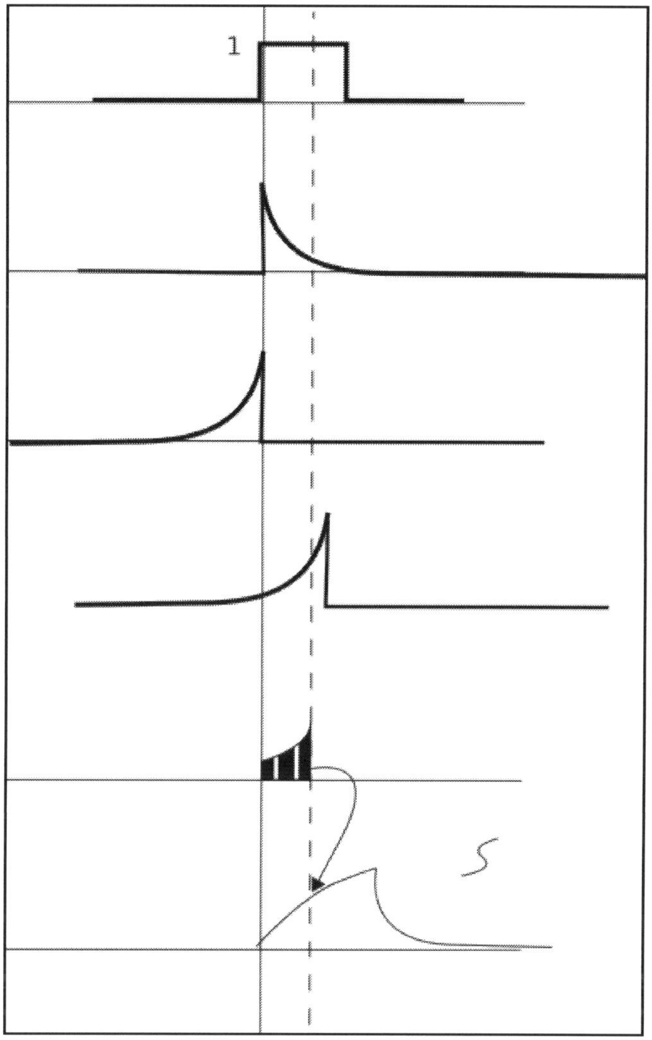
1
S

Discrete convolution

The convolution can be translated into a discrete domain and described in discrete terms for discrete functions:

$$(f * g)[n] = \sum_{m=-\infty}^{\infty} f(m) g(n-m)$$

Kernels and convolutions

When applying the concept of convolution in the discrete domain, kernels are used quite frequently.

Kernels can be defined as *nxm*-dimensional matrices, which are normally a few elements long in all dimensions and usually, $m = n$.

The convolution operation consists of multiplying the corresponding pixels with the kernel, one pixel at a time, and summing the values for the purpose of assigning that value to the central pixel.

The same operation will then be applied, shifting the convolution matrix to the left until all possible pixels are visited.

In the following example, we have an image of many pixels and a kernel of size 3×3, which is particularly common in image processing:

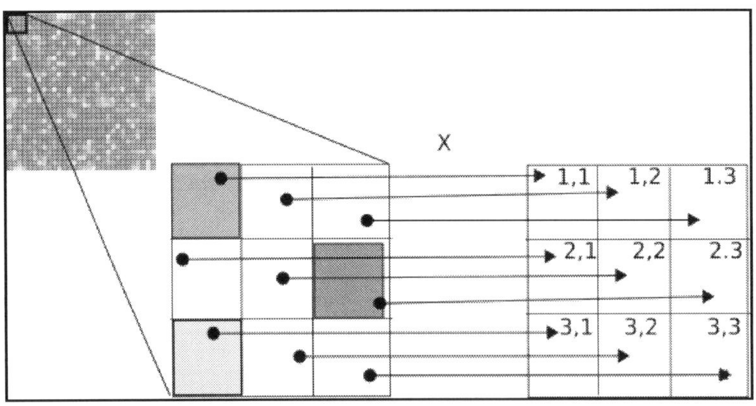

Interpretation of the convolution operations

Having reviewed the main characteristics of the convolution operation for continuous and discrete fields, let's now look at the use of this operation in machine learning.

The convolution kernels highlight or hide patterns. Depending on the trained (or in the example, manually set) parameters, we can begin to discover parameters, such as orientation and edges in different dimensions. We may also cover some unwanted details or outliers by means such as blurring kernels.

As *LeCun* in his *fundational* paper stated:

> *"Convolutional networks can be seen as synthesizing their own feature extractor."*

This characteristic of convolutional neural networks is the main advantage over previous data processing techniques; we can determine with great flexibility the primary components of a determined dataset and represent further samples as a combination of these basic building blocks.

Applying convolution in TensorFlow

TensorFlow provides a variety of methods for convolution. The canonical form is applied by the `conv2d` operation. Lets have a look at the usage of this operation:

```
tf.nn.conv2d(input, filter, strides, padding, use_cudnn_on_gpu,
data_format, name=None)
```

The parameters we use are as follows:

- `input`: This is the original tensor to which the operation will be applied. It has a definite format of four dimensions, and the default dimension order is shown next.
- `[batch, in_height, in_width, in_channels]`: Batch is a dimension that allows you to have a collection of images. This order is called**NHWC**. The other option is **NCWH**.

  For example, a single *100×100* pixel color image will have the following shape:

  ```
  [1,100,100,3]
  ```

- `filter`: This is a tensor representing a `kernel` or `filter`. It has a very generic method:

```
[filter_height, filter_width, in_channels, out_channels]
```

- `strides`: This is a list of four `int` tensor datatypes, which indicate the sliding windows for each dimension.
- `Padding`: This can be `SAME` or `VALID`. `SAME` will try to conserve the initial tensor dimension, but `VALID` will allow it to grow in case the output size and padding are computed.
- `use_cudnn_on_gpu`: This indicates whether or not to use the `CUDA GPU CNN` library to accelerate calculations.
- `data_format`: This specifies the order in which data is organized (NHWC or NCWH).

Other convolutional operations

TensorFlow provides a number of ways of applying convolutions, which are listed as follows:

- `tf.nn.conv2d_transpose`: This applies the transpose (gradient) of `conv2d` and is used in deconvolutional networks
- `tf.nn.conv1d`: This performs 1D convolution, given a 3D input and `filter` tensors
- `tf.nn.conv3d`: This performs 3D convolution, given a 5D input and `filter` tensors

Sample code – applying convolution to a grayscale image

In this sample code, we will read a grayscale image in the GIF format, which will generate a three-channel tensor but with the same RGB values per pixel. We will then transform the tensor into a real grayscale matrix, apply a `kernel`, and retrieve the results in an output image in the JPEG format.

Note that you can tune the parameter in the `kernel` variable to observe the effects of the changes in the image.

The following is the sample code:

```
import tensorflow as tf

#Generate the filename queue, and read the gif files contents
filename_queue =
tf.train.string_input_producer(tf.train.match_filenames_once("data/test.gif
"))
reader = tf.WholeFileReader()
key, value = reader.read(filename_queue)
image=tf.image.decode_gif(value)

#Define the kernel parameters
kernel=tf.constant(
[
[[[-1.]],[[-1.]],[[-1.]]],
[[[-1.]],[[8.]],[[-1.]]],
[[[-1.]],[[-1.]],[[-1.]]]
]
)

#Define the train coordinator
coord = tf.train.Coordinator()

with tf.Session() as sess:
tf.initialize_all_variables().run()
threads = tf.train.start_queue_runners(coord=coord)
#Get first image
image_tensor = tf.image.rgb_to_grayscale(sess.run([image])[0])
#apply convolution, preserving the image size
imagen_convoluted_tensor=tf.nn.conv2d(tf.cast(image_tensor,
tf.float32),kernel,[1,1,1,1],"SAME")
#Prepare to save the convolution option
file=open ("blur2.jpeg", "wb+")
#Cast to uint8 (0..255), previous scalation, because the convolution could
alter the scale of the final image
out=tf.image.encode_jpeg(tf.reshape(tf.cast(imagen_convoluted_tensor/tf.red
uce_max(imagen_convoluted_tensor)*255.,tf.uint8),
tf.shape(imagen_convoluted_tensor.eval()[0]).eval()))
file.close()
coord.request_stop()
coord.join(threads)
```

Sample kernels results

In the following figure, you can observe how the changes in the parameters affect the outcome of the image. The first image is the original one.

The filter types are from left to right and top to bottom-blur, bottom Sobel (a kind of filter searching from top to bottom edges), emboss (which highlights the corner edges), and outline (which outlines the exterior limits of the figures).

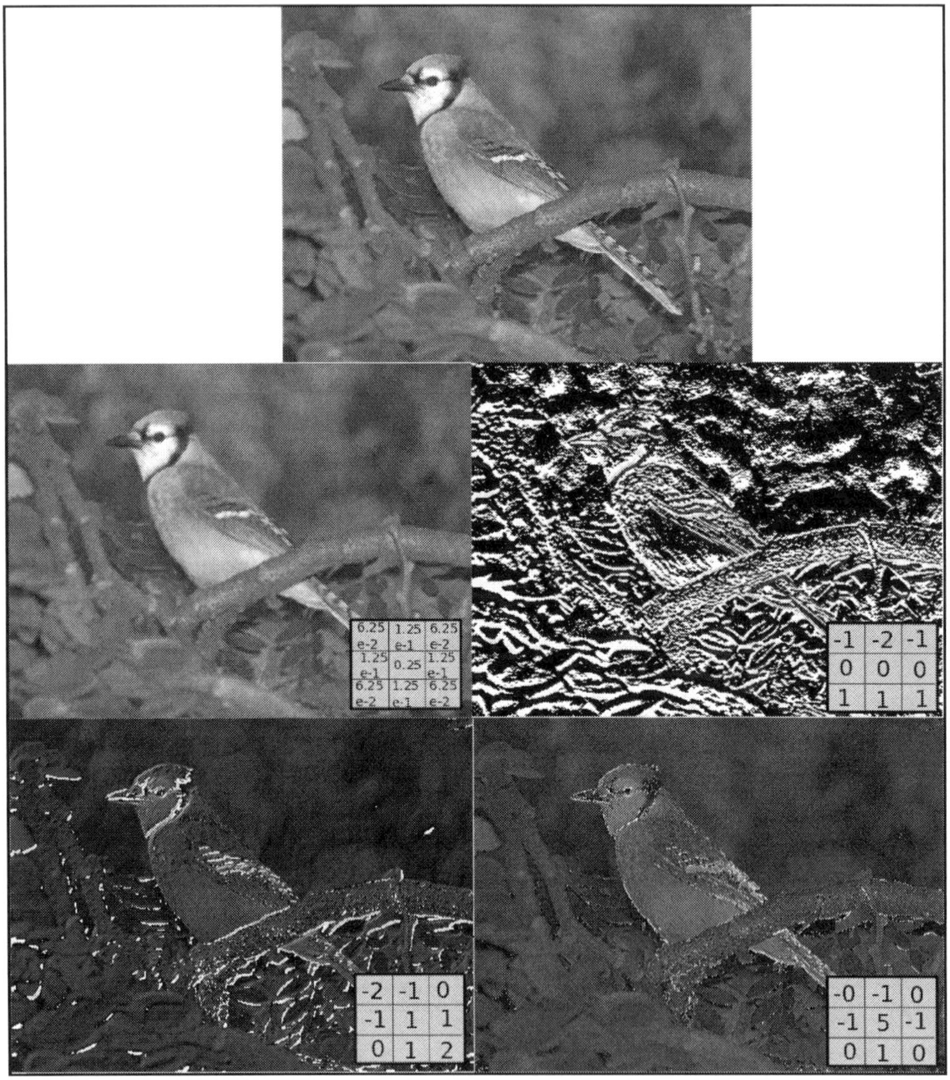

Subsampling operation – pooling

The subsampling operation is performed in TensorFlow by means of an operation called pool. The idea is to apply a kernel (of varying dimensions) and extract one of the elements covered by the kernel, the `max_pool` and `avg_pool` being a few of the most well known, which get only the maximum and the average of the elements for an applied kernel.

In the following figure, you can see the action of applying a 2×2 kernel to a one-channel, 16×16 matrix. It just keeps the maximum value of the internal zone it covers.

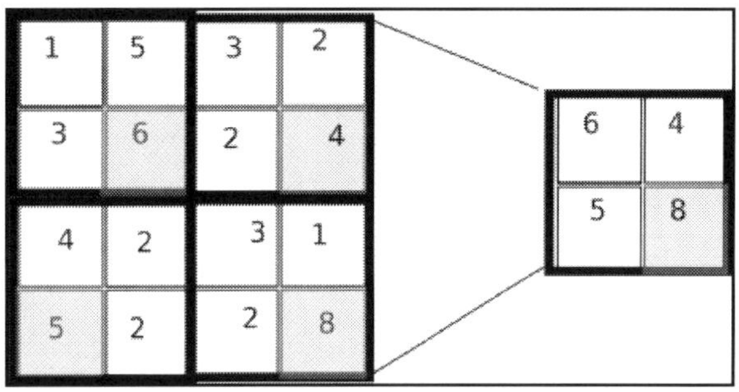

The type of pooling operations that can be made are also varied; for example, in *LeCun's* paper, the operation applied to the original pixels has to multiply them for a trainable parameter and add an additional trainable `bias`.

Properties of subsampling layers

The main purpose of subsampling layers is more or less the same as that of convolutional layers; to reduce the quantity and complexity of information while retaining the most important information elements. They build a compact representation of the underlying information.

Invariance property

Subsampling layers also allow important parts of the information to be translated from a detailed to a simpler representation of the data. By sliding the filter across the image, we translate the detected features to more significant image parts, eventually reaching a 1-pixel image, with the feature represented by that pixel value. Conversely, this property could also produce the model to lose the locality of feature detection.

Subsampling layers implementation performance.

Subsampling layers are much faster to implement because the elimination criterion for unused data elements is really simple; it just needs a couple of comparisons, in general.

Applying pool operations in TensorFlow

First we will analyze the most commonly used `pool` operation, `max_pool`. It has the following signature:

```
tf.nn.max_pool(value, ksize, strides, padding, data_format, name)
```

This method is similar to `conv2d`, and the parameters are as follows:

- `value`: This is a 4D tensor of `float32` elements and shape (batch length, height, width, channels)
- `ksize`: This is a list of ints representing the window size on each dimension
- `strides`: This is the step of the moving windows on each dimension
- `data_format`: This sets the data dimensions
- `ordering`: NHWC, or NCHW
- `padding`: `VALID` or `SAME`

Other pool operations

- `tf.nn.avg_pool`: This returns a reduced tensor with the avg of each window
- `tf.nn.max_pool_with_argmax`: This returns the `max_pool` tensor and a tensor with the flattened index of the `max_value`
- `tf.nn.avg_pool3d`: This performs an `avg_pool` operation with a cubic-like window; the input has an additional depth
- `tf.nn.max_pool3d`: This performs the same function as `(...)` but applies the `max` operation

Sample code

In the following sample code, we will take an original:

```
import tensorflow as tf

#Generate the filename queue, and read the gif files contents
filename_queue =
tf.train.string_input_producer(tf.train.match_filenames_once("data/test.gif
"))
reader = tf.WholeFileReader()
key, value = reader.read(filename_queue)
image=tf.image.decode_gif(value)

#Define the  coordinator
coord = tf.train.Coordinator()

def normalize_and_encode (img_tensor):
    image_dimensions = tf.shape(img_tensor.eval()[0]).eval()
    return tf.image.encode_jpeg(tf.reshape(tf.cast(img_tensor, tf.uint8),
image_dimensions))

with tf.Session() as sess:
    maxfile=open ("maxpool.jpeg", "wb+")
    avgfile=open ("avgpool.jpeg", "wb+")
    tf.initialize_all_variables().run()
    threads = tf.train.start_queue_runners(coord=coord)

    image_tensor = tf.image.rgb_to_grayscale(sess.run([image])[0])

    maxed_tensor=tf.nn.avg_pool(tf.cast(image_tensor,
tf.float32),[1,2,2,1],[1,2,2,1],"SAME")
    averaged_tensor=tf.nn.avg_pool(tf.cast(image_tensor,
tf.float32),[1,2,2,1],[1,2,2,1],"SAME")

    maxfile.write(normalize_and_encode(maxed_tensor).eval())
    avgfile.write(normalize_and_encode(averaged_tensor).eval())
    coord.request_stop()
    maxfile.close()
    avgfile.close()
coord.join(threads)
```

In the following figure, we see the original image and the reduced-size image, first with the `max_pool` and then the `avg_pool`. As you can see, the two images seem equal, but if we draw the image differences between them, we see that there is a subtle difference if we take the maximum value instead of the mean, which is always lower or equal.

Improving efficiency – dropout operation

One of the main advantages observed during the training of large neural networks is overfitting, that is, generating very good approximations for the training data but emitting noise for the zones between single points.

In case of overfitting, the model is specifically adjusted to the training dataset, so it will not be useful for generalization. Therefore, although it performs well on the training set, its performance on the test dataset and subsequent tests is poor because it lacks the generalization property.

For this reason, the dropout operation was introduced. This operation reduces the value of some randomly selected weights to zero, making null the subsequent layers.

The main advantage of this method is that it avoids all neurons in a layer to synchronously optimize their weights. This adaptation made in random groups avoids all the neurons converging to the same goals, thus decorrelating the adapted weights.

A second property discovered in the dropout application is that the activation of the hidden units becomes sparse, which is also a desirable characteristic.

In the following figure, we have a representation of an original fully connected multilayer neural network and the associated network with the dropout linked:

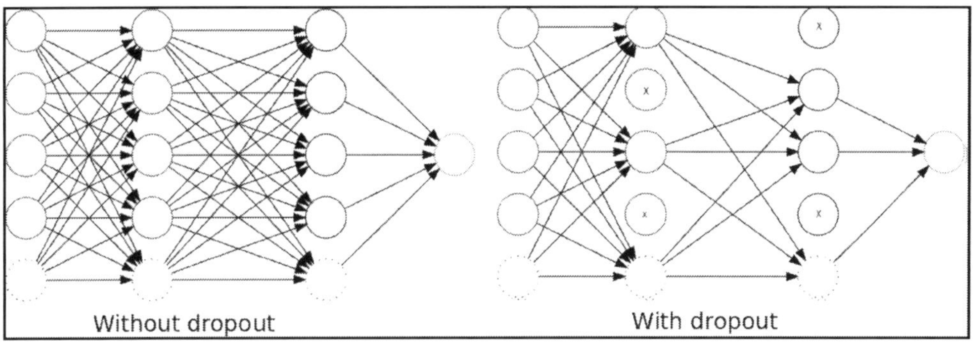

Applying the dropout operation in TensorFlow

In order to apply the `dropout` operation, TensorFlows implements the `tf.nn.dropout` method, which works as follows:

```
tf.nn.dropout (x, keep_prob, noise_shape, seed, name)
```

The parameters are as follows:

- `x`: This is the original tensor
- `keep_prob`: This is the probability of keeping a neuron and the factor by which the remaining nodes are multiplied
- `noise_shape`: This is a four-element list that determines whether a dimension will apply zeroing independently or not

Sample code

In this sample, we will apply the dropout operation to a sample vector. Dropout will also work on transmitting the dropout to all the architecture-dependent units.

In the following example, you can see the results of applying dropout to the `x` variable, with a 0.5 probability of zeroing, and in the cases in which it didn't occur, the values were doubled (multiplied by 1/1.5, the dropout probability):

```
>>> import tensorflow as tf
>>> x=[1.0,.5,.75,.25,.2,.8, .4, .6]
>>> dropout=tf.nn.dropout(x,0.5)
>>> with tf.Session() as sess:
...     print sess.run(dropout)
...
[ 0.          0.          1.5         0.5         0.40000001  1.60000002
  0.          1.20000005]
```

It's clear that approximately half of the input was zeroed (this example was chosen to show that probabilities will not always give the expected four zeroes).

One factor that could have surprised you is the scale factor applied to the non-dropped elements. This technique is used to maintain the same network, and restore it to the original architecture when training, using `keep_prob` as 1.

Convolutional type layer building methods

In order to build convolutional neural networks layers, there exist some common practices and methods, which can be considered quasi-canonical in the way deep neural networks are built.

In order to facilitate the building of convolutional layers, we will look at some some simple utility functions.

Convolutional layer

This is an example of a convolutional layer, which concatenates a convolution, adds a `bias` parameter sum, and finally returns the activation function we have chosen for the whole layer (in this case, the `relu` operation, which is a frequently used one).

```
def conv_layer(x_in, weights, bias, strides=1):
x = tf.nn.conv2d(x, weights, strides=[1, strides, strides, 1],
padding='SAME')
x = tf.nn.bias_add(x_in, bias)
return tf.nn.relu(x)
```

Subsampling layer

A subsampling layer can normally be represented by a `max_pool` operation by maintaining the initial parameters of the layer:

```
def maxpool2d(x, k=2):
return tf.nn.max_pool(x, ksize=[1, k, k, 1], strides=[1, k, k, 1],
padding='SAME')
```

Example 1 – MNIST digit classification

In this section, we will work for the first time on one of the most well-known datasets for pattern recognition. It was initially developed in order to train neural networks for character recognition of handwritten digits on checks.

The original dataset has 60,000 different digits for training and 10,000 for testing, and it was a subset of the original employed dataset when it was used.

In the following diagram, we show the LeNet-5 architecture, which was the first well-known convolutional architecture published regarding that problem.

Here, you can see the dimensions of the layers and the last result representation:

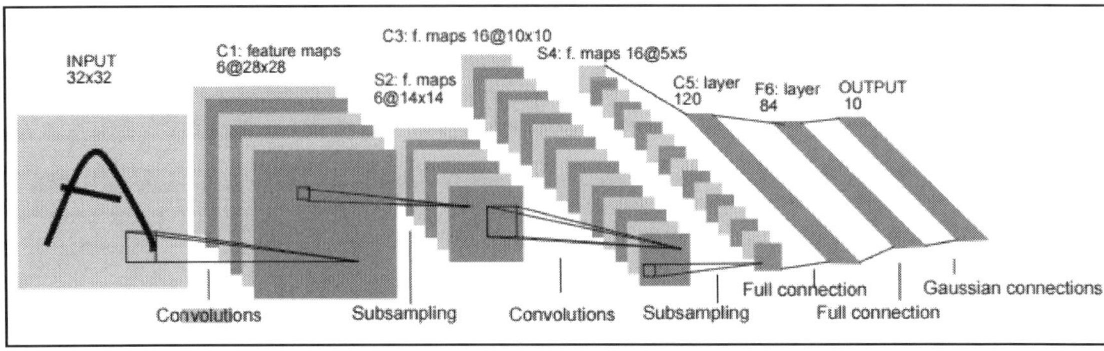

Dataset description and loading

MNIST as a dataset that is easy to understand and read but difficult to master. Currently, there are a number of good algorithms for solving this problem. In our case, we will look to build a model sufficiently good to be quite far from the 10% random results.

In order to access the MNIST dataset, we will be using some utility classes developed for the MNIST tutorials of TensorFlow.

These two lines are all we need to have a complete MNIST dataset available to work.

In the following figure, we can see an approximation of the data structures of the dataset object:

With this code, we will open and explore the MNIST dataset:

```
In [1]: from tensorflow.examples.tutorials.mnist import input_data

In [2]: mnist = input_data.read_data_sets("/tmp/data/", one_hot=True)
Extracting /tmp/data/train-images-idx3-ubyte.gz
Extracting /tmp/data/train-labels-idx1-ubyte.gz
Extracting /tmp/data/t10k-images-idx3-ubyte.gz
Extracting /tmp/data/t10k-labels-idx1-ubyte.gz

In [3]: mnist
Out[3]: Datasets(train=<tensorflow.contrib.learn.python.learn.datasets.mnist.DataSet object at 0x7f20f0
3f5bd0>, validation=<tensorflow.contrib.learn.python.learn.datasets.mnist.DataSet object at 0x7f20f03f5
c50>, test=<tensorflow.contrib.learn.python.learn.datasets.mnist.DataSet object at 0x7f20f03f5c90>)

In [4]: mnist.train.images
Out[4]:
array([[ 0.,  0.,  0., ...,  0.,  0.,  0.],
       [ 0.,  0.,  0., ...,  0.,  0.,  0.],
       [ 0.,  0.,  0., ...,  0.,  0.,  0.],
       ...,
       [ 0.,  0.,  0., ...,  0.,  0.,  0.],
       [ 0.,  0.,  0., ...,  0.,  0.,  0.],
       [ 0.,  0.,  0., ...,  0.,  0.,  0.]], dtype=float32)

In [5]: mnist.train.labels
Out[5]:
array([[ 0.,  0.,  0., ...,  1.,  0.,  0.],
       [ 0.,  0.,  0., ...,  0.,  0.,  0.],
       [ 0.,  0.,  0., ...,  0.,  0.,  0.],
       ...,
       [ 0.,  0.,  0., ...,  0.,  0.,  0.],
       [ 0.,  0.,  0., ...,  0.,  0.,  0.],
       [ 0.,  0.,  0., ...,  0.,  1.,  0.]])

In [6]:
```

To print a character (in the Jupyter Notebook) we will reshape the linear way the image is represented, form a square matrix of *28×28*, assign a grayscale colormap, and draw the resulting data structure using the following line:

```
plt.imshow(mnist.train.images[0].reshape((28, 28), order='C'),
cmap='Greys', interpolation='nearest')
```

The following figure shows the results of this line applied to different dataset elements:

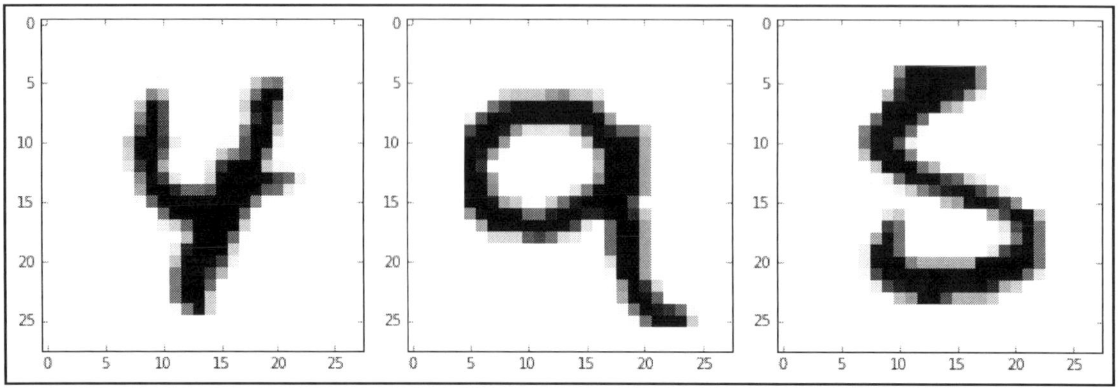

Dataset preprocessing

In this example, we won't be doing any preprocessing; we will just mention that better classification scores can be achieved just by augmenting the dataset examples with linearly transformed existing samples, such as translated, rotated, and skewed samples.

Modelling architecture

Here, we will look at the different layers that we have chosen for this particular architecture.

It begins generating a dictionary of weights with names:

```
'wc1': tf.Variable(tf.random_normal([5, 5, 1, 32])),
'wc2': tf.Variable(tf.random_normal([5, 5, 32, 64])),
'wd1': tf.Variable(tf.random_normal([7*7*64, 1024])),
'out': tf.Variable(tf.random_normal([1024, n_classes]))
```

For each weight, a `bias` will be also added to account for constants.

Then we define the connected layers, integrating one after another:

```
conv_layer_1 = conv2d(x_in, weights['wc1'], biases['bc1'])

conv_layer_1 = subsampling(conv_layer_1, k=2)
```

```
conv_layer_2 = conv2d(conv_layer_1, weights['wc2'], biases['bc2'])

conv_layer_2 = subsampling(conv_layer_2, k=2)


fully_connected_layer = tf.reshape(conv_layer_2, [-1,
weights['wd1'].get_shape().as_list()[0]])
fully_connected_layer = tf.add(tf.matmul(fully_connected_layer,
weights['wd1']), biases['bd1'])
fully_connected_layer = tf.nn.relu(fully_connected_layer)

fully_connected_layer = tf.nn.dropout(fully_connected_layer, dropout)


prediction_output = tf.add(tf.matmul(fully_connected_layer,
weights['out']), biases['out'])
```

Loss function description

The loss function will be the mean of the cross entropy error function, typical of softmax functions for classification.

```
cost = tf.reduce_mean(tf.nn.softmax_cross_entropy_with_logits(pred, y))
```

Loss function optimizer

For this example, we will use the improved`AdamOptimizer`, with a configurable learning rate, which we define at 0.001.

```
optimizer = tf.train.AdamOptimizer
           (learning_rate=learning_rate).minimize(cost)
```

Accuracy test

The accuracy test calculates the mean of the comparison between the label and the results, obtaining a value between `0` and `1`.

```
correct_pred = tf.equal(tf.argmax(pred, 1), tf.argmax(y, 1))
accuracy = tf.reduce_mean(tf.cast(correct_pred, tf.float32))
```

Result description

The results of this example are succinct, and given that we train with only 10,000 samples, the accuracy is not stellar but clearly separated from one-tenth of the random sampling results:

```
Optimization Finished!
Testing Accuracy: 0.382812
```

Full source code

The following is the source code:

```
import tensorflow as tf
%matplotlib inline
import matplotlib.pyplot as plt
# Import MINST data
from tensorflow.examples.tutorials.mnist import input_data
mnist = input_data.read_data_sets("/tmp/data/", one_hot=True)
# Parameters
learning_rate = 0.001
training_iters = 2000
batch_size = 128
display_step = 10

# Network Parameters
n_input = 784 # MNIST data input (img shape: 28*28)
n_classes = 10 # MNIST total classes (0-9 digits)
dropout = 0.75 # Dropout, probability to keep units

# tf Graph input
x = tf.placeholder(tf.float32, [None, n_input])
y = tf.placeholder(tf.float32, [None, n_classes])
keep_prob = tf.placeholder(tf.float32) #dropout (keep probability)

#plt.imshow(X_train[1202].reshape((20, 20), order='F'), cmap='Greys',
interpolation='nearest')

# Create some wrappers for simplicity
def conv2d(x, W, b, strides=1):
    # Conv2D wrapper, with bias and relu activation
    x = tf.nn.conv2d(x, W, strides=[1, strides, strides, 1],
padding='SAME')
    x = tf.nn.bias_add(x, b)
    return tf.nn.relu(x)
def maxpool2d(x, k=2):
```

```
    # MaxPool2D wrapper
    return tf.nn.max_pool(x, ksize=[1, k, k, 1], strides=[1, k, k, 1],
                          padding='SAME')
# Create model
def conv_net(x, weights, biases, dropout):
    # Reshape input picture
    x = tf.reshape(x, shape=[-1, 28, 28, 1])

    # Convolution Layer
    conv1 = conv2d(x, weights['wc1'], biases['bc1'])
    # Max Pooling (down-sampling)
    conv1 = maxpool2d(conv1, k=2)

    # Convolution Layer
    conv2 = conv2d(conv1, weights['wc2'], biases['bc2'])
    # Max Pooling (down-sampling)
    conv2 = maxpool2d(conv2, k=2)

    # Fully connected layer
    # Reshape conv2 output to fit fully connected layer input
    fc1 = tf.reshape(conv2, [-1, weights['wd1'].get_shape().as_list()[0]])
    fc1 = tf.add(tf.matmul(fc1, weights['wd1']), biases['bd1'])
    fc1 = tf.nn.relu(fc1)
    # Apply Dropout
    fc1 = tf.nn.dropout(fc1, dropout)

    # Output, class prediction
    out = tf.add(tf.matmul(fc1, weights['out']), biases['out'])
    return out
# Store layers weight & bias
weights = {
# 5x5 conv, 1 input, 32 outputs
'wc1': tf.Variable(tf.random_normal([5, 5, 1, 32])),
# 5x5 conv, 32 inputs, 64 outputs
'wc2': tf.Variable(tf.random_normal([5, 5, 32, 64])),
# fully connected, 7*7*64 inputs, 1024 outputs
'wd1': tf.Variable(tf.random_normal([7*7*64, 1024])),
# 1024 inputs, 10 outputs (class prediction)
'out': tf.Variable(tf.random_normal([1024, n_classes]))
}

biases = {
'bc1': tf.Variable(tf.random_normal([32])),
'bc2': tf.Variable(tf.random_normal([64])),
'bd1': tf.Variable(tf.random_normal([1024])),
'out': tf.Variable(tf.random_normal([n_classes]))
}
```

```
# Construct model
pred = conv_net(x, weights, biases, keep_prob)

# Define loss and optimizer
cost = tf.reduce_mean(tf.nn.softmax_cross_entropy_with logits(pred, y))
optimizer =
tf.train.AdamOptimizer(learning_rate=learning_rate).minimize(cost)

# Evaluate model
correct_pred = tf.equal(tf.argmax(pred, 1), tf.argmax(y, 1))
accuracy = tf.reduce_mean(tf.cast(correct_pred, tf.float32))

# Initializing the variables
init = tf.initialize_all_variables()

# Launch the graph
with tf.Session() as sess:
    sess.run(init)
    step = 1
    # Keep training until reach max iterations
    while step * batch_size < training_iters:
        batch_x, batch_y = mnist.train.next_batch(batch_size)
        test = batch_x[0]
        fig = plt.figure()
        plt.imshow(test.reshape((28, 28), order='C'), cmap='Greys',
        interpolation='nearest')
        print (weights['wc1'].eval()[0])
        plt.imshow(weights['wc1'].eval()[0][0].reshape(4, 8), cmap='Greys',
interpolation='nearest')
        # Run optimization op (backprop)
        sess.run(optimizer, feed_dict={x: batch_x, y: batch_y,
                                       keep_prob: dropout})
        if step % display_step == 0:
            # Calculate batch loss and accuracy
            loss, acc = sess.run([cost, accuracy], feed_dict={x: batch_x,
                                                              y: batch_y,
                                                            keep_prob: 1.})
            print "Iter " + str(step*batch_size) + ", Minibatch Loss= " + \
                  "{:.6f}".format(loss) + ", Training Accuracy= " + \
                  "{:.5f}".format(acc)
        step += 1
    print "Optimization Finished!"

    # Calculate accuracy for 256 mnist test images
    print "Testing Accuracy:", \
        sess.run(accuracy, feed_dict={x: mnist.test.images[:256],
                                      y: mnist.test.labels[:256],
                                      keep_prob: 1.})
```

Example 2 – image classification with the CIFAR10 dataset

In this example, we will be working on one of the most extensively used datasets in image comprehension, one which is used as a simple but general benchmark. In this example, we will build a simple CNN model to have an idea of the general structure of computations needed to tackle this type of classification problem.

Dataset description and loading

This dataset consists of 40,000 images of *32×32* pixels, representing the following categories: airplane, automobile, bird, cat, deer, dog, frog, horse, ship, and truck. In this example, we will just take the first of the 10,000 image bundles to work on.

Here are some examples of the images you can find in the dataset:

Dataset preprocessing

We must make some data-structure adjustments to the original dataset, first by transforming it into a `[10000, 3, 32, 32]` multidimensional array and then moving the channel dimension to the last order.

```
datadir='data/cifar-10-batches-bin/'
plt.ion()
G = glob.glob (datadir + '*.bin')
A = np.fromfile(G[0],dtype=np.uint8).reshape([10000,3073])
labels = A [:,0]
images = A [:,1:].reshape([10000,3,32,32]).transpose (0,2,3,1)
plt.imshow(images[14])
print labels[11]
images_unroll = A [:,1:]
```

Modelling architecture

Here, we will define our modeling function, which is a succession of convolution and pooling operations, with a final flattened layer and a logistic regression applied in order to determine the class probability of the current sample.

```
def conv_model (X, y):
X= tf. reshape(X, [-1, 32, 32, 3])
    with tf.variable_scope('conv_layer1'):
        h_conv1=tf.contrib.layers.conv2d(X, num_outputs=16,
kernel_size=[5,5],  activation_fn=tf.nn.relu)#print (h_conv1)
        h_pool1=max_pool_2x2(h_conv1)#print (h_pool1)
with tf.variable_scope('conv_layer2'):
        h_conv2=tf.contrib.layers.conv2d(h_pool1, num_outputs=16,
kernel_size=[5,5], activation_fn=tf.nn.relu)
    #print (h_conv2)
    h_pool2=max_pool_2x2(h_conv2)
    h_pool2_flat = tf.reshape(h_pool2,  [-1,8*8*16 ])
    h_fc1 = tf.contrib.layers.stack(h_pool2_flat,
tf.contrib.layers.fully_connected ,[96,48], activation_fn=tf.nn.relu )

return skflow.models.logistic_regression(h_fc1,y)
```

Loss function description and optimizer

The following is the function:

```
classifier = skflow.TensorFlowEstimator(model_fn=conv_model, n_classes=10,
batch_size=100, steps=2000, learning_rate=0.01)
```

Training and accuracy tests

With these two commands, we start the fitting of the model and producing the scoring of the trained model, using the image set:

```
%time classifier.fit(images, labels, logdir='/tmp/cnn_train/')
%time score =metrics.accuracy_score(labels, classifier.predict(images))
```

Results description

The following is the result:

Parameter	Result 1	Result 2
CPU times	user 35min 6s	user 39.8 s
sys	1min 50s	7.19 s
total	36min 57s	47 s
Wall time	25min 3s	32.5 s
Accuracy	0.612200	

Full source code

The following is the complete source code:

```
import glob
import numpy as np
import matplotlib.pyplot as plt
import tensorflow as tf
import tensorflow.contrib.learn as skflow
from sklearn import metrics
from tensorflow.contrib import learn

datadir='data/cifar-10-batches-bin/'
```

```
plt.ion()
G = glob.glob (datadir + '*.bin')
A = np.fromfile(G[0],dtype=np.uint8).reshape([10000,3073])
labels = A [:,0]
images = A [:,1:].reshape([10000,3,32,32]).transpose (0,2,3,1)
plt.imshow(images[15])
print labels[11]
images_unroll = A [:,1:]
def max_pool_2x2(tensor_in):
    return tf.nn.max_pool(tensor_in,  ksize= [1,2,2,1], strides= [1,2,2,1],
padding='SAME')

def conv_model (X, y):
    X= tf. reshape(X, [-1, 32, 32, 3])
    with tf.variable_scope('conv_layer1'):
        h_conv1=tf.contrib.layers.conv2d(X, num_outputs=16,
kernel_size=[5,5],  activation_fn=tf.nn.relu)#print (h_conv1)
        h_pool1=max_pool_2x2(h_conv1)#print (h_pool1)
    with tf.variable_scope('conv_layer2'):
        h_conv2=tf.contrib.layers.conv2d(h_pool1, num_outputs=16,
kernel_size=[5,5], activation_fn=tf.nn.relu)
    #print (h_conv2)
    h_pool2=max_pool_2x2(h_conv2)
    h_pool2_flat = tf.reshape(h_pool2,  [-1,8*8*16 ])
    h_fc1 = tf.contrib.layers.stack(h_pool2_flat,
tf.contrib.layers.fully_connected ,[96,48], activation_fn=tf.nn.relu )
    return skflow.models.logistic_regression(h_fc1,y)

images = np.array(images,dtype=np.float32)
classifier = skflow.TensorFlowEstimator(model_fn=conv_model, n_classes=10,
batch_size=100, steps=2000, learning_rate=0.01)

%time classifier.fit(images, labels, logdir='/tmp/cnn_train/')
%time score =metrics.accuracy_score(labels, classifier.predict(images))
```

Summary

In this chapter, we learned about one of the building blocks of the most advanced neural network architectures: convolutional neural networks. With this new tool, we worked on more complex datasets and concept abstractions, and so we will be able to understand state-of-the-art-models.

In the next chapter, we will be working with another new form of neural network and a part of a more recent neural network architecture: recurrent neural networks.

7
Recurrent Neural Networks and LSTM

Reviewing what we know about the more traditional neural networks models, we observe that the train and prediction phases are normally expressed in a static manner, where an input is feed, and we get an output, but we don't just take in account the sequence in which the events occur. Unlike the prediction models reviewed so far, recurrent neural networks predictions depends on the current input vector and also the values of previous ones.

The topics we will cover in this chapter are as follow:

- Getting an idea of how recurrent neural networks works, and the main operation types used in building them
- Explain the ideas implemented in more advanced models, like LSTM
- Applying an LSTM model in TensorFlow to predict energy consumption cycles
- Compose new music, starting with a series of studies from J.S Bach

Recurrent neural networks

Knowledge doesn't normally appear from a void. Many new ideas are born as a combination of previous knowledge, and so that's a useful behaviour to emulate. Traditional neural networks don't include any mechanism translating previous seen elements to the current state.

Trying to implement this concepts, we have recurrent neural networks, or RNN. Recurrent neural networks can be defined a sequential model of neural networks, which have the property of reusing information already given. One of their main assumptions is that the current information has a dependency on previous data. In the following figure, we observe a simplified diagram of a RNN basic element, called Cell:

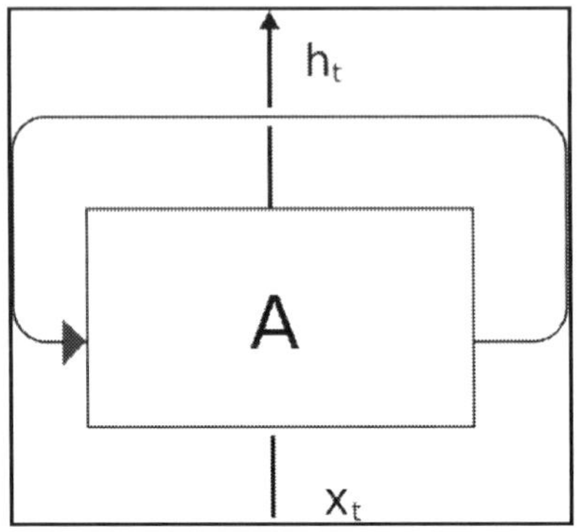

The main information elements of a cell are the input (**Xt**), an state, and an output (**ht**). But as we said before, cells have not an independent state, so it stores also state information. In the following figure we will show an "unrolled" RNN cell, showing how it goes from the initial state, to outputting the final $\mathbf{h}_n$ value, with some intermediate states in between.

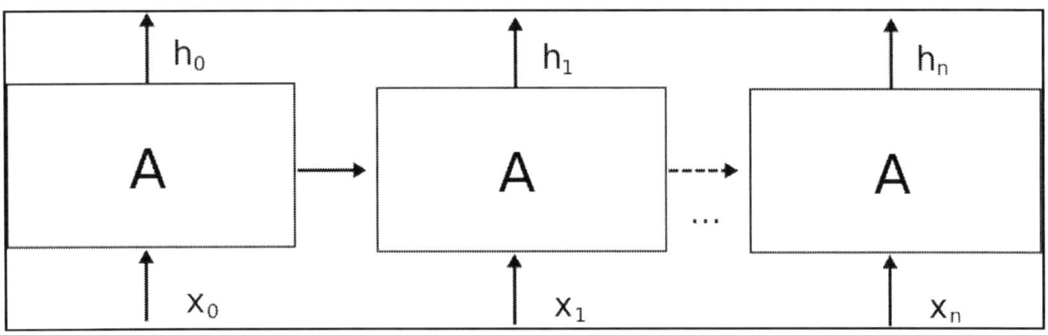

Once we define the dynamics of the cell, the next objective would be to investigate the contents of what makes or defines an RNN cell. In the most common case of standard RNN, there is simply a neural network layer, which takes the input, and the previous state as inputs, applies the tanh operation, and outputs the new state *h(t+1)*.

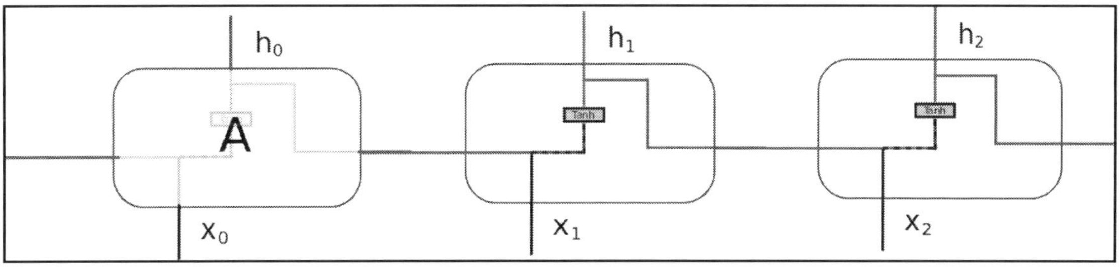

This simple setup is able to sum up information as the epochs pass, but further experimentation showed that for complex knowledge, the sequence distance makes difficult to relate some contexts (For example, *The architect knows about designing beautiful buildings*) seems like a simple structure to remember, but the context needed for them for being associated, requires an increasing sequence to be able to relate both concepts. This also brings the associated issue of exploding and vanishing gradients.

Exploding and vanishing gradients

One of the main problems of recurrent neural networks happens in the back propagation stages, given its recurrent nature, the number of steps that the back propagation of the errors has is one corresponding to a very deep network. This cascade of gradient calculations could lead to a very non significant value on the last stages, or in the contrary, to ever increasing and unbounded parameter. Those phenomena receive the name of vanishing and exploding gradients. This is one of the reasons for which LSTM architecture was created.

LSTM neural networks

The **Long Short—Term Memory** (**LSTM**) is a specific RNN architecture whose special architecture allows them to represent long term dependencies. Moreover, they are specifically designed to remember information patterns and information over long periods of time.

The gate operation – a fundamental component

In order to better understand the building blocks of the internal of the lstm cell, we will describe the main operational block of the LSTM: the gate operation.

This operation basically has a multivariate input, and in this block we decide to let some of the inputs go trough, and block the other. We can think of it as an information filter, and contributes mainly to allow for getting and remembering the needed information elements.

In order to implement this function, we take a multivariate control vector (marked with an arrow), which is connected with a neural network layer with a sigmoid activation function. Applying the control vector and passing through the sigmoid function, we will get a binary like vector.

We will represent this function with many switch signs:

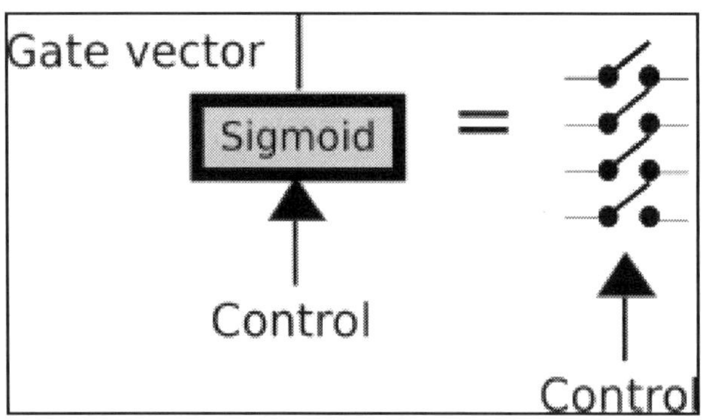

After defining that binary vector, we will multiply the input function with the vector so we will filter it, letting only parts of the information to get through. We will represent this operation with a triangle, pointing in the direction to which the information goes.

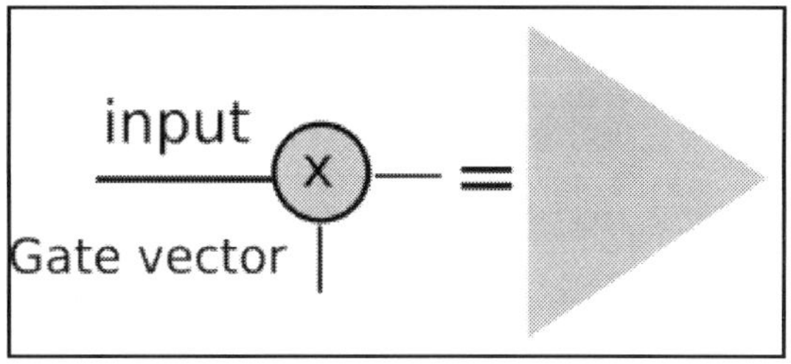

General LSTM cell structure

In the following picture, we represent the general structure of a LSTM Cell. It mainly consist of three of the the mentioned gate operations, to protect and control the cell state.

This operation will allow both discard (Hopefully not important) low state data, and incorporate (Hopefully important) new data to the state.

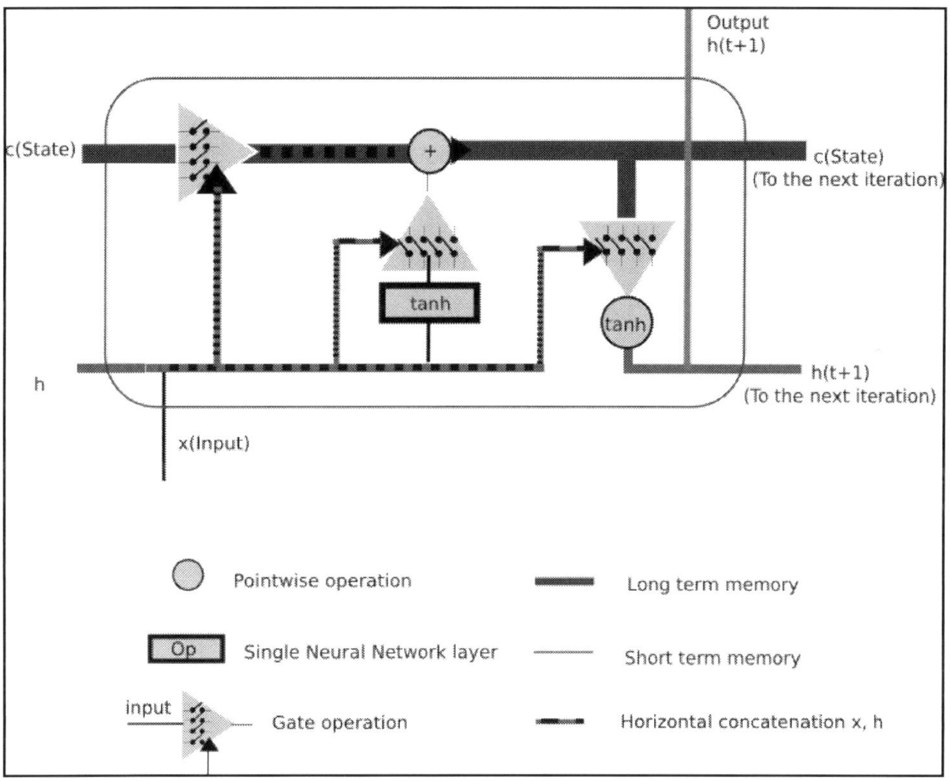

The previous figure tries to show all concepts going on on the operation of one LSTM Cell.

As the inputs we have:

- The cell state, which will store long term information, because it carries on the optimized weights from the starting coming from the origin of the cell training, and
- The short term state, *h(t)*, which will be used directly combined with the current input on each iteration, and so it will have a much bigger influence from the latest values of the inputs

And as outputs, we have, the result of combining the application of all the gate operations.

Operation steps

In this section we will describe a generalization of all the different substeps that the information will do for each loop steps of its operation.

Part 1 – set values to forget (input gate)

In this section, we will take the values coming from the short term, combined with the input itself, and this values will set the values for a binary fuction, represented by a multivariable sigmoid. Depending on the input and short term memory values, the sigmoid output will allow or restrict some of the previous Knowledge or weights contained on the cell state.

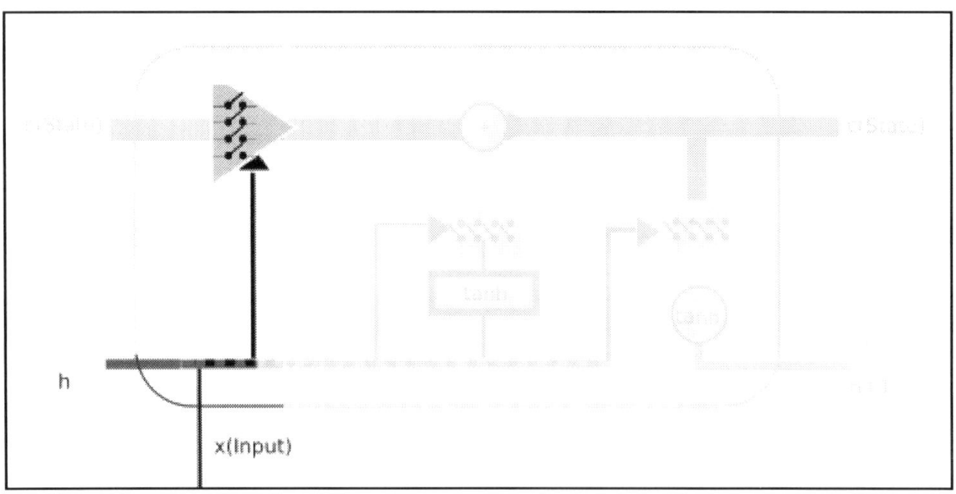

Part 2 – set values to keep, change state

Then is time to set the filter which will allow or reject the incorporation of new and short term memory to the cell semi-permanent state.

So in this stage, we will determine how much of the new and semi-new information will be incorporated in the new cell state. Additionally, we will finally pass through the information filter we have been configuring, and as a result, we will have an updated long term state.

In order to normalize the new and short term information, we pass the new and short term info via a neural network with *tanh* activation, this will allow to feed the new information in a normalized (*-1,1*) range.

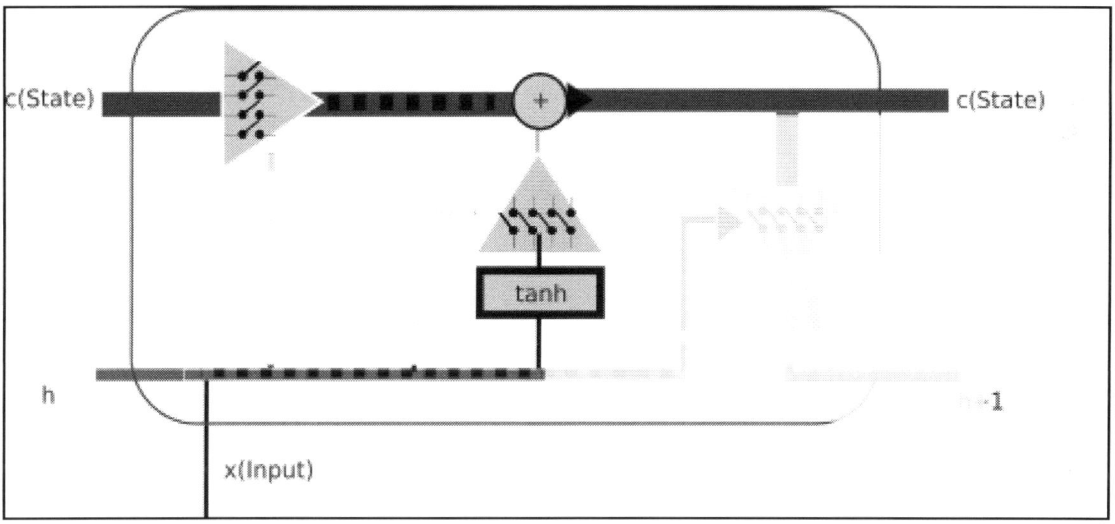

Part 3 – output filtered cell state

Now its the turn of the short term state. It will also use the new and previous short term state to allow new information to pass, but the input will be the long term status, dot multiplied multiplied by a tanh function, again to normalize the input to a (*-1,1*) range.

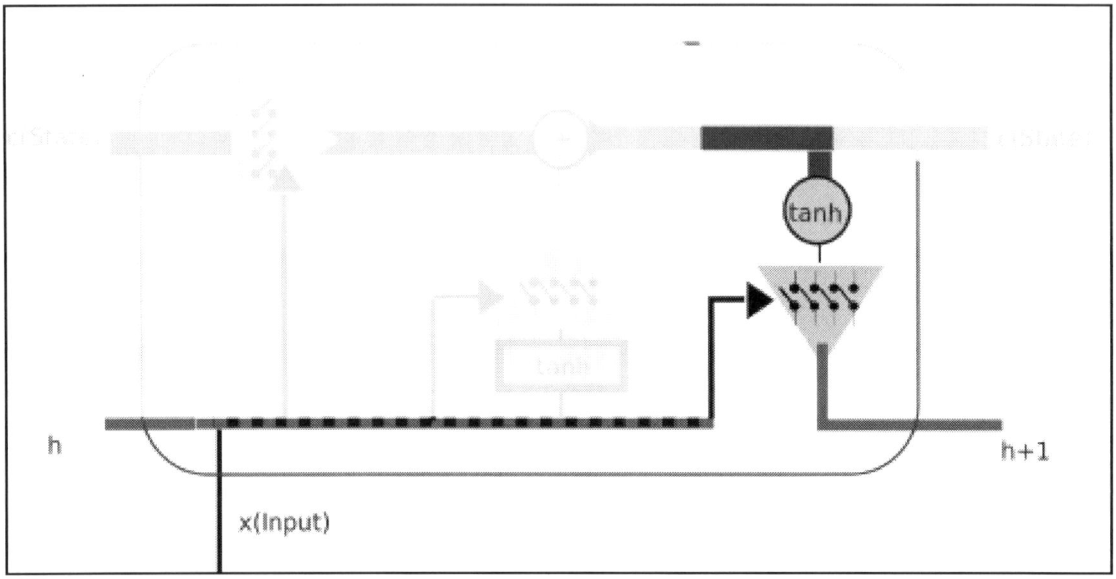

Other RNN architectures

In this chapter in general, and assuming the field of RNN is much more general that the we will be focusing on the LSTM type of recurrent neural network cells. There are also other variations of the RNN that are being employed and add advantages to the field, for example.

- **LSTM with peepholes**: In this networks the cell gates are connected to the cell state
- **Gate Recurring Unit**: It's a simpler model which combines the forget and input gates, merges the state and hidden state of the cell, and so simplifies a lot the training of the net

TensorFlow LSTM useful classes and methods

In this section, we will review the main classes and methods that we can use to build a LSTM layer, which we will use in the examples of the book.

class tf.nn.rnn_cell.BasicLSTMCell

This class basic LSTM recurrent network cell, with a forget bias, and no fancy characteristics of other related types, like peep-holes, that allow the cell to take a look on the cell state even on stages where it's not supposed to have an influence on the results.

The following are the main parameters:

- **num_units**: Int, the number of units of the LSTM cell
- **forget_bias**: Float, This bias (default *1*) is added to the forget gates in order to allow the first iterations to reduce the loss of information for the initial training steps.
- **activation**: Is the activation function of the inner states (The default is the standard *tanh*)

class MultiRNNCell(RNNCell)

In the architectures we will be using for this particular example, we won't be using a single cell to take in account the historical values. In this case we will be using a stack of connected cells. For this reason we will be instantiating the `MultiRNNCell` class.

```
MultiRNNCell(cells, state_is_tuple=False)
```

Thisis the constructor for the `multiRNNCell`, the main argument of this method is cells, which will be an instance of `RNNCells` we want to stack.

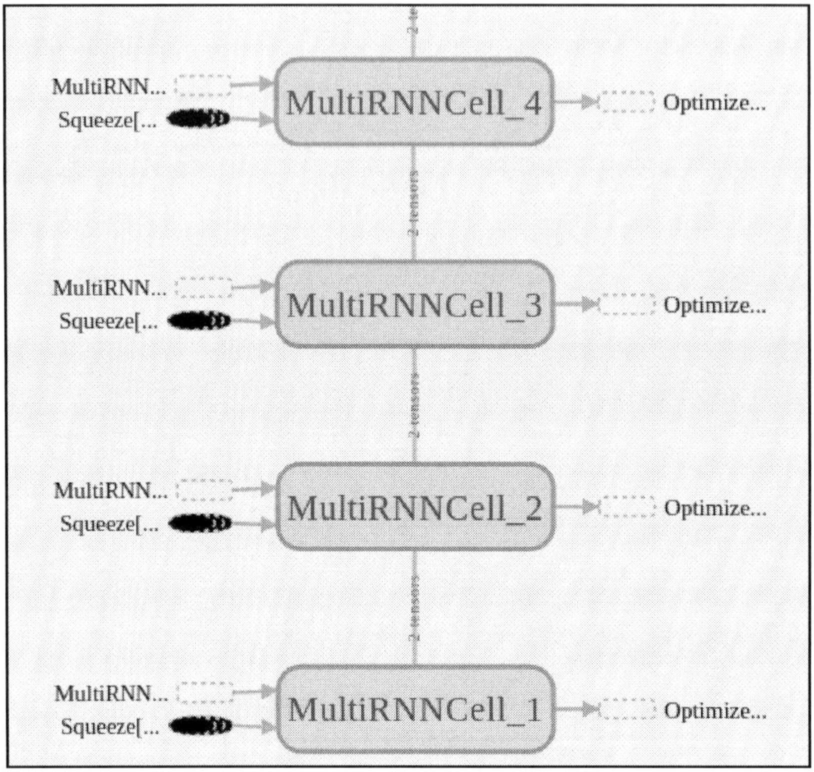

learn.ops.split_squeeze(dim, num_split, tensor_in)

This function split the input on a dimension, and then it squeezes the previous dimension the splitted tensor belonged. It takes the dimension to cut, the number of ways to split, and then tensor to split. It return the same tensor but with one dimension reduced.

Example 1 – univariate time series prediction with energy consumption data

In this example, we will be solving a problem of the domain of regression. The dataset we will be working on is a compendium of many measurements of power consumption of one home, throughout a period of time. As we could infer, this kind of behaviour can easily follow patterns (It increases when the persons uses the microwave to prepare breakfast, and computers after the wake up hour, can decrease a bit in the afternoon, and then increase at night with all the lights, decreasing to zero starting from midnight until next wake up hour).

So let's try to model for this behavior in a sample case.

Dataset description and loading

In this example we will be using the *Electricity Load Diagrams Data Sets*, from *Artur Trindade* (site: `https://archive.ics.uci.edu/ml/datasets/ElectricityLoadDiagrams20112014`).

This is the description of the original dataset:

> *Data set has no missing values.*
> *Values are in kW of each 15 min. To convert values in kWh values must be divided by 4.*
> *Each column represent one client. Some clients were created after 2011. In these cases consumption were considered zero.*
> *All time labels report to Portuguese hour. However all days present 96 measures (24*15). Every year in March time change day (which has only 23 hours) the values between 1:00 am and 2:00 am are zero for all points. Every year in October time change day (which has 25 hours) the values between 1:00 am and 2:00 am aggregate the consumption of two hours.*

In order to simplify our model description, we took just one client complete measurements, and converted its format to standard CSV. It is located on the data subfolder of this chapter code folder

With this code lines, we will open and represent the client's data:

```
import pandas as pd
from matplotlib import pyplot as plt
df = pd.read_csv("data/elec_load.csv", error_bad_lines=False)
plt.subplot()
plot_test, = plt.plot(df.values[:1500], label='Load')
plt.legend(handles=[plot_test])
```

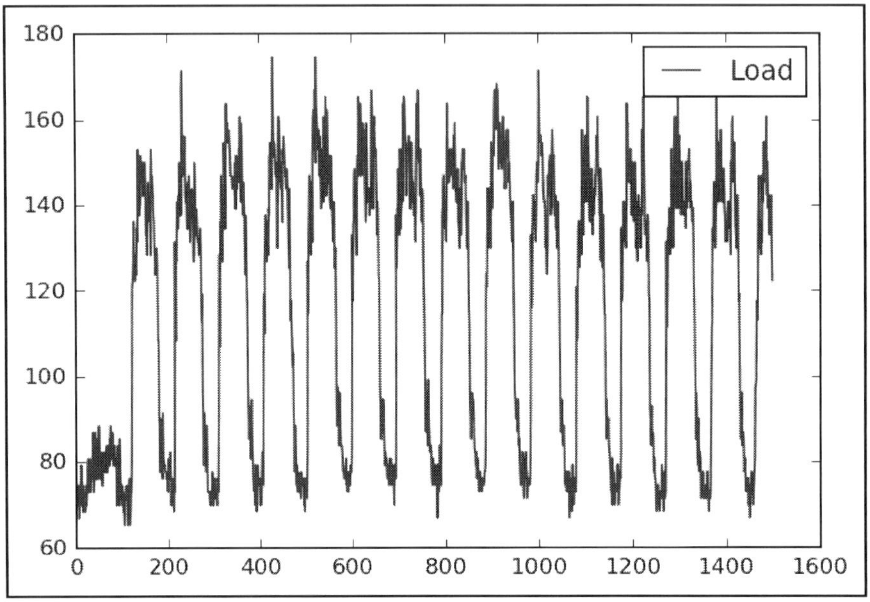

I we take a look at this representation (We look to the first *1500* samples) we see an initial transient state, probable when the measurements were put in place, and then we see a really clear cycle of high and low consumption levels.

From simple observation we also see that the cicles are more or less of *100* samples, pretty close to the *96* samples per day this dataset has.

Dataset preprocessing

In order to assure a better convergency of the back propagation methods, we should try to normalize the input data.

So we will be applying the classic scale and centering technique, substracting the mean value, and scaling by the floor of the maximum value.

To get the needed values, we use the pandas the `describe()` method.

```
                Load
count  140256.000000
mean      145.332503
std        48.477976
min         0.000000
25%       106.850998
50%       151.428571
75%       177.557604
max       338.218126
```

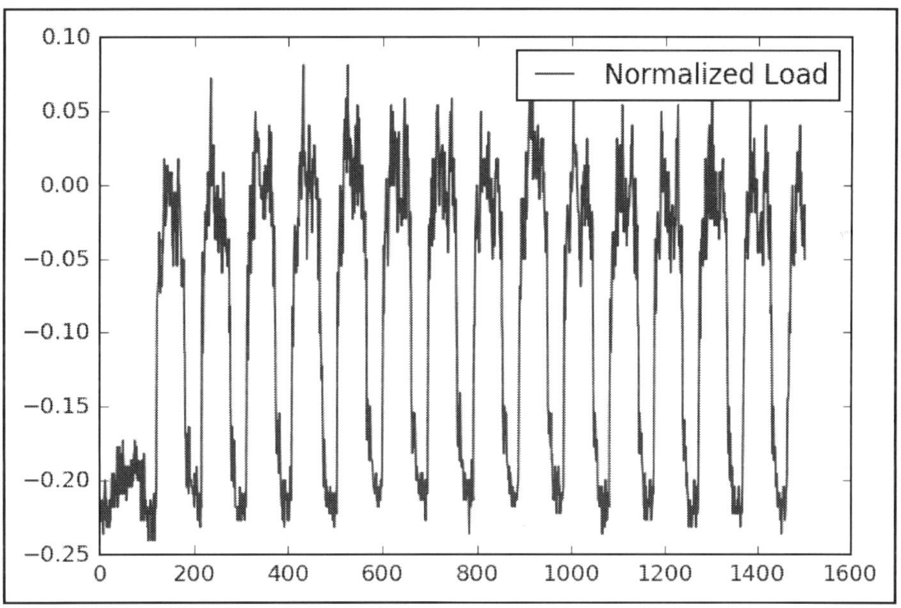

Modelling architecture

Here we will succinctly describe the architecture that will try to model the variations on electricity consumption:

The resulting architecture basically consists on a 10 member serial connected LSTM multicell, which has a linear regress or variable at the end, which will transform the results of the output of the linear array of cells, to a final real number, for a given history of values (in this case we have to input the last 5 values to predict the next one).

```
def lstm_model(time_steps, rnn_layers, dense_layers=None):
    def lstm_cells(layers):
        return
[tf.nn.rnn_cell.BasicLSTMCell(layer['steps'],state_is_tuple=True)
                for layer in layers]

    def dnn_layers(input_layers, layers):
            return input_layers

    def _lstm_model(X, y):
        stacked_lstm = tf.nn.rnn_cell.MultiRNNCell(lstm_cells(rnn_layers),
state_is_tuple=True)
        x_ = learn.ops.split_squeeze(1, time_steps, X)
        output, layers = tf.nn.rnn(stacked_lstm, x_, dtype=dtypes.float32)
        output = dnn_layers(output[-1], dense_layers)
        return learn.models.linear_regression(output, y)

    return _lstm_model
```

The following figure shows the main blocks, complemented later by the learn module, there you can see the RNN stage, the optimizer, and the final linear regression before the output.

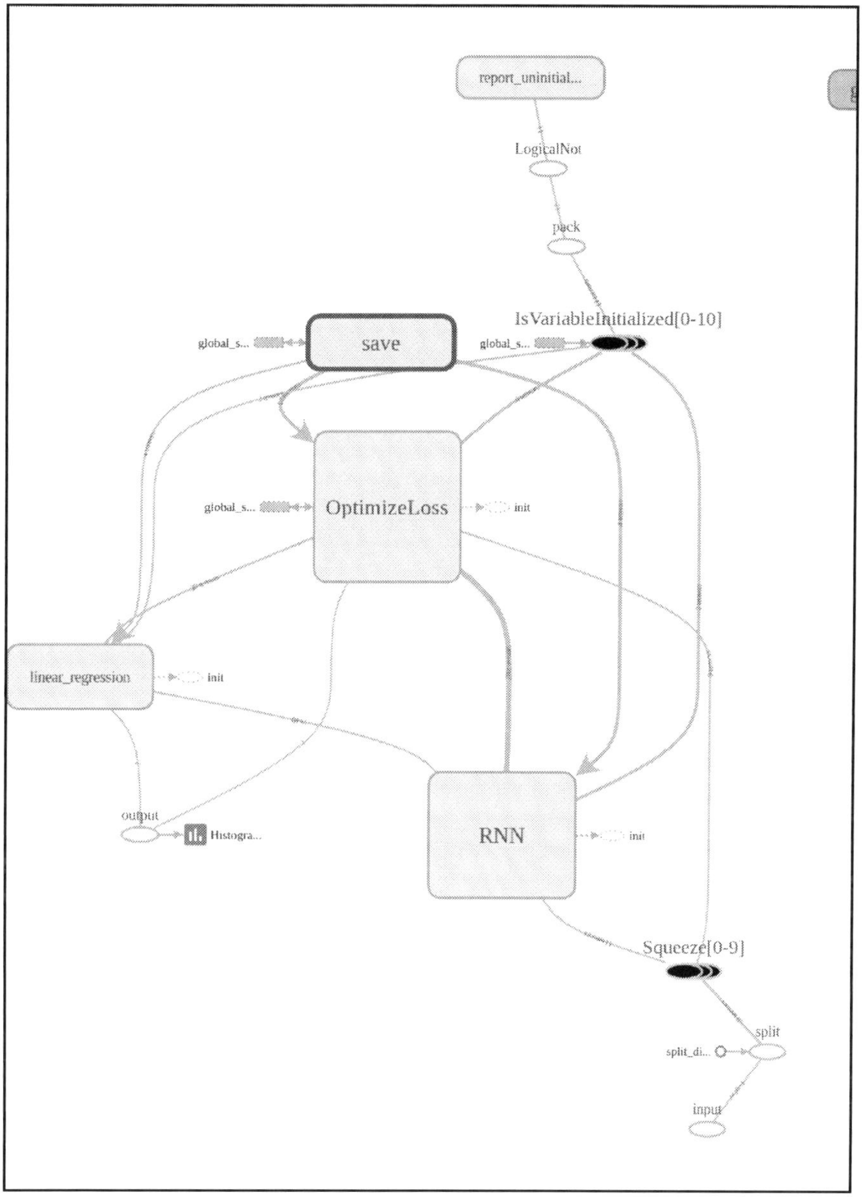

In this picture we take a look at the RNN stage, there we can observe the cascade of individual LSTM cells, with the input squeeze, and all the complementary operations that the learn package adds.

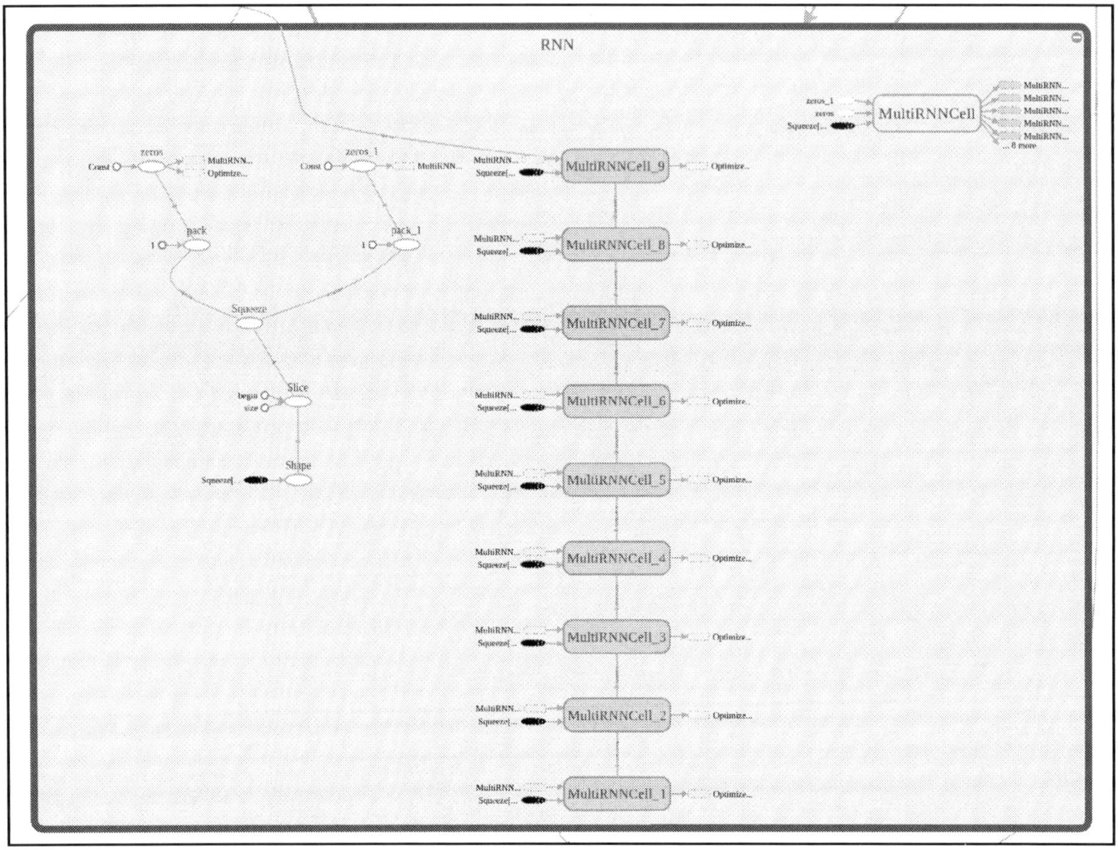

And then we will complete the definition of the model with the regressor:

```
regressor = learn.TensorFlowEstimator(model_fn=lstm_model(
                                    TIMESTEPS, RNN_LAYERS, DENSE_LAYERS),
n_classes=0,
                                      verbose=2,  steps=TRAINING_STEPS,
optimizer='Adagrad',
                                      learning_rate=0.03,
batch_size=BATCH_SIZE)
```

Loss function description

For the loss function, the classical regression parameter mean squared error will do:

```
rmse = np.sqrt(((predicted - y['test']) ** 2).mean(axis=0))
```

Convergency test

Here we will run the fit function for the current model:

```
regressor.fit(X['train'], y['train'], monitors=[validation_monitor],
logdir=LOG_DIR)
```

And will obtain the following (Very good)! error rates. One exercise we could do is to avoid normalizing the data, and see if the mean error is the same (NB: It's not, its much worse)

This is the simple console output we will get:

```
MSE: 0.001139
```

And this is the generated loss/mean graphic that tells us how the error is decaying with every iteration:

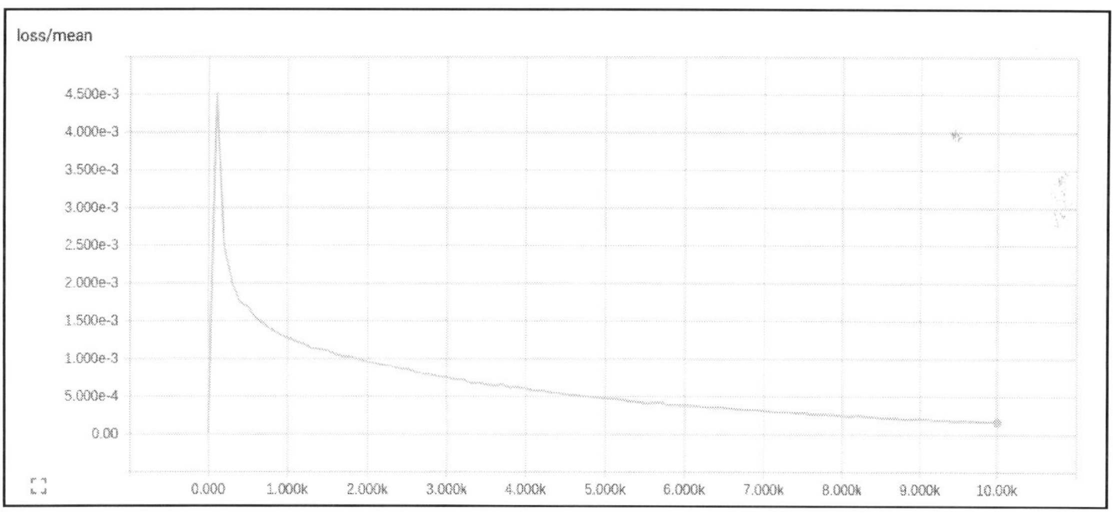

Results description

Now we can get a graphic of the real test values, and the predicted one, where we see that the mean error indicates a very good predicting capabilities of our recurrent model:

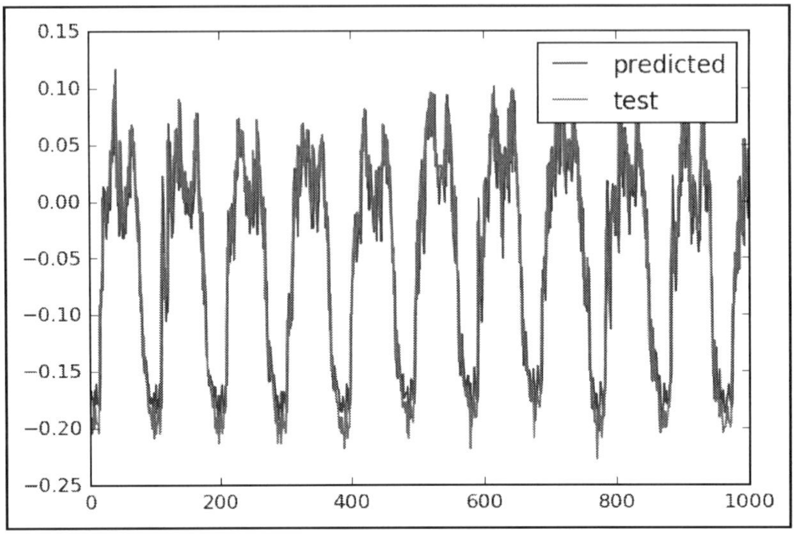

Full source code

The following is the complete source code:

```
import numpy as np
import pandas as pd
import tensorflow as tf
from matplotlib import pyplot as plt


from tensorflow.python.framework import dtypes
from tensorflow.contrib import learn

import logging
logging.basicConfig(level=logging.INFO)


from tensorflow.contrib import learn
from sklearn.metrics import mean_squared_error
```

```
LOG_DIR = './ops_logs'
TIMESTEPS = 5
RNN_LAYERS = [{'steps': TIMESTEPS}]
DENSE_LAYERS = None
TRAINING_STEPS = 10000
BATCH_SIZE = 100
PRINT_STEPS = TRAINING_STEPS / 100

def lstm_model(time_steps, rnn_layers, dense_layers=None):
    def lstm_cells(layers):
        return
[tf.nn.rnn_cell.BasicLSTMCell(layer['steps'],state_is_tuple=True)
                for layer in layers]

    def dnn_layers(input_layers, layers):
            return input_layers

    def _lstm_model(X, y):
        stacked_lstm = tf.nn.rnn_cell.MultiRNNCell(lstm_cells(rnn_layers),
state_is_tuple=True)
        x_ = learn.ops.split_squeeze(1, time_steps, X)
        output, layers = tf.nn.rnn(stacked_lstm, x_, dtype=dtypes.float32)
        output = dnn_layers(output[-1], dense_layers)
        return learn.models.linear_regression(output, y)

    return _lstm_model


regressor = learn.TensorFlowEstimator(model_fn=lstm_model(TIMESTEPS,
RNN_LAYERS, DENSE_LAYERS), n_classes=0,
                                      verbose=2,  steps=TRAINING_STEPS,
optimizer='Adagrad',
                                      learning_rate=0.03,
batch_size=BATCH_SIZE)

df = pd.read_csv("data/elec_load.csv", error_bad_lines=False)
plt.subplot()
plot_test, = plt.plot(df.values[:1500], label='Load')
plt.legend(handles=[plot_test])


print df.describe()
array=(df.values- 147.0) /339.0
plt.subplot()
plot_test, = plt.plot(array[:1500], label='Normalized Load')
plt.legend(handles=[plot_test])
```

```
listX = []
listy = []
X={}
y={}

for i in range(0,len(array)-6):
    listX.append(array[i:i+5].reshape([5,1]))
    listy.append(array[i+6])

arrayX=np.array(listX)
arrayy=np.array(listy)


X['train']=arrayX[0:12000]
X['test']=arrayX[12000:13000]
X['val']=arrayX[13000:14000]

y['train']=arrayy[0:12000]
y['test']=arrayy[12000:13000]
y['val']=arrayy[13000:14000]


# print y['test'][0]
# print y2['test'][0]


#X1, y2 = generate_data(np.sin, np.linspace(0, 100, 10000), TIMESTEPS,
seperate=False)
# create a lstm instance and validation monitor
validation_monitor = learn.monitors.ValidationMonitor(X['val'], y['val'],
every_n_steps=PRINT_STEPS,
early_stopping_rounds=1000)

regressor.fit(X['train'], y['train'], monitors=[validation_monitor],
logdir=LOG_DIR)

predicted = regressor.predict(X['test'])
rmse = np.sqrt(((predicted - y['test']) ** 2).mean(axis=0))
score = mean_squared_error(predicted, y['test'])
print ("MSE: %f" % score)

#plot_predicted, = plt.plot(array[:1000], label='predicted')

plt.subplot()
plot_predicted, = plt.plot(predicted, label='predicted')

plot_test, = plt.plot(y['test'], label='test')
plt.legend(handles=[plot_predicted, plot_test])
```

Example 2 – writing music "a la" Bach

In this example, we will work with a recurrent neural network specialized in character sequences, or the char RNN model.

We will feed this neural network with a series of musical tunes, the Bach Goldberg Variations, expressed in a character based format, and write a sample piece of music based on the learned structures.

Note that this examples owes many ideas and concepts to the paper *Visualizing and Understanding Recurrent Networks* (`https://arxiv.org/abs/1506.02078`) and the article titled *The Unreasonable Effectiveness of recurrent neural networks*, available at (`http://karpathy.github.io/2015/05/21/rnn-effectiveness/`).

Character level models

As we previously saw, Char RNN models work with character sequences. This category of inputs can represent a vast array of possible languages. The following, are a few examples:

- Programming code
- Different human languages (modeling of the writing style of certain author)
- Scientific papers (tex) and so on

Character sequences and probability representation

The input contents of an RNN need a clear and straightforward way of representation. For this reason, the one hot representation is chosen, which is convenient to use directly for the characterization of an output of a limited quantity of possible outcomes (the number of limited characters is finite and in tens), and use it to directly compare with a `Sotmax` function value.

So the input of the model is a sequence of characters, and the output of the model will be a sequence of an array per instance. The length of the array will be the same as the vocabulary size, so each of the array positions will represent the probability of the current character being in this sequence position, given the previously entered sequence characters.

In the following figure, we observe a very simplified model of the setup, with the encoded input word and the model predicting the word *TEST* as the expected output:

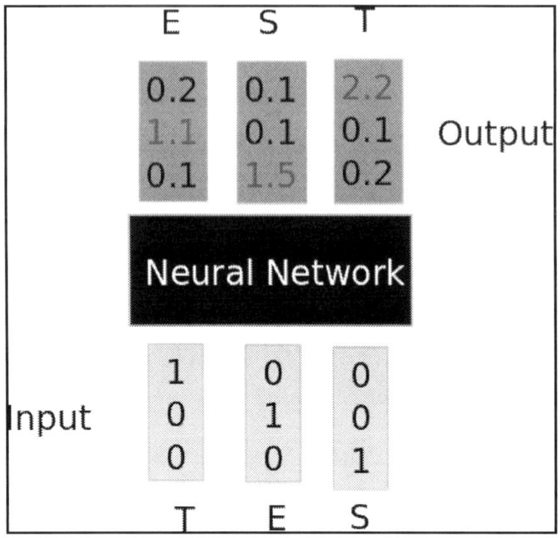

Encoding music as characters – the ABC music format

When searching for a format to represent the input data, it is important to choose the one that is more simple but structurally homogeneous, if possible.

Regarding music representation, the ABC format is a suitable candidate because it has a very simple structure and uses a limited number of characters, and it is a subset of the ASCII charset.

ABC format data organization

An ABC format page has mainly two components: a header and the notes.

- **Header**: A header contains some key: value rows, such as `X:[Reference number]`, `T:[Title]`, `M:[Meter]`, `K:[Key]`, `C[Composer]`.
- **Notes**: The notes start after the K header key and list the different notes of each bar, separated by the `|` character.

There are other elements, but with the following example, you will have an idea of how the format works, even with no music training:

The original sample is as follows:

```
X:1
T:Notes
M:C
L:1/4
K:C
C, D, E, F,|G, A, B, C|D E F G|A B c d|e f g a|b c' d' e'|f' g' a' b'|]
```

The final representation is as follows:

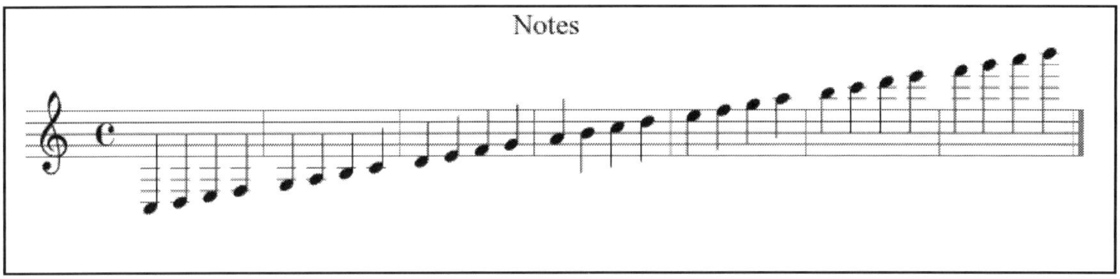

Bach Goldberg variations:

The Bach Goldberg variations is a set of an original aria and 30 works based on it, named after a Bach disciple, *Johann Gottlieb Goldberg,* who was probably its main interpreter.

In the next listing and figure, we will represent the first part of the variation *Nr 1* so you have an idea of the document structure we will try to emulate:

```
X:1
T:Variation no. 1
C:J.S.Bach
M:3/4
L:1/16
Q:500
V:2 bass
K:G
[V:1]GFG2- GDEF GAB^c |d^cd2- dABc defd |gfg2- gfed ^ceAG|
[V:2]G,,2B,A, B,2G,2G,,2G,2 |F,,2F,E, F,2D,2F,,2D,2 |E,,2E,D,
E,2G,2A,,2^C2|
%  (More parts with V:1 and V:2)
```

Useful libraries and methods

In this section, we will learn the new functionalities we will be using in this example.

Saving and restoring variables and models

One very important feature for real world applications is the ability to save and retrieve whole models. TensorFlow provides this ability through the `tf.train.Saver` object.

The main methods of this object are the following:

- `tf.train.Saver(args)`: This is the constructor. This is a list of the main parameters:
    - `var_list`: This is a list containing the list of all variables to save. For example, {`firstvar: var1, secondvar: var2`}. If none, save all the objects.
    - `max_to_keep`: This denotes the maximum number of checkpoints to maintain.
    - `write_version`: This is the file format version, actually only 1 is valid.
- `tf.train.Saver.save`: This method runs the ops added by the constructor for saving variables. This requires a current session and all variables to have been initialized. The main parameters are as follows:
    - `session`: This is a session to save the variables
    - `save_path`: This is the path to the checkpoint filename
    - `global_step`: This is a unique step identifier

  This methods returns the path where the checkpoint was saved.

- `tf.train.Saver.restore`: This method restores the previously saved variables. The main parameters are as follows:
    - `session`: The session is where the variables are to be restored
    - `save_path`: This is a variable previously returned by the save method, a call to the latest_checkpoint(), or a provided one

Loading and saving pseudocode

Here, we will build with some sample code a minimal structure for saving and retrieving two sample variables.

Variable saving

The following is the code to create variables:

```
# Create some variables.
simplevar = tf.Variable(..., name="simple")
anothervar = tf.Variable(..., name="another")
```

```
...
# Add ops to save and restore all the variables.
saver = tf.train.Saver()
# Later, launch the model, initialize the variables, do some work, save the
# variables to disk.
with tf.Session() as sess:
  sess.run(tf.initialize_all_variables())
  # Do some work with the model.
  ..
  # Save the variables to disk.
  save_path = saver.save(sess, "/tmp/model.ckpt")
```

Variable restoring

The following is the code for restoring the variables:

```
saver = tf.train.Saver()
# Later, launch the model, use the saver to restore variables from disk,
and
# do some work with the model.
with tf.Session() as sess:
#Work with the restored model....
```

Dataset description and loading

For this dataset, we start with the 30 works, and then we generate a list of `1000` instances of theirs, randomly distributed:

```
import random
input = open('input.txt', 'r').read().split('X:')
for i in range (1,1000):
    print "X:" + input[random.randint(1,30)] +
"\n_____________________________________________\n"
```

Network Training

The original material for the network training will be the `30` works in the ABC format.

Note that the original ABC file was located at `http://www.barfly.dial.pipex.com/Goldbergs.abc`.

Then we use this little program ().

For this dataset, we start with the `30` works, and then we generate a list of `1000` instances of theirs, randomly distributed:

```
import random
input = open('original.txt', 'r').read().split('X:')
for i in range (1,1000):
    print "X:" + input[random.randint(1,30)] +
"\n_______________________________________________\n"
```

And then we execute the following to get the data set:

```
python generate_dataset.py > input.txt
```

Dataset preprocessing

The generated dataset needs a bit of information before being useful. First, it needs the definition of the vocabulary.

Vocabulary definition

The first step in the process is to find all the different characters that can be found in the original text in order to be able to dimension and fill the one-hot encoded inputs later.

In the following figure, we represent the different characters found in the ABC music format. Here you can see what's represented in the standard, with normal and special punctuation characters:

```
(,|  |2|||G|/|B|A|:|z|F|D|E|\u000a|[|]|_|e|d|C|c|3|^|V|4|a|g|-|f|=|b|
(|1|s|K|6|%|t|r|l|.|8|'|n|i|)|o|M|h|P|0|T|m|L|J|Q|S|X|~|O|5|u|>|7|9|
p|N|w|H|<|I|v|"|{|}|#|?|\u005c|q|y|x|tp1|.|
```

Modelling architecture

The model for this RNN is described in the following lines, and it is a multilayer LSTM with initial zero state:

```
        cell_fn = rnn_cell.BasicLSTMCell
        cell = cell_fn(args.rnn_size, state_is_tuple=True)
        self.cell = cell = rnn_cell.MultiRNNCell([cell] * args.num_layers,
state_is_tuple=True)
        self.input_data = tf.placeholder(tf.int32, [args.batch_size,
args.seq_length])
        self.targets = tf.placeholder(tf.int32, [args.batch_size,
args.seq_length])
        self.initial_state = cell.zero_state(args.batch_size, tf.float32)
        with tf.variable_scope('rnnlm'):
            softmax_w = tf.get_variable("softmax_w", [args.rnn_size,
args.vocab_size])
            softmax_b = tf.get_variable("softmax_b", [args.vocab_size])
            with tf.device("/cpu:0"):
                embedding = tf.get_variable("embedding", [args.vocab_size,
args.rnn_size])
                inputs = tf.split(1, args.seq_length,
tf.nn.embedding_lookup(embedding, self.input_data))
                inputs = [tf.squeeze(input_, [1]) for input_ in inputs]
        def loop(prev, _):
            prev = tf.matmul(prev, softmax_w) + softmax_b
            prev_symbol = tf.stop_gradient(tf.argmax(prev, 1))
            return tf.nn.embedding_lookup(embedding, prev_symbol)
        outputs, last_state = seq2seq.rnn_decoder(inputs,
self.initial_state, cell, loop_function=loop if infer else None,
scope='rnnlm')
        output = tf.reshape(tf.concat(1, outputs), [-1, args.rnn_size])
```

Loss function description

The loss function is defined by the losss_by_example function. This is based on a measure called perplexity, which measures how well a probability distribution predicts a sample. This measure is used extensively in language models:

```
self.logits = tf.matmul(output, softmax_w) + softmax_b
self.probs = tf.nn.softmax(self.logits)
loss = seq2seq.sequence_loss_by_example([self.logits],
        [tf.reshape(self.targets, [-1])],
        [tf.ones([args.batch_size * args.seq_length])],
        args.vocab_size)
self.cost = tf.reduce_sum(loss) / args.batch_size / args.seq_length
```

Stop condition

The program will iterate until the number of epochs and the batch number is reached. Here is the condition block:

```
if (e==args.num_epochs-1 and b == data_loader.num_batches-1)
```

Results description

In order to run the program, first you run the training script using the following code:

```
python train.py
```

Then you run the sample program with the following code:

```
python sample.py
```

Configuring a prime of `X:1\n`, which is a plausible initialization character sequence, we obtain, depending on the depth (recommended 3) and the length (recommended 512) of the RNN, almost an recognizable complete composition.

The following music sheet was obtained copying the resulting character sequence at `http://www.drawthedots.com/` and applying simple character corrections, based on on-site diagnostics:

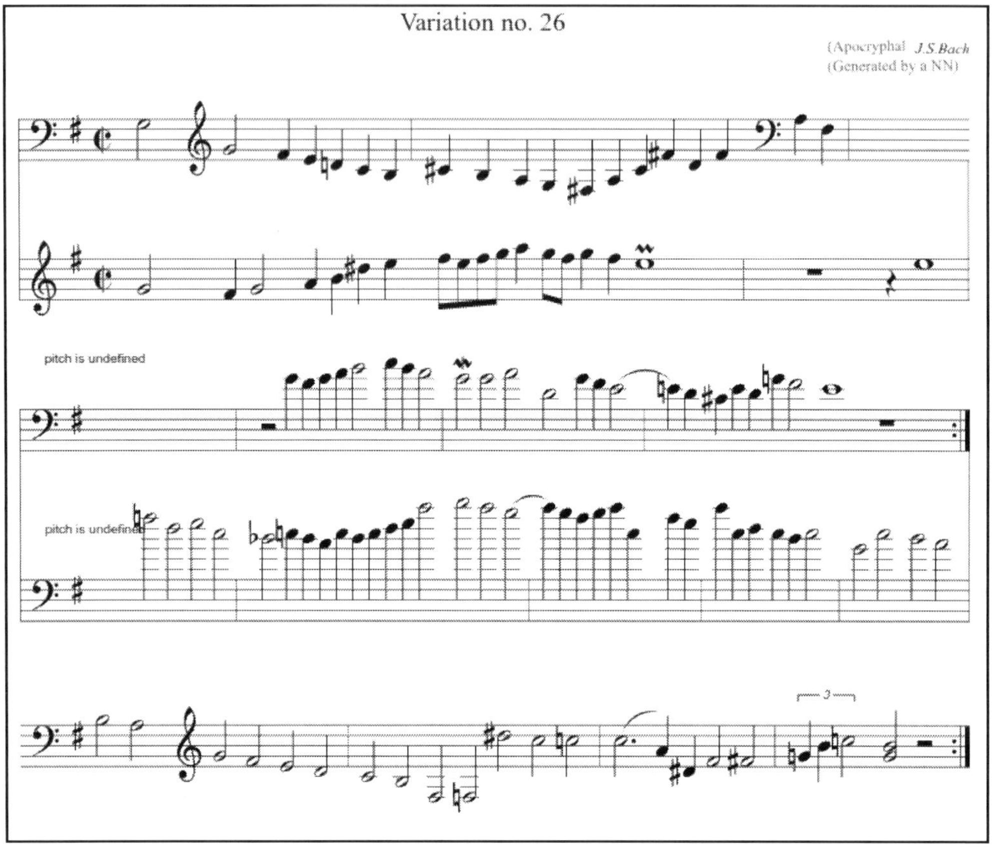

Full source code

The following is the complete source code(`train.py`):

```
from __future__ import print_function
import numpy as np
import tensorflow as tf

import argparse
import time
import os
```

```
from six.moves import cPickle
from utils import TextLoader
from model import Model
class arguments:
    def __init__(self):
        return
def main():
    args = arguments()
    train(args)
def train(args):
    args.data_dir='data/'; args.save_dir='save'; args.rnn_size =64;
    args.num_layers=1;  args.batch_size=50;args.seq_length=50
    args.num_epochs=5;args.save_every=1000; args.grad_clip=5.
    args.learning_rate=0.002; args.decay_rate=0.97
    data_loader = TextLoader(args.data_dir, args.batch_size,
args.seq_length)
    args.vocab_size = data_loader.vocab_size
    with open(os.path.join(args.save_dir, 'config.pkl'), 'wb') as f:
        cPickle.dump(args, f)
    with open(os.path.join(args.save_dir, 'chars_vocab.pkl'), 'wb') as f:
        cPickle.dump((data_loader.chars, data_loader.vocab), f)
    model = Model(args)
    with tf.Session() as sess:
        tf.initialize_all_variables().run()
        saver = tf.train.Saver(tf.all_variables())
        for e in range(args.num_epochs):
            sess.run(tf.assign(model.lr, args.learning_rate *
(args.decay_rate ** e)))
            data_loader.reset_batch_pointer()
            state = sess.run(model.initial_state)
            for b in range(data_loader.num_batches):
                start = time.time()
                x, y = data_loader.next_batch()
                feed = {model.input_data: x, model.targets: y}
                for i, (c, h) in enumerate(model.initial_state):
                    feed[c] = state[i].c
                    feed[h] = state[i].h
                train_loss, state, _ = sess.run([model.cost,
model.final_state, model.train_op], feed)
                end = time.time()
                print("{}/{} (epoch {}), train_loss = {:.3f}, time/batch =
{:.3f}" \
                    .format(e * data_loader.num_batches + b,
                            args.num_epochs * data_loader.num_batches,
                            e, train_loss, end - start))
                if (e==args.num_epochs-1 and b ==
data_loader.num_batches-1): # save for the last result
                    checkpoint_path = os.path.join(args.save_dir,
```

```
'model.ckpt')
                        saver.save(sess, checkpoint_path, global_step = e *
data_loader.num_batches + b)
                        print("model saved to {}".format(checkpoint_path))

if __name__ == '__main__':
    main()
```

The following is the complete source code (`model.py`):

```
import tensorflow as tf
from tensorflow.python.ops import rnn_cell
from tensorflow.python.ops import seq2seq
import numpy as np

class Model():
    def __init__(self, args, infer=False):
        self.args = args
        if infer: #When we sample, the batch and sequence lenght are = 1
            args.batch_size = 1
            args.seq_length = 1
        cell_fn = rnn_cell.BasicLSTMCell #Define the internal cell
structure
        cell = cell_fn(args.rnn_size, state_is_tuple=True)
        self.cell = cell = rnn_cell.MultiRNNCell([cell] * args.num_layers,
state_is_tuple=True)
        #Build the inputs and outputs placeholders, and start with a zero
internal values
        self.input_data = tf.placeholder(tf.int32, [args.batch_size,
args.seq_length])
        self.targets = tf.placeholder(tf.int32, [args.batch_size,
args.seq_length])
        self.initial_state = cell.zero_state(args.batch_size, tf.float32)
        with tf.variable_scope('rnnlm'):
            softmax_w = tf.get_variable("softmax_w", [args.rnn_size,
args.vocab_size]) #Final w
            softmax_b = tf.get_variable("softmax_b", [args.vocab_size])
#Final bias
            with tf.device("/cpu:0"):
                embedding = tf.get_variable("embedding", [args.vocab_size,
args.rnn_size])
                inputs = tf.split(1, args.seq_length,
tf.nn.embedding_lookup(embedding, self.input_data))
                inputs = [tf.squeeze(input_, [1]) for input_ in inputs]
        def loop(prev, _):
            prev = tf.matmul(prev, softmax_w) + softmax_b
            prev_symbol = tf.stop_gradient(tf.argmax(prev, 1))
```

```
            return tf.nn.embedding_lookup(embedding, prev_symbol)
        outputs, last_state = seq2seq.rnn_decoder(inputs,
self.initial_state, cell, loop_function=loop if infer else None,
scope='rnnlm')
        output = tf.reshape(tf.concat(1, outputs), [-1, args.rnn_size])
        self.logits = tf.matmul(output, softmax_w) + softmax_b
        self.probs = tf.nn.softmax(self.logits)
        loss = seq2seq.sequence_loss_by_example([self.logits],
            [tf.reshape(self.targets, [-1])],
            [tf.ones([args.batch_size * args.seq_length])],
            args.vocab_size)
        self.cost = tf.reduce_sum(loss) / args.batch_size / args.seq_length
        self.final_state = last_state
        self.lr = tf.Variable(0.0, trainable=False)
        tvars = tf.trainable_variables()
        grads, _ = tf.clip_by_global_norm(tf.gradients(self.cost,
 tvars),
        args.grad_clip)
        optimizer = tf.train.AdamOptimizer(self.lr)
        self.train_op = optimizer.apply_gradients(zip(grads, tvars))
    def sample(self, sess, chars, vocab, num=200, prime='START',
sampling_type=1):
        state = sess.run(self.cell.zero_state(1, tf.float32))
        for char in prime[:-1]:
            x = np.zeros((1, 1))
            x[0, 0] = vocab[char]
            feed = {self.input_data: x, self.initial_state:state}
            [state] = sess.run([self.final_state], feed)
        def weighted_pick(weights):
            t = np.cumsum(weights)
            s = np.sum(weights)
            return(int(np.searchsorted(t, np.random.rand(1)*s)))
        ret = prime
        char = prime[-1]
        for n in range(num):
            x = np.zeros((1, 1))
            x[0, 0] = vocab[char]
            feed = {self.input_data: x, self.initial_state:state}
            [probs, state] = sess.run([self.probs, self.final_state], feed)
            p = probs[0]
            sample = weighted_pick(p)
            pred = chars[sample]
            ret += pred
            char = pred
        return ret
```

The following is the complete source code(`sample.py`):

```
from __future__ import print_function

import numpy as np
import tensorflow as tf
import time
import os
from six.moves import cPickle
from utils import TextLoader
from model import Model
from six import text_type

class arguments: #Generate the arguments class
    save_dir= 'save'
    n=1000
    prime='x:1\n'
    sample=1

def main():
    args = arguments()
    sample(args)   #Pass the argument object

def sample(args):
    with open(os.path.join(args.save_dir, 'config.pkl'), 'rb') as f:
        saved_args = cPickle.load(f) #Load the config from the standard
file
    with open(os.path.join(args.save_dir, 'chars_vocab.pkl'), 'rb') as f:

        chars, vocab = cPickle.load(f) #Load the vocabulary
    model = Model(saved_args, True) #Rebuild the model
    with tf.Session() as sess:
        tf.initialize_all_variables().run()
        saver = tf.train.Saver(tf.all_variables())
        ckpt = tf.train.get_checkpoint_state(args.save_dir) #Retrieve the
chkpoint
        if ckpt and ckpt.model_checkpoint_path:
            saver.restore(sess, ckpt.model_checkpoint_path) #Restore the
model
            print(model.sample(sess, chars, vocab, args.n, args.prime,
args.sample))
            #Execute the model, generating a n char sequence
            #starting with the prime sequence
if __name__ == '__main__':
    main()
```

The following is the complete source code(`utils.py`):

```
import codecs
import os
import collections
from six.moves import cPickle
import numpy as np

class TextLoader():
    def __init__(self, data_dir, batch_size, seq_length, encoding='utf-8'):
        self.data_dir = data_dir
        self.batch_size = batch_size
        self.seq_length = seq_length
        self.encoding = encoding

        input_file = os.path.join(data_dir, "input.txt")
        vocab_file = os.path.join(data_dir, "vocab.pkl")
        tensor_file = os.path.join(data_dir, "data.npy")

        if not (os.path.exists(vocab_file) and
os.path.exists(tensor_file)):
            print("reading text file")
            self.preprocess(input_file, vocab_file, tensor_file)
        else:
            print("loading preprocessed files")
            self.load_preprocessed(vocab_file, tensor_file)
        self.create_batches()
        self.reset_batch_pointer()

    def preprocess(self, input_file, vocab_file, tensor_file):
        with codecs.open(input_file, "r", encoding=self.encoding) as f:
            data = f.read()
        counter = collections.Counter(data)
        count_pairs = sorted(counter.items(), key=lambda x: -x[1])
        self.chars, _ = zip(*count_pairs)
        self.vocab_size = len(self.chars)
        self.vocab = dict(zip(self.chars, range(len(self.chars))))
        with open(vocab_file, 'wb') as f:
            cPickle.dump(self.chars, f)
        self.tensor = np.array(list(map(self.vocab.get, data)))
        np.save(tensor_file, self.tensor)

    def load_preprocessed(self, vocab_file, tensor_file):
        with open(vocab_file, 'rb') as f:
            self.chars = cPickle.load(f)
        self.vocab_size = len(self.chars)
        self.vocab = dict(zip(self.chars, range(len(self.chars))))
        self.tensor = np.load(tensor_file)
```

```
        self.num_batches = int(self.tensor.size / (self.batch_size *
                                                   self.seq_length))

    def create_batches(self):
        self.num_batches = int(self.tensor.size / (self.batch_size *
                                                   self.seq_length))

        self.tensor = self.tensor[:self.num_batches * self.batch_size *
self.seq_length]
        xdata = self.tensor
        ydata = np.copy(self.tensor)
        ydata[:-1] = xdata[1:]
        ydata[-1] = xdata[0]
        self.x_batches = np.split(xdata.reshape(self.batch_size, -1),
self.num_batches, 1)
        self.y_batches = np.split(ydata.reshape(self.batch_size, -1),
self.num_batches, 1)


    def next_batch(self):
        x, y = self.x_batches[self.pointer], self.y_batches[self.pointer]
        self.pointer += 1
        return x, y

    def reset_batch_pointer(self):
        self.pointer = 0
```

Summary

In this chapter, we reviewed one of the most recent neural networks architectures, recurrent neural networks, completing the panorama of the mainstream approaches in the machine learning field.

In the following chapter, we will research the different neural network layer type combinations appearing in state of the art implementations and cover some new interesting experimental models.

8
Deep Neural Networks

In this chapter, we will be reviewing one of the most state of the art, and most prolifically studied fields in Machine Learning, Deep neural networks.

Deep neural network definition

This is an area which is experiencing a blast on news techniques, and every day we hear of successful experiments applying DNN in solving new problems, for example, in computer vision, autonomous car driving, speech and text understanding, and so on.

In the previous chapters, we were using techniques that can be related with DNN, especially in the one covering Convolutional Neural Network.

For practical reasons, we will be referring to Deep Learning and Deep Neural Networks, to the architectures where the number of layers is significantly superior to a couple of similar layer, we will be referring to the Neural Network architectures with like tens of layer, or combinations of complex constructs.

Deep network architectures through time

In this section, we will be reviewing the milestone architectures that appeared throughout the history of deep learning, starting with LeNet5.

LeNet 5

The field of neural networks had been quite silent during the *1980*s and the *1990*s. There were some efforts, but the architectures were quite simple, and a big (and often not available) machine power was needed to try more complex approaches.

Around 1998, in Bells Labs, during research around the classification of hand written check digits, Ian LeCun started a new trend implementing the bases of what is considered *Deep Learning – The Convolutional Neural Networks*, which we have already studied in `Chapter 5`, *Simple FeedForward Neural Networks* .

In those years, SVM and other much more rigorously defined techniques were used to tackle those kinds of problems, but the fundamental paper on CNN, shows that Neural Networks could have a comparable or better performance compared to the then state of the art methods.

Alexnet

After some more years of hiatus (even though LeCun continued applying his networks to other tasks, such as face and object recognition), the exponential growth of both available structured data, and raw processing power, allowed the teams to grow and tune the models, to an extent that could have been considered impossible, and thus the complexity of the models could be increased without the risk of waiting months for training.

Computer research teams from a number of technological firms and universities began competing on some very difficult tasks, including image recognition. For one of these challenges, the Imagenet Classification Challenge, the Alexnet architecture was developed:

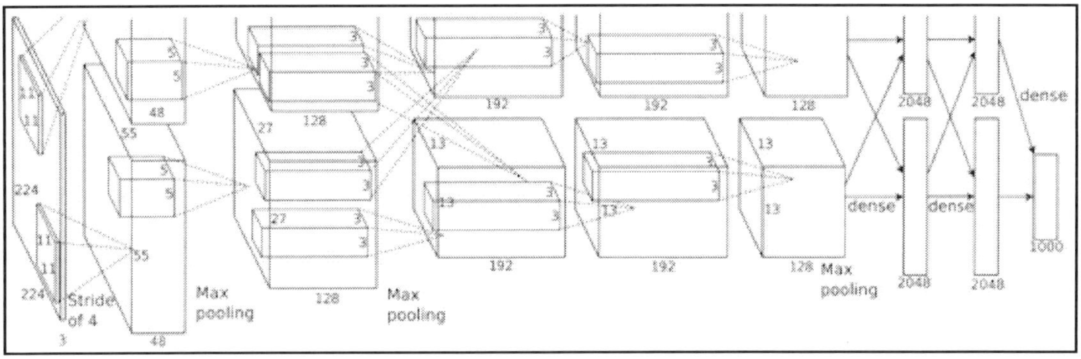

Alexnet architecture

Main features

Alexnet can be seen as an augmented LeNet5, in the sense that its first layers with convolution operations. but add the not so used max pooling layers, and then a series of dense connected layers, building a last output class probability layer. The **Visual Geometry Group** (**VGG**) model

One of the other main contenders of the image classification challenge was the VGGof the University of Oxford.

The main characteristic of the VGG network architecture is that they reduced the size of the convolutional filters, to a simple 3×3, and combined them in sequences.

This idea of tiny convolutional kernels was disruptive to the initial ideas of the LeNet and its successor Alexnet, which used filters of up to 11×11 filters, much more complex and low in performance. This change in filter size was the beginning of a trend that is still current:

ConvNet Configuration					
A	A-LRN	B	C	D	E
11 weight layers	11 weight layers	13 weight layers	16 weight layers	16 weight layers	19 weight layers
input (224 × 224 RGB image)					
conv3-64	conv3-64 **LRN**	conv3-64 **conv3-64**	conv3-64 conv3-64	conv3-64 conv3-64	conv3-64 conv3-64
maxpool					
conv3-128	conv3-128	conv3-128 **conv3-128**	conv3-128 conv3-128	conv3-128 conv3-128	conv3-128 conv3-128
maxpool					
conv3-256 conv3-256	conv3-256 conv3-256	conv3-256 conv3-256	conv3-256 conv3-256 **conv1-256**	conv3-256 conv3-256 **conv3-256**	conv3-256 conv3-256 conv3-256 **conv3-256**
maxpool					
conv3-512 conv3-512	conv3-512 conv3-512	conv3-512 conv3-512	conv3-512 conv3-512 **conv1-512**	conv3-512 conv3-512 **conv3-512**	conv3-512 conv3-512 conv3-512 **conv3-512**
maxpool					
conv3-512 conv3-512	conv3-512 conv3-512	conv3-512 conv3-512	conv3-512 conv3-512 **conv1-512**	conv3-512 conv3-512 **conv3-512**	conv3-512 conv3-512 conv3-512 **conv3-512**
maxpool					
FC-4096					
FC-4096					
FC-1000					
soft-max					

Table 2: **Number of parameters** (in millions).

Network	A,A-LRN	B	C	D	E
Number of parameters	133	133	134	138	144

Summary of the parameter number per layer in VGG

However, this positive change of using a series of small convolution weights, the total setup amounted to a really big number of parameters (in the order of many millions) and so it had to be limited by a number of measures.

The original inception model

After two main research cycles dominated by Alexnet and VGG, Google disrupted the challenges with a very powerful architecture, Inception, which has several iterations.

The first of these iterations, started with its own version of Convolutional Neural Network layer-based architecture, called GoogLeNet, an architecture with a name reminiscent to the network approach that started it all.

GoogLenet (Inception V1)

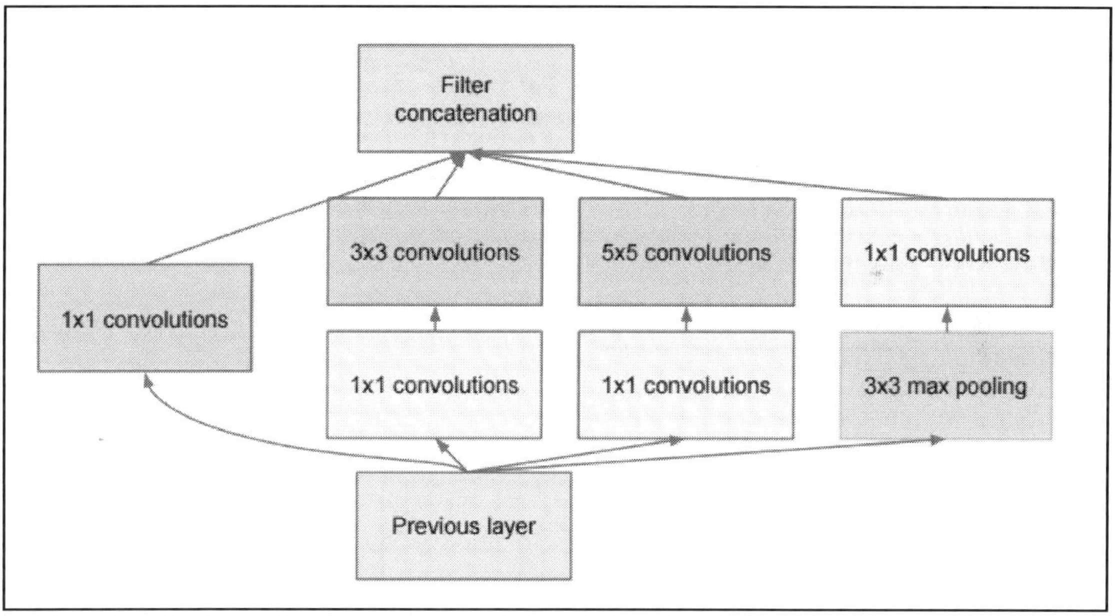

lInception module

GoogLeNet was the first iteration of this effort, and as you will see in the following figure, it has a very deep architecture, but it has the chilling sum of nine chained inception modules, with little or no modification:

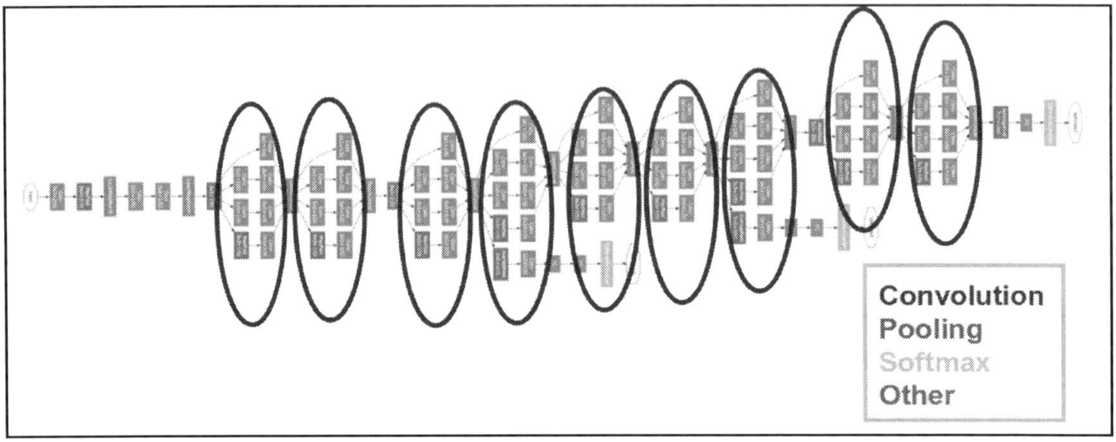

Inception original architecture

Even being so complex, it managed to reduce the needed parameter number, and increased the accuracy, compared to Alexnet, which had been released just two years before.

The comprehension and scalability of this complex architecture is improved nevertheless, by the fact that almost all the structure consists of a determined arrangement and repetition of the same original structural layer building blocks.

Batch normalized inception (V2)

The state of the art neural networks of 2015, while improving iteration over iteration, were having a problem of training instability.

In order to understand how the problems consisted, first we will remember the simple normalization steps that we applied in the previous examples. It basically consisted of centering the values on zero, and dividing by the maximum value, or the standard deviation, in order to have a good baseline for the gradients of the back propagations.

What occurs during the training of really large datasets, is that after a number of training examples, the different value oscillations begin to amplify the mean parameter value, like in a resonance phenomenon. What we very simply described is called a co variance shift.

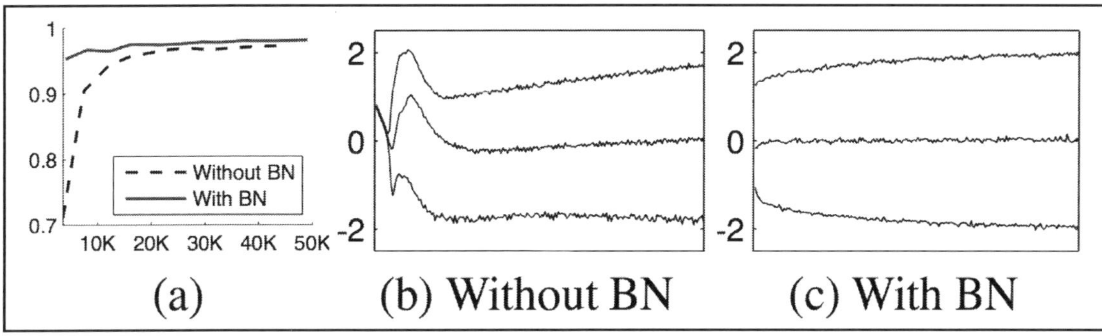

Performance comparison with and without Batch Normalization

This is the main reason why the Batch Normalization techniques had been developed.

Again simplifying the process description, it consists of applying normalizations not only to the original input values, it also normalizes the output values at each layer, avoiding the instabilities appearing between layers, before they begin to affect or drift the values.

This is the main feature that Google shipped in its improved implementation of GoogLeNet, released in February 2015, and it is also called Inception V2.

Inception v3

Fast forward to December 2015, and there is a new iteration of the Inception architecture. The difference of months between releases gives us an idea of the pace of development of the new iterations.

The basic adaptations for this architecture are:

- Reduce the number of convolutions to maximum 3×3
- Increase the general depth of the networks
- Use the width increase technique at each layer to improve feature combination

The following diagram illustrates how the improved inception module can be interpreted:

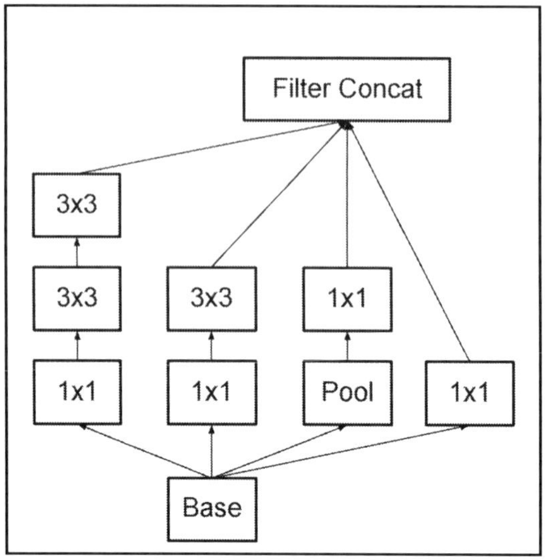

Inception V3 base module

And this is a representation of the whole V3 architecture, with many instances of the common building module:

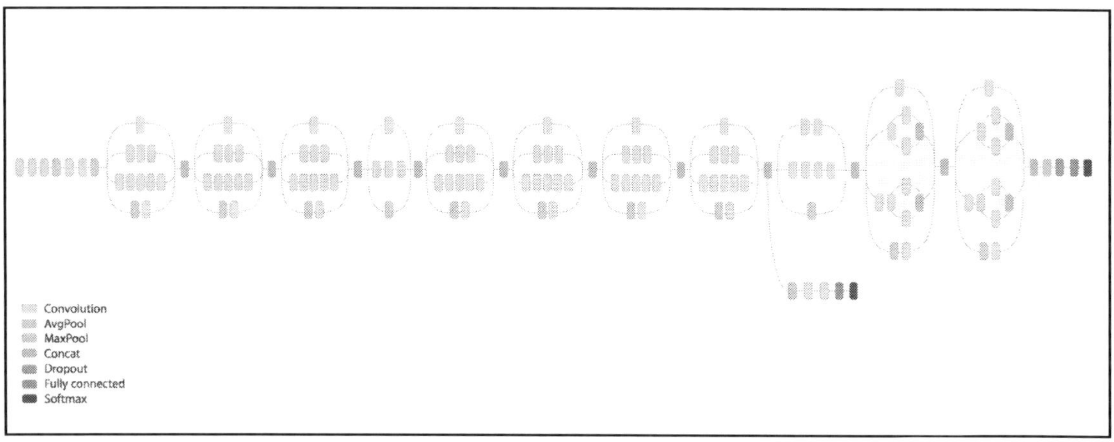

Inception V3 general diagram

Residual Networks (ResNet)

The Residual Network architecture appears in December 2015 (more or less the same time as the Inception V3), and it brought a simple but novel idea: not only use the output of each constitutional layer, but also combine the output of the layer with the original input.

In the following diagram, we observe a simplified view of one of the ResNet modules; it clearly shows the sum operation at the end of the Convolutional layer stack, and a final **relu** operation:

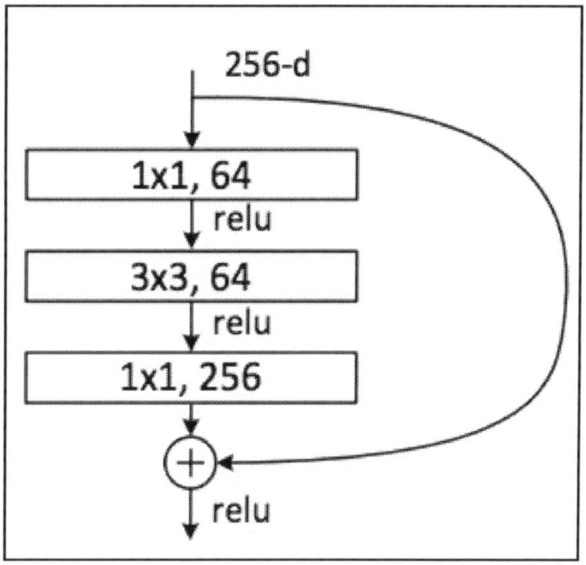

ResNet general architecture

The convolutional part of the module includes a feature reduction from 256 to 64 values, a 3×3 filter layer maintaining the features number, and then a feature augmenting 1×1 layer, from 64 x 256 values. In recent developments, ResNet is also used in a depth of less than 30 layers, with a wide distribution.

Other deep neural network architectures

There are a big number of recently developed neural network architectures; in fact, the field is so dynamic that we have more or less a new outstanding architecture apparition every year. A list of the most promising neural network architectures are:

- **SqueezeNet**: This architecture is an effort at reducing the parameter number and complexity of Alexnet, claiming a 50x parameter number reduction
- **Efficient Neural Network (Enet)**: Aims to build a simpler, low latency, number of floating point operations, neural networks with real-time results
- **Fractalnet**: Its main characteristics are the implementation of very deep networks, without requiring the residual architecture, organizing the structural layout as a truncated fractal

Example – painting with style – VGG style transfer

In this example, we will work with the implementation of the paper*A Neural Algorithm of Artistic Style* from *Leon Gatys*.

The original code for this exercise was kindly provided by *Anish Athalye* (`http://www.anishathalye.com/`).

We have to note that this exercise does not have a training part. We will just be loading a pretrained coefficient matrix, provided by VLFeat, a database of pre trained models, which can be used to work on models, avoiding the normally computationally intensive training:

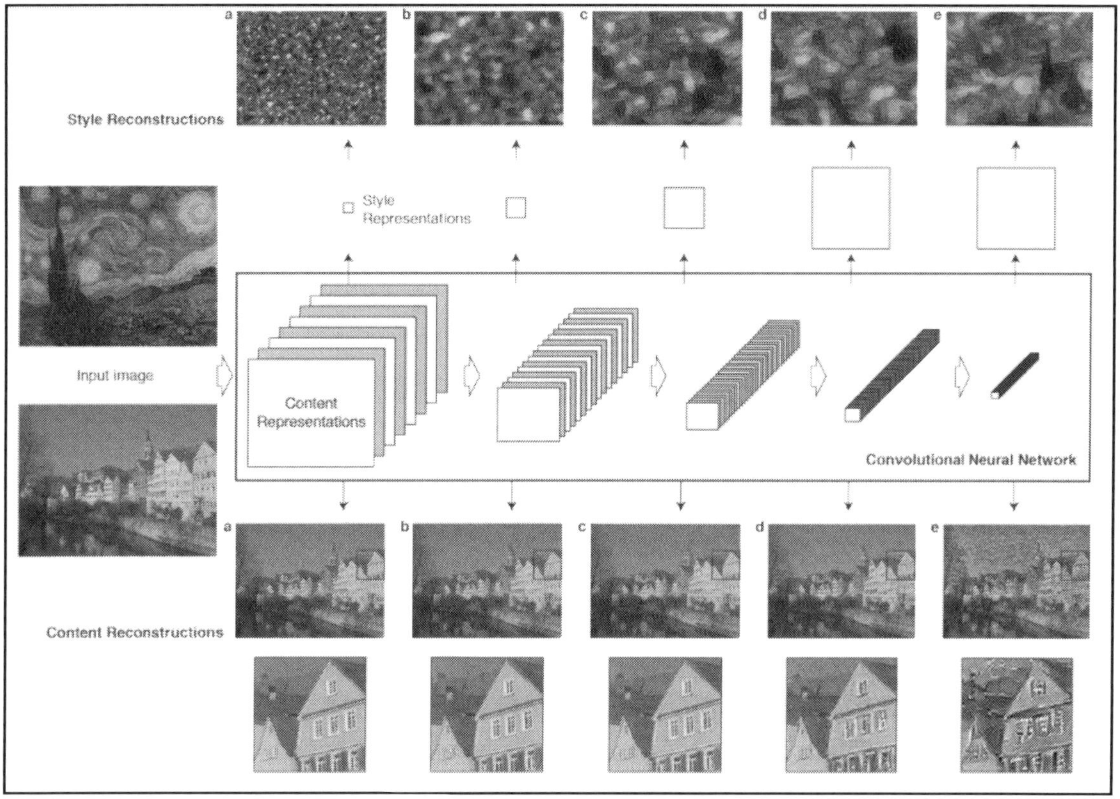

Style transfer main concepts

Useful libraries and methods

- **Loading parameters files with scipy.io.loadmat**
    - The first useful library that we will be using is the scipy io module, to load the coefficient data, which is saved as a matlab mat format.
- **Usage of the preceding parameter**:

```
scipy.io.loadmat(file_name, mdict=None, appendmat=True, **kwargs)
```

- **Returns of the preceding parameter**:

    `mat_dict : dict :dictionary` with variable names as keys, and loaded matrices as values. If the `mdict` parameter is filled, the results will be assigned to it.

Dataset description and loading

For the solution of this problem, we will be using a pre-trained dataset, that is, the retrained coefficients of a VGG neural network, with the Imagenet dataset.

Starry night, Vincent van Gogh   Colosseum, Roma

Dataset preprocessing

Given that the coefficients are given in the loaded parameter matrix, there is not much work to do regarding the initial dataset.

Modeling architecture

The modeling architecture is divided mainly in two parts: the style and the content.

For the generation of the final images, a VGG network without the final fully connected layer is used.

Loss functions

This architecture defines two different loss functions to optimize the two different aspects of the final image, one for the content and one for the style.

Content loss function

The code for `content_loss` function is as follows:

```
# content loss
      content_loss = content_weight * (2 * tf.nn.l2_loss(
             net[CONTENT_LAYER] - content_features[CONTENT_LAYER]) /
             content_features[CONTENT_LAYER].size)
```

Style loss function

Loss optimization loop

The code for loss optimization loop is as follows:

```
      best_loss = float('inf')
      best = None
      with tf.Session() as sess:
          sess.run(tf.initialize_all_variables())
          for i in range(iterations):
              last_step = (i == iterations - 1)
              print_progress(i, last=last_step)
              train_step.run()

              if (checkpoint_iterations and i % checkpoint_iterations ==
0) or last_step:
                  this_loss = loss.eval()
                  if this_loss < best_loss:
                      best_loss = this_loss
                      best = image.eval()
                  yield (
                      (None if last_step else i),
                      vgg.unprocess(best.reshape(shape[1:]), mean_pixel)
                  )
```

Convergency test

In this example, we will just check for the number of indicated iterations (the iterations parameter).

Program execution

For the execution of this program for a good (around 1000) iteration number, we recommend to have at least 8GB of RAM memory available:

```
python neural_style.py --content examples/2-content.jpg --styles
examples/2-style1.jpg  --checkpoint-iterations=100 --iterations=1000 --
checkpoint-output=out%s.jpg --output=outfinal
```

The results for the preceding command is as follows:

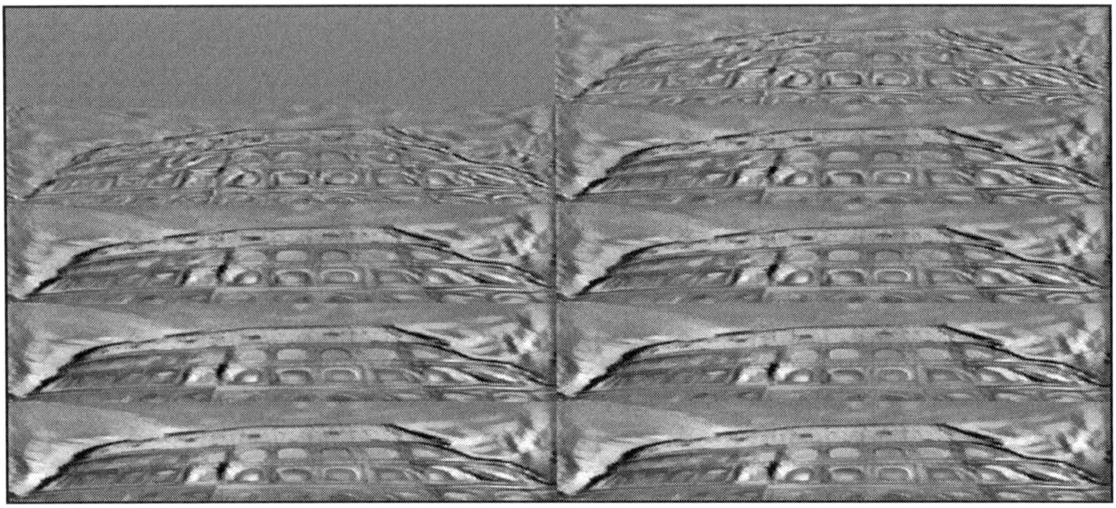

Style transfer steps

The console output is as follows:

```
Iteration 1/1000
Iteration 2/1000
Iteration 3/1000
Iteration 4/1000
...
Iteration 999/1000
Iteration 1000/1000
  content loss: 908786
    style loss: 261789
       tv loss: 25639.9
    total loss: 1.19621e+06
```

Full source code

The code for `neural_style.py` is as follows:

```
import os

import numpy as np
import scipy.misc

from stylize import stylize

import math
from argparse import ArgumentParser

# default arguments
CONTENT_WEIGHT = 5e0
STYLE_WEIGHT = 1e2
TV_WEIGHT = 1e2
LEARNING_RATE = 1e1
STYLE_SCALE = 1.0
ITERATIONS = 100
VGG_PATH = 'imagenet-vgg-verydeep-19.mat'


def build_parser():
    parser = ArgumentParser()
    parser.add_argument('--content',
            dest='content', help='content image',
            metavar='CONTENT', required=True)
    parser.add_argument('--styles',
            dest='styles',
            nargs='+', help='one or more style images',
            metavar='STYLE', required=True)
    parser.add_argument('--output',
            dest='output', help='output path',
            metavar='OUTPUT', required=True)
    parser.add_argument('--checkpoint-output',
            dest='checkpoint_output', help='checkpoint output format',
            metavar='OUTPUT')
    parser.add_argument('--iterations', type=int,
            dest='iterations', help='iterations (default %(default)s)',
            metavar='ITERATIONS', default=ITERATIONS)
    parser.add_argument('--width', type=int,
            dest='width', help='output width',
            metavar='WIDTH')
    parser.add_argument('--style-scales', type=float,
            dest='style_scales',
            nargs='+', help='one or more style scales',
```

```
            metavar='STYLE_SCALE')
    parser.add_argument('--network',
            dest='network', help='path to network parameters (default
%(default)s)',
            metavar='VGG_PATH', default=VGG_PATH)
    parser.add_argument('--content-weight', type=float,
            dest='content_weight', help='content weight (default
%(default)s)',
            metavar='CONTENT_WEIGHT', default=CONTENT_WEIGHT)
    parser.add_argument('--style-weight', type=float,
            dest='style_weight', help='style weight (default %(default)s)',
            metavar='STYLE_WEIGHT', default=STYLE_WEIGHT)
    parser.add_argument('--style-blend-weights', type=float,
            dest='style_blend_weights', help='style blending weights',
            nargs='+', metavar='STYLE_BLEND_WEIGHT')
    parser.add_argument('--tv-weight', type=float,
            dest='tv_weight', help='total variation regularization weight
(default %(default)s)',
            metavar='TV_WEIGHT', default=TV_WEIGHT)
    parser.add_argument('--learning-rate', type=float,
            dest='learning_rate', help='learning rate (default
%(default)s)',
            metavar='LEARNING_RATE', default=LEARNING_RATE)
    parser.add_argument('--initial',
            dest='initial', help='initial image',
            metavar='INITIAL')
    parser.add_argument('--print-iterations', type=int,
            dest='print_iterations', help='statistics printing frequency',
            metavar='PRINT_ITERATIONS')
    parser.add_argument('--checkpoint-iterations', type=int,
            dest='checkpoint_iterations', help='checkpoint frequency',
            metavar='CHECKPOINT_ITERATIONS')
    return parser


def main():
    parser = build_parser()
    options = parser.parse_args()

    if not os.path.isfile(options.network):
        parser.error("Network %s does not exist. (Did you forget to
download it?)" % options.network)

    content_image = imread(options.content)
    style_images = [imread(style) for style in options.styles]

    width = options.width
    if width is not None:
```

```
        new_shape = (int(math.floor(float(content_image.shape[0]) /
                content_image.shape[1] * width)), width)
        content_image = scipy.misc.imresize(content_image, new_shape)
    target_shape = content_image.shape
    for i in range(len(style_images)):
        style_scale = STYLE_SCALE
        if options.style_scales is not None:
            style_scale = options.style_scales[i]
        style_images[i] = scipy.misc.imresize(style_images[i], style_scale
*
                target_shape[1] / style_images[i].shape[1])

    style_blend_weights = options.style_blend_weights
    if style_blend_weights is None:
        # default is equal weights
        style_blend_weights = [1.0/len(style_images) for _ in style_images]
    else:
        total_blend_weight = sum(style_blend_weights)
        style_blend_weights = [weight/total_blend_weight
                               for weight in style_blend_weights]

    initial = options.initial
    if initial is not None:
        initial = scipy.misc.imresize(imread(initial),
content_image.shape[:2])

    if options.checkpoint_output and "%s" not in options.checkpoint_output:
        parser.error("To save intermediate images, the checkpoint output "
                     "parameter must contain `%s` (e.g. `foo%s.jpg`)")

    for iteration, image in stylize(
        network=options.network,
        initial=initial,
        content=content_image,
        styles=style_images,
        iterations=options.iterations,
        content_weight=options.content_weight,
        style_weight=options.style_weight,
        style_blend_weights=style_blend_weights,
        tv_weight=options.tv_weight,
        learning_rate=options.learning_rate,
        print_iterations=options.print_iterations,
        checkpoint_iterations=options.checkpoint_iterations
    ):
        output_file = None
        if iteration is not None:
            if options.checkpoint_output:
                output_file = options.checkpoint_output % iteration
```

```
        else:
            output_file = options.output
        if output_file:
            imsave(output_file, image)


def imread(path):
    return scipy.misc.imread(path).astype(np.float)


def imsave(path, img):
    img = np.clip(img, 0, 255).astype(np.uint8)
    scipy.misc.imsave(path, img)


if __name__ == '__main__':
    main()
```

The code for `Stilize.py` is as follows:

```
import vgg

import tensorflow as tf
import numpy as np

from sys import stderr

CONTENT_LAYER = 'relu4_2'
STYLE_LAYERS = ('relu1_1', 'relu2_1', 'relu3_1', 'relu4_1', 'relu5_1')


try:
    reduce
except NameError:
    from functools import reduce


def stylize(network, initial, content, styles, iterations,
        content_weight, style_weight, style_blend_weights, tv_weight,
        learning_rate, print_iterations=None, checkpoint_iterations=None):
    """
    Stylize images.

    This function yields tuples (iteration, image); `iteration` is None
    if this is the final image (the last iteration).  Other tuples are
yielded
    every `checkpoint_iterations` iterations.
```

```
    :rtype: iterator[tuple[int|None,image]]
    """
    shape = (1,) + content.shape
    style_shapes = [(1,) + style.shape for style in styles]
    content_features = {}
    style_features = [{} for _ in styles]

    # compute content features in feedforward mode
    g = tf.Graph()
    with g.as_default(), g.device('/cpu:0'), tf.Session() as sess:
        image = tf.placeholder('float', shape=shape)
        net, mean_pixel = vgg.net(network, image)
        content_pre = np.array([vgg.preprocess(content, mean_pixel)])
        content_features[CONTENT_LAYER] = net[CONTENT_LAYER].eval(
                feed_dict={image: content_pre})

    # compute style features in feedforward mode
    for i in range(len(styles)):
        g = tf.Graph()
        with g.as_default(), g.device('/cpu:0'), tf.Session() as sess:
            image = tf.placeholder('float', shape=style_shapes[i])
            net, _ = vgg.net(network, image)
            style_pre = np.array([vgg.preprocess(styles[i], mean_pixel)])
            for layer in STYLE_LAYERS:
                features = net[layer].eval(feed_dict={image: style_pre})
                features = np.reshape(features, (-1, features.shape[3]))
                gram = np.matmul(features.T, features) / features.size
                style_features[i][layer] = gram

    # make stylized image using backpropogation
    with tf.Graph().as_default():
        if initial is None:
            noise = np.random.normal(size=shape, scale=np.std(content) *
0.1)
            initial = tf.random_normal(shape) * 0.256
        else:
            initial = np.array([vgg.preprocess(initial, mean_pixel)])
            initial = initial.astype('float32')
        image = tf.Variable(initial)
        net, _ = vgg.net(network, image)

        # content loss
        content_loss = content_weight * (2 * tf.nn.l2_loss(
                net[CONTENT_LAYER] - content_features[CONTENT_LAYER]) /
                content_features[CONTENT_LAYER].size)
        # style loss
        style_loss = 0
        for i in range(len(styles)):
```

```
            style_losses = []
            for style_layer in STYLE_LAYERS:
                layer = net[style_layer]
                _, height, width, number = map(lambda i: i.value,
layer.get_shape())
                size = height * width * number
                feats = tf.reshape(layer, (-1, number))
                gram = tf.matmul(tf.transpose(feats), feats) / size
                style_gram = style_features[i][style_layer]
                style_losses.append(2 * tf.nn.l2_loss(gram - style_gram) /
style_gram.size)
            style_loss += style_weight * style_blend_weights[i] *
reduce(tf.add, style_losses)
        # total variation denoising
        tv_y_size = _tensor_size(image[:,1:,:,:])
        tv_x_size = _tensor_size(image[:,:,1:,:])
        tv_loss = tv_weight * 2 * (
                (tf.nn.l2_loss(image[:,1:,:,:] - image[:,:shape[1]-1,:,:])
/
                    tv_y_size) +
                (tf.nn.l2_loss(image[:,:,1:,:] - image[:,:,:shape[2]-1,:])
/
                    tv_x_size))
        # overall loss
        loss = content_loss + style_loss + tv_loss

        # optimizer setup
        train_step = tf.train.AdamOptimizer(learning_rate).minimize(loss)

        def print_progress(i, last=False):
            stderr.write('Iteration %d/%d\n' % (i + 1, iterations))
            if last or (print_iterations and i % print_iterations == 0):
                stderr.write('  content loss: %g\n' % content_loss.eval())
                stderr.write('    style loss: %g\n' % style_loss.eval())
                stderr.write('       tv loss: %g\n' % tv_loss.eval())
                stderr.write('    total loss: %g\n' % loss.eval())

        # optimization
        best_loss = float('inf')
        best = None
        with tf.Session() as sess:
            sess.run(tf.initialize_all_variables())
            for i in range(iterations):
                last_step = (i == iterations - 1)
                print_progress(i, last=last_step)
                train_step.run()

                if (checkpoint_iterations and i % checkpoint_iterations ==
```

```
0) or last_step:
                    this_loss = loss.eval()
                    if this_loss < best_loss:
                        best_loss = this_loss
                        best = image.eval()
                    yield (
                        (None if last_step else i),
                        vgg.unprocess(best.reshape(shape[1:]), mean_pixel)
                    )


def _tensor_size(tensor):
    from operator import mul
    return reduce(mul, (d.value for d in tensor.get_shape()), 1)
 vgg.py
import tensorflow as tf
import numpy as np
import scipy.io


def net(data_path, input_image):
    layers = (
        'conv1_1', 'relu1_1', 'conv1_2', 'relu1_2', 'pool1',

        'conv2_1', 'relu2_1', 'conv2_2', 'relu2_2', 'pool2',

        'conv3_1', 'relu3_1', 'conv3_2', 'relu3_2', 'conv3_3',
        'relu3_3', 'conv3_4', 'relu3_4', 'pool3',

        'conv4_1', 'relu4_1', 'conv4_2', 'relu4_2', 'conv4_3',
        'relu4_3', 'conv4_4', 'relu4_4', 'pool4',

        'conv5_1', 'relu5_1', 'conv5_2', 'relu5_2', 'conv5_3',
        'relu5_3', 'conv5_4', 'relu5_4'
    )

    data = scipy.io.loadmat(data_path)
    mean = data['normalization'][0][0][0]
    mean_pixel = np.mean(mean, axis=(0, 1))
    weights = data['layers'][0]

    net = {}
    current = input_image
    for i, name in enumerate(layers):
        kind = name[:4]
        if kind == 'conv':
            kernels, bias = weights[i][0][0][0][0]
            # matconvnet: weights are [width, height, in_channels,
```

```
out_channels]
            # tensorflow: weights are [height, width, in_channels,
out_channels]
            kernels = np.transpose(kernels, (1, 0, 2, 3))
            bias = bias.reshape(-1)
            current = _conv_layer(current, kernels, bias)
        elif kind == 'relu':
            current = tf.nn.relu(current)
        elif kind == 'pool':
            current = _pool_layer(current)
        net[name] = current

    assert len(net) == len(layers)
    return net, mean_pixel

def _conv_layer(input, weights, bias):
    conv = tf.nn.conv2d(input, tf.constant(weights), strides=(1, 1, 1, 1),
            padding='SAME')
    return tf.nn.bias_add(conv, bias)

def _pool_layer(input):
    return tf.nn.max_pool(input, ksize=(1, 2, 2, 1), strides=(1, 2, 2, 1),
            padding='SAME')


def preprocess(image, mean_pixel):
    return image - mean_pixel


def unprocess(image, mean_pixel):
    return image + mean_pixel
```

Summary

In this chapter, we have been learning about the different Deep Neural Network architectures.

We learned about building one of the most well known architectures of recent years, VGG, and how to employ it to generate images that translate artistic style.

In the next chapter, we will be using one of the most useful technologies in Machine Learning: Graphical Processing Units. We will review the steps needed to install TensorFlow with GPU support and train models with it, comparing execution times with the CPU as the only model running.

9
Running Models at Scale – GPU and Serving

Until now, we have been running code that runs on the host computer's main CPU. This implies that, at most, we use all the different processor cores (2 or 4 for low-end processors, up to 16 in more advanced processors).

In the last decade, the **General Processing Unit**, or **GPU**, has become a ubiquitous part of any high performance computing setup. Its massive, intrinsic parallelism is very well suited for the high dimension matrix multiplications and other operations required in machine learning model training and running.

Nevertheless, even having really powerful computing nodes there is a large number of tasks with which even the most powerful individual server can't cope.

For this reason, a distributed way of training and running a model had to be developed. This is the original function of distributed TensorFlow.

In this chapter, you will:

- Learn how to discover the available computing resources TensorFlow has available
- Learn how to assign tasks to any of the different computing units in a computing node
- Learn how to log the GPU operations
- Learn how to distribute the computing not only in the main host computer, but across a cluster of many distributed units

GPU support on TensorFlow

TensorFlow has native support for at least two computing capabilities: CPU and GPU. For this, it implements one version of each operation for each kind of computing device it supports:

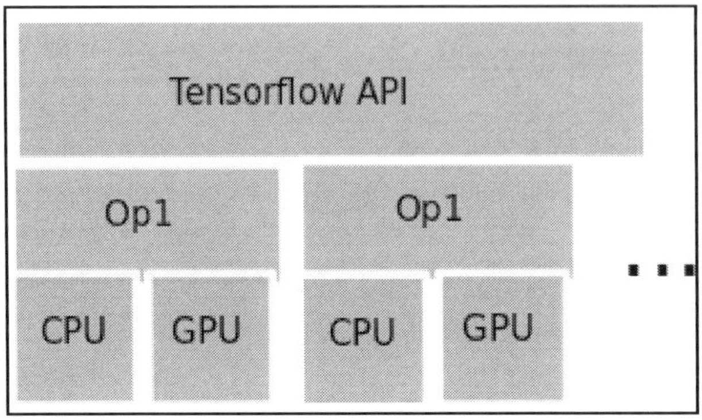

Log device placement and device capabilities

Before trying to perform calculations, TensorFlow allows you to log all the available resources. In this way we can apply operations only in existing computing types.

Querying the computing capabilities

In order to obtain a log of the computing elements on a machine, we can use the `log_device_placement` flag when we create a TensorFlow session, in this way:

```
python
>>>Import tensorflow as tf
>>>sess = tf.Session(config=tf.ConfigProto(log_device_placement=True))
```

This is the output of the commands:

```
$ python
Python 2.7.12 (default, Jul  1 2016, 15:12:24)
[GCC 5.4.0 20160609] on linux2
Type "help", "copyright", "credits" or "license" for more information.
>>> import tensorflow as tf
I tensorflow/stream_executor/dso_loader.cc:108] successfully opened CUDA library libcublas.so
locally
I tensorflow/stream_executor/dso_loader.cc:108] successfully opened CUDA library libcudnn.so.5
 locally
I tensorflow/stream_executor/dso_loader.cc:108] successfully opened CUDA library libcufft.so l
ocally
I tensorflow/stream_executor/dso_loader.cc:108] successfully opened CUDA library libcuda.so.1
locally
I tensorflow/stream_executor/dso_loader.cc:108] successfully opened CUDA library libcurand.so
locally
>>> sess = tf.Session(config=tf.ConfigProto(log_device_placement=True))
I tensorflow/stream_executor/cuda/cuda_gpu_executor.cc:925] successful NUMA node read from Sys
FS had negative value (-1), but there must be at least one NUMA node, so returning NUMA node z
ero
I tensorflow/core/common_runtime/gpu/gpu_init.cc:102] Found device 0 with properties:
name: GRID K520
major: 3 minor: 0 memoryClockRate (GHz) 0.797
pciBusID 0000:00:03.0
Total memory: 4.00GiB
Free memory: 3.95GiB
I tensorflow/core/common_runtime/gpu/gpu_init.cc:126] DMA: 0
I tensorflow/core/common_runtime/gpu/gpu_init.cc:136] 0:   Y
I tensorflow/core/common_runtime/gpu/gpu_device.cc:840] Creating TensorFlow device (/gpu:0) ->
 (device: 0, name: GRID K520, pci bus id: 0000:00:03.0)
Device mapping:
/job:localhost/replica:0/task:0/gpu:0 -> device: 0, name: GRID K520, pci bus id: 0000:00:03.0
I tensorflow/core/common_runtime/direct_session.cc:175] Device mapping:
/job:localhost/replica:0/task:0/gpu:0 -> device: 0, name: GRID K520, pci bus id: 0000:00:03.0
```

Selecting a GPU to run code

This long output mainly shows the loading of the different needed `CUDA` library, and then the name (`GRID K520`) and the computing capabilities of the GPU.

Selecting a CPU for computing

If we have a GPU available, but still want to continue working with the CPU, we can select one via the method, `tf.Graph.device`.

The method call is the following:

```
tf.Graph.device(device_name_or_function) :
```

This function receives a processing unit string, a function returning a processing unit string, or none, and returns a context manager with the processing unit assigned.

If the parameter is a function, each operation will call this function to decide in which processing unit it will execute, a useful element to combine all operations.

Device naming

To specify which computing unit we are referring to when specifying a device, TensorFlow uses a simple scheme with the following format:

/[device type]:[device index]

Device ID format

Example device identification includes:

- **"/cpu:0"**: The first CPU of your machine
- **"/gpu:0"**: The GPU of your machine, if you have one
- **"/gpu:1"**: The second GPU of your machine, and so on

When available, if nothing is indicated to the contrary, the first GPU device is used.

Example 1 – assigning an operation to the GPU

In this example, we will create two tensors, locate the existing GPU as the default location, and will execute the tensor sum on it on a server configured with the CUDA environment (which you will learn to install in Appendix A – *Library Installation and Additional Tips*).

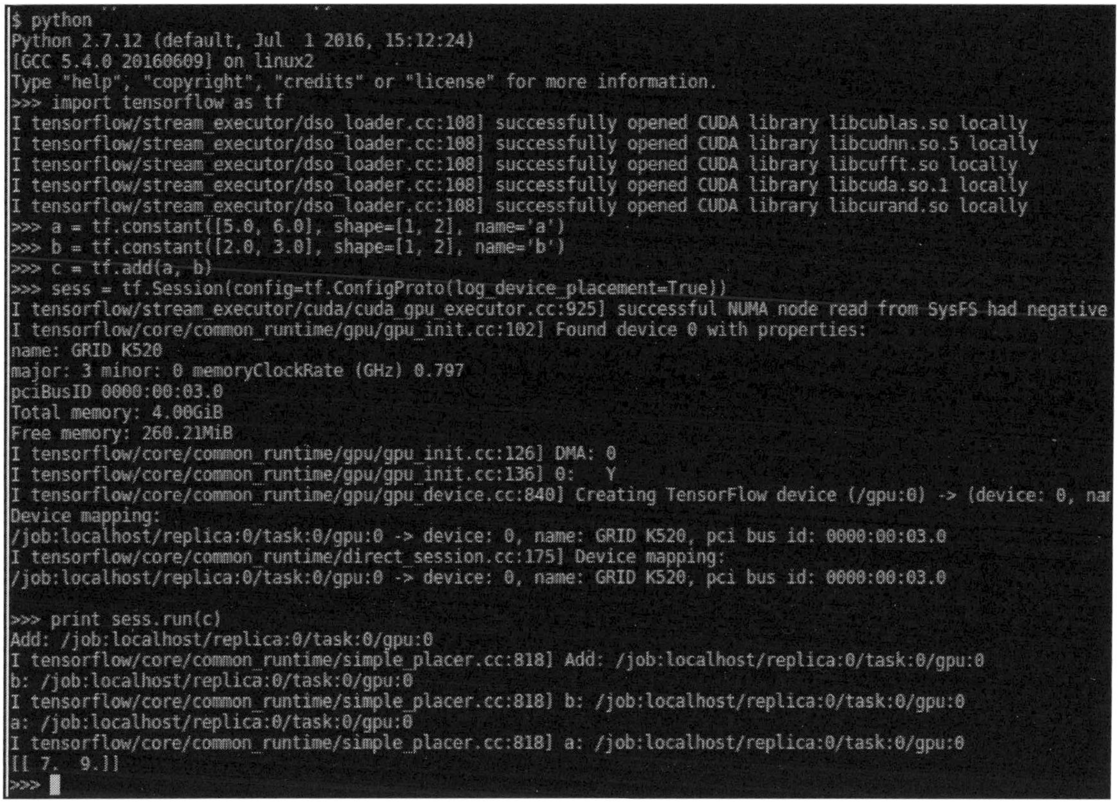

```
$ python
Python 2.7.12 (default, Jul  1 2016, 15:12:24)
[GCC 5.4.0 20160609] on linux2
Type "help", "copyright", "credits" or "license" for more information.
>>> import tensorflow as tf
I tensorflow/stream_executor/dso_loader.cc:108] successfully opened CUDA library libcublas.so locally
I tensorflow/stream_executor/dso_loader.cc:108] successfully opened CUDA library libcudnn.so.5 locally
I tensorflow/stream_executor/dso_loader.cc:108] successfully opened CUDA library libcufft.so locally
I tensorflow/stream_executor/dso_loader.cc:108] successfully opened CUDA library libcuda.so.1 locally
I tensorflow/stream_executor/dso_loader.cc:108] successfully opened CUDA library libcurand.so locally
>>> a = tf.constant([5.0, 6.0], shape=[1, 2], name='a')
>>> b = tf.constant([2.0, 3.0], shape=[1, 2], name='b')
>>> c = tf.add(a, b)
>>> sess = tf.Session(config=tf.ConfigProto(log_device_placement=True))
I tensorflow/stream_executor/cuda/cuda_gpu_executor.cc:925] successful NUMA node read from SysFS had negative
I tensorflow/core/common_runtime/gpu/gpu_init.cc:102] Found device 0 with properties:
name: GRID K520
major: 3 minor: 0 memoryClockRate (GHz) 0.797
pciBusID 0000:00:03.0
Total memory: 4.00GiB
Free memory: 260.21MiB
I tensorflow/core/common_runtime/gpu/gpu_init.cc:126] DMA: 0
I tensorflow/core/common_runtime/gpu/gpu_init.cc:136] 0:   Y
I tensorflow/core/common_runtime/gpu/gpu_device.cc:840] Creating TensorFlow device (/gpu:0) -> (device: 0, na
Device mapping:
/job:localhost/replica:0/task:0/gpu:0 -> device: 0, name: GRID K520, pci bus id: 0000:00:03.0
I tensorflow/core/common_runtime/direct_session.cc:175] Device mapping:
/job:localhost/replica:0/task:0/gpu:0 -> device: 0, name: GRID K520, pci bus id: 0000:00:03.0

>>> print sess.run(c)
Add: /job:localhost/replica:0/task:0/gpu:0
I tensorflow/core/common_runtime/simple_placer.cc:818] Add: /job:localhost/replica:0/task:0/gpu:0
b: /job:localhost/replica:0/task:0/gpu:0
I tensorflow/core/common_runtime/simple_placer.cc:818] b: /job:localhost/replica:0/task:0/gpu:0
a: /job:localhost/replica:0/task:0/gpu:0
I tensorflow/core/common_runtime/simple_placer.cc:818] a: /job:localhost/replica:0/task:0/gpu:0
[[ 7.  9.]]
>>>
```

Here we see that both the constants and the sum operation are built on the `/gpu:0` server. This is because the GPU is the preferred computing device type when available.

Example 2 – calculating Pi number in parallel

This example will serve as an introduction of parallel processing, implementing the Monte Carlo approximation of Pi.

Monte Carlo utilizes a random number sequence to perform an approximation.

In order to solve this problem, we will throw many random samples, knowing that the ratio of samples inside the circle over the ones on the square, is the same as the area ratio.

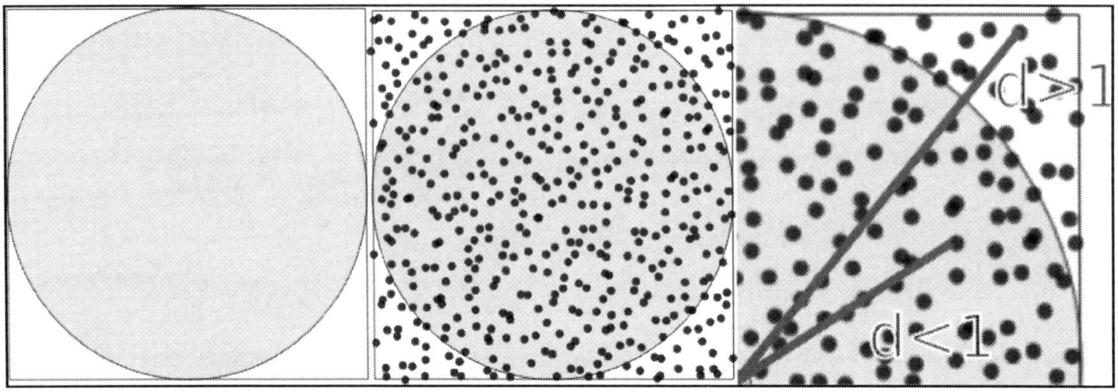

Random area calculation techniques

The calculation assumes that if the probability distribution is uniform, the number of samples assigned is proportional to the area of the figures.

We use the following proportion:

$$\rho = \frac{\text{Area of Circle}}{\text{Area of Square}} = \frac{\pi r^2}{(2r)^2} = \frac{\pi}{4} = \frac{3.1415926535897932}{4} = 0.7853981633974483$$

Area proportion for Pi calculation

From the aforementioned proportion, we infer that number of sample in the circle/number of sample of square is also **0.78**.

An additional fact is that the more random samples we can generate for the calculation, the more approximate the answer. This is when incrementing the number of GPUs will give us more samples and accuracy.

A further reduction that we do is that we generate (X,Y) coordinates, ranging from (0..1), so the random number generation is more direct. So the only criteria we need to determine if a sample belongs to the circle is `distance = d < 1.0` (radius of the circle).

Solution implementation

This solution will be based around the CPU; it will manage the GPU resources that we have in the server (in this case, **4**) and then we will receive the results, doing the final sample sum.

Note: This method has a really slow convergence rate of $O(n^{1/2})$, but will be used as an example, given its simplicity.

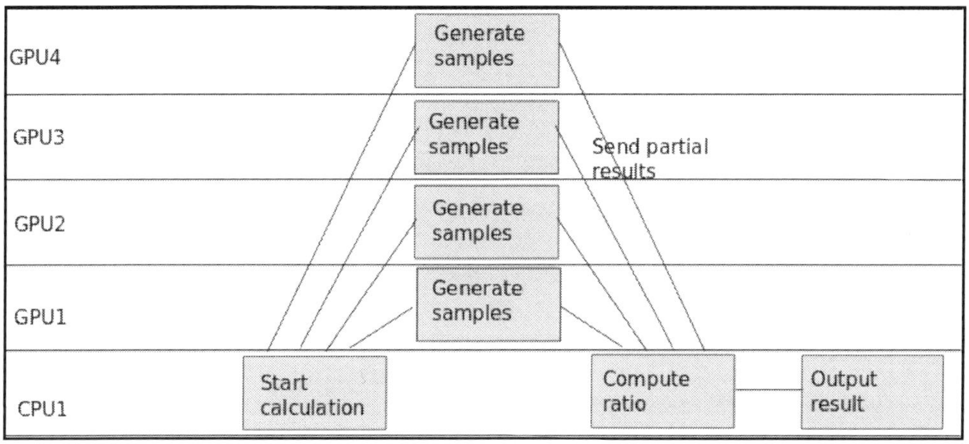

Computing tasks timeline

In the preceding figure, we see the parallel behavior of the calculation, being the sample generation and counting the main activity.

Source code

The source code is as follows:

```
import tensorflow as tf
import numpy as np
c = []
#Distribute the work between the GPUs
for d in ['/gpu:0', '/gpu:1', '/gpu:2', '/gpu:3']:
    #Generate the random 2D samples
    i=tf.constant(np.random.uniform(size=10000), shape=[5000,2])
    with tf.Session() as sess:
        tf.initialize_all_variables()
```

```
        #Calculate the euclidean distance to the origin
        distances=tf.reduce_sum(tf.pow(i,2),1)
        #Sum the samples inside the circle
        tempsum =
sess.run(tf.reduce_sum(tf.cast(tf.greater_equal(tf.cast(1.0,tf.float64),dis
tances),tf.float64)))
        #append the current result to the results array
        c.append( tempsum)
    #Do the final ratio calculation on the CPU
    with tf.device('/cpu:0'):
        with tf.Session() as sess:
            sum = tf.add_n(c)
            print (sess.run(sum/20000.0)*4.0)
```

Distributed TensorFlow

Distributed TensorFlow is a complementary technology, which aims to easily and efficiently create clusters of computing nodes, and to distribute the jobs between nodes in a seamless way.

It is the standard way to create distributed computing environments, and to execute the training and running of models at a massive scale, so it's very important to be able to do the main task found in production, high volume data setups.

Technology components

In this section, we will describe all the components on a distributed TensorFlow computing setup, from the most fine-grained task elements, to the whole cluster description.

Jobs

Jobs define a group of homogeneous tasks, normally aimed to the same subset of the problem-solving area.

Examples of job distinctions are:

- A parameter server job which will store the model parameters in an individual job, and will be in charge of distributing to all the distributed nodes the initial and current parameter values
- A worker job, where all the computing intensive tasks are performed

Tasks

Tasks are subdivisions of jobs, which perform the different steps or parallel work units to solve the problem area of its job, and are normally attached to a single process.

Every job has a number of tasks, and they are identified by an index. Normally the task with the index 0, is considered the main or coordinator task.

Servers

Server are logical objects representing a set of physical devices dedicated to implementing tasks. A server will be exclusively assigned to a single task.

Combined overview

In the following figure, we will represent all the participating parts in a cluster computing setup:

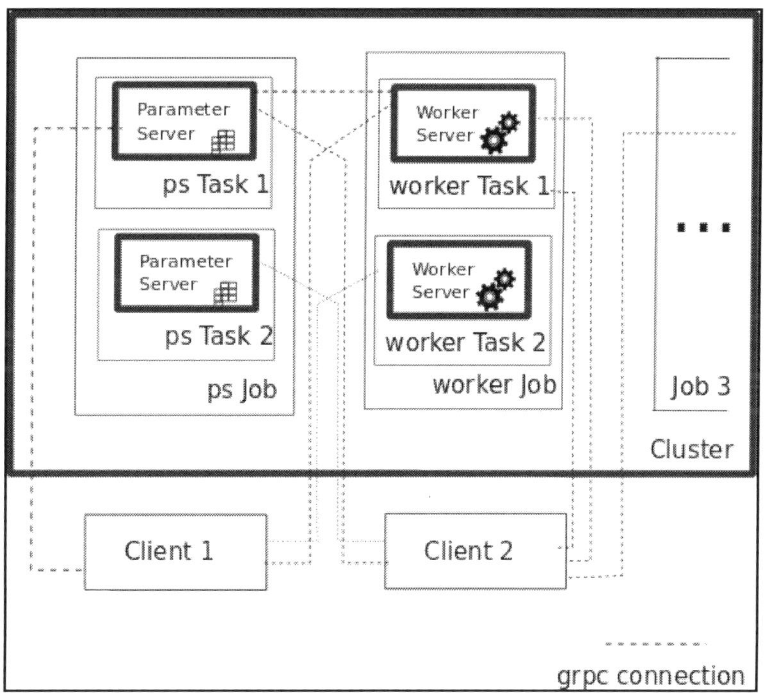

TensorFlow cluster setup elements

The figure contains the two jobs represented by the **ps** and the worker jobs, and the grpc communication channels (covered in Appendix A – *Library Installation and Additional Tips*) that can be created from the clients for them. For every job type, there are servers implementing different tasks, which solve subsets of the job's domain problem.

Creating a TensorFlow cluster

The first task for a distributed cluster program will be defining and creating a ClusterSpec object, which contains the real server instance's addresses and ports, which will be a part of the cluster.

The two main ways of defining this ClusterSpec are:

- Create a `tf.train.ClusterSpec` object, which specifies all cluster tasks
- Passing the mentioned ClusterSpec object, when creating a `tf.train.Server`, and relating the local task with a job name plus task index

ClusterSpec definition format

ClusterSpec objects are defined using the protocol buffer format, which is a special format based on JSON.

The format is the following:

```
{
    "job1 name": [
        "task0 server uri",
        "task1 server uri"
         ...
    ]
...
    "jobn name"[
        "task0 server uri",
        "task1 server uri"
    ]})
...
```

So this would be the function call to create a cluster with a parameter server task server and three worker task servers:

```
tf.train.ClusterSpec({
    "worker": [
        "wk0.example.com:2222",
        "wk1.example.com:2222",
```

```
        "wk2.example.com:2222"
    ],
    "ps": [
        "ps0.example.com:2222",
    ]})
```

Creating tf.Train.Server

After we create the ClusterSpec, we now have an exact idea of the cluster configuration, in the runtime. We will proceed to create the local server instance, creating an instance of `tf.train.Server`:

This is a sample server creation, which takes a cluster object, a job name, and a task index as a parameter:

```
server = tf.train.Server(cluster, job_name="local", task_index=[Number of
server])
```

Cluster operation – sending computing methods to tasks

In order to begin learning the operation of the cluster, we need to learn the addressing of the computing resources.

First of all, we suppose we have already created a cluster, with its different resources of jobs and tasks. The ID string for any of the resources has the following form:

/job:[job name]/tasks:[task id]

And the normal invocation of the resource in a context manager is the with keyword, with the following structure.

```
with tf.device("/job:ps/task:1"):
  [Code Block]
```

The with keyword indicates that whenever a task identifier is needed, the one specified in the context manager directive will be used.

The following figure illustrates a sample cluster setup, with the addressing names of all the different parts of the setup:

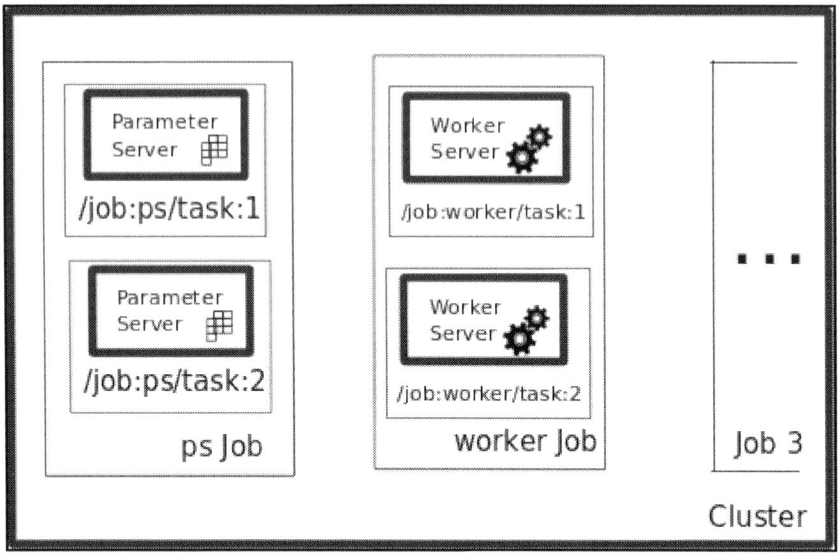

Server elements naming

Sample distributed code structure

This sample code will show you the approximate structure of a program addressing different tasks in a cluster, specifically a parameter server and a worker job:

```
#Address the Parameter Server task
with tf.device("/job:ps/task:1"):
  weights = tf.Variable(...)
  bias = tf.Variable(...)

#Address the Parameter Server task
with tf.device("/job:worker/task:1"):
    #... Generate and train a model
  layer_1 = tf.nn.relu(tf.matmul(input, weights_1) + biases_1)
  logits = tf.nn.relu(tf.matmul(layer_1, weights_2) + biases_2)
  train_op = ...

#Command the main task of the cluster
with tf.Session("grpc://worker1.cluster:2222") as sess:
  for i in range(100):
    sess.run(train_op)
```

Example 3 – distributed Pi calculation

In this example, we will change the perspective, going from one server with several computing resources, to a cluster of servers with a number of resources for each one.

The execution of the distributed version will have a different setup, explained in the following figure:

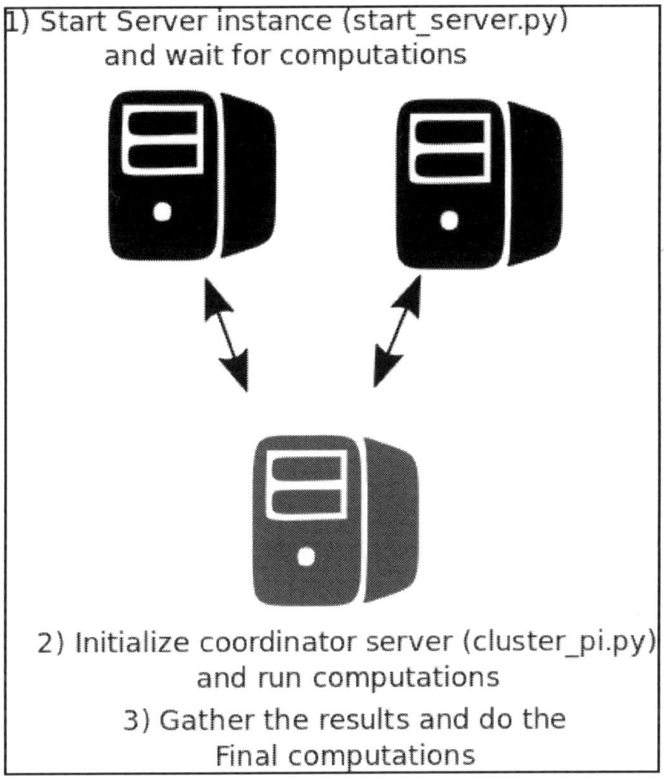

Distributed coordinated running

Server script

This script will be executed on each one of the computation nodes, which will generate a batch of samples, augmenting the number of generated random numbers by the number of available servers. In this case, we will use two servers and we suppose we initiate them in the localhost, indicating in the command-line the index number. If you want to run them in separate nodes, you just have to replace the localhost addresses in the ClusterSpec definition (and the name if you want it to be more representative).

The source code for the script is as follows:

```
import tensorflow as tf
tf.app.flags.DEFINE_string("index", "0","Server index")
FLAGS = tf.app.flags.FLAGS
print FLAGS.index
cluster = tf.train.ClusterSpec({"local": ["localhost:2222",
"localhost:2223"]})
server = tf.train.Server(cluster, job_name="local",
task_index=int(FLAGS.index))
server.join()
```

The command lines for executing this script in localhost are as follows:

```
python start_server.py -index=0 #Server  task 0
python start_server.py -index=1 #Server task 1
```

This is the expected output for one of the servers:

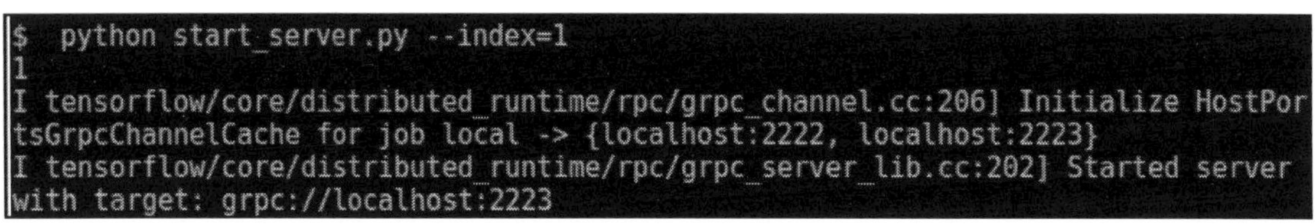

Individual server starting command line

Client script

Then we have the client script which will send the random number creation tasks to the cluster members, and will do the final Pi calculations, almost in the same way as the GPU example.

Full source code

The source code is as follows:

```
import tensorflow as tf
import numpy as np

tf.app.flags.DEFINE_integer("numsamples", "100","Number of samples per
server")
FLAGS = tf.app.flags.FLAGS

print ("Sample number per server: " + str(FLAGS.numsamples)  )
cluster = tf.train.ClusterSpec({"local": ["localhost:2222",
"localhost:2223"]})
#This is the list containing the sumation of samples on any node
c=[]

def generate_sum():
        i=tf.constant(np.random.uniform(size=FLAGS.numsamples*2),
shape=[FLAGS.numsamples,2])
        distances=tf.reduce_sum(tf.pow(i,2),1)
        return
(tf.reduce_sum(tf.cast(tf.greater_equal(tf.cast(1.0,tf.float64),distances),
tf.int32)))


with tf.device("/job:local/task:0"):
        test1= generate_sum()

with tf.device("/job:local/task:1"):
        test2= generate_sum()
#If your cluster is local, you must replace localhost by the address of the
first node
with tf.Session("grpc://localhost:2222") as sess:
      result = sess.run(tf.cast(test1 +
test2,tf.float64)/FLAGS.numsamples*2.0)
      print(result)
```

Example 4 – running a distributed model in a cluster

This very simple example will serve us as an example of how the pieces of a distributed TensorFlow setup work.

In this sample, we will do a very simple task, which nevertheless takes all the needed steps in a machine learning process.

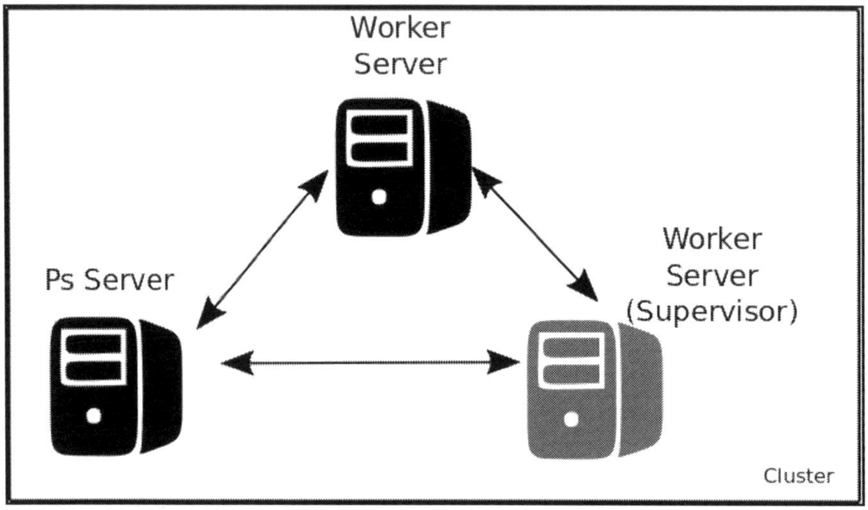

Distributed training cluster setup

The **Ps Server** will contain the different parameters of the linear function to solve (in this case just `x` and `b0`), and the two worker servers will do the training of the variable, which will constantly update and improve upon the last one, working on a collaboration mode.

Sample code

The sample code is as follows:

```
import tensorflow as tf
import numpy as np
from sklearn.utils import shuffle

# Here we define our cluster setup via the command line
tf.app.flags.DEFINE_string("ps_hosts", "",
```

```
                           "Comma-separated list of hostname:port pairs")
tf.app.flags.DEFINE_string("worker_hosts", "",
                           "Comma-separated list of hostname:port pairs")

# Define the characteristics of the cluster node, and its task index
tf.app.flags.DEFINE_string("job_name", "", "One of 'ps', 'worker'")
tf.app.flags.DEFINE_integer("task_index", 0, "Index of task within the
job")

FLAGS = tf.app.flags.FLAGS


def main(_):
  ps_hosts = FLAGS.ps_hosts.split(",")
  worker_hosts = FLAGS.worker_hosts.split(",")

  # Create a cluster following the command line paramaters.
  cluster = tf.train.ClusterSpec({"ps": ps_hosts, "worker": worker_hosts})
  # Create the local task.
  server = tf.train.Server(cluster,
                           job_name=FLAGS.job_name,
                           task_index=FLAGS.task_index)

  if FLAGS.job_name == "ps":
    server.join()
  elif FLAGS.job_name == "worker":

    # Assigns ops to the local worker by default.
    with tf.device(tf.train.replica_device_setter(
        worker_device="/job:worker/task:%d" % FLAGS.task_index,
        cluster=cluster)):

      #Define the training set, and the model parameters, loss function and
training operation
      trX = np.linspace(-1, 1, 101)
      trY = 2 * trX + np.random.randn(*trX.shape) * 0.4 + 0.2 # create a y
value
      X = tf.placeholder("float", name="X") # create symbolic variables
      Y = tf.placeholder("float", name = "Y")

      def model(X, w, b):
        return tf.mul(X, w) + b # We just define the line as X*w + b0

      w = tf.Variable(-1.0, name="b0") # create a shared variable
      b = tf.Variable(-2.0, name="b1") # create a shared variable
      y_model = model(X, w, b)

      loss = (tf.pow(Y-y_model, 2)) # use sqr error for cost function
```

```
      global_step = tf.Variable(0)

      train_op = tf.train.AdagradOptimizer(0.8).minimize(
          loss, global_step=global_step)

    #Create a saver, and a summary and init operation
      saver = tf.train.Saver()
      summary_op = tf.merge_all_summaries()
      init_op = tf.initialize_all_variables()

    # Create a "supervisor", which oversees the training process.
    sv = tf.train.Supervisor(is_chief=(FLAGS.task_index == 0),
                             logdir="/tmp/train_logs",
                             init_op=init_op,
                             summary_op=summary_op,
                             saver=saver,
                             global_step=global_step,
                             save_model_secs=600)

    # The supervisor takes care of session initialization, restoring from
    # a checkpoint, and closing when done or an error occurs.
    with sv.managed_session(server.target) as sess:
      # Loop until the supervisor shuts down
      step = 0
      while not sv.should_stop() :
        # Run a training step asynchronously.
        # See `tf.train.SyncReplicasOptimizer` for additional details on
how to
        # perform *synchronous* training.
        for i in range(100):
          trX, trY = shuffle (trX, trY, random_state=0)
          for (x, y) in zip(trX, trY):
              _, step = sess.run([train_op, global_step],feed_dict={X: x,
Y: y})
          #Print the partial results, and the current node doing the
calculation
          print ("Partial result from node: " + str(FLAGS.task_index) + ",
w: " + str(w.eval(session=sess))+ ", b0: " + str(b.eval(session=sess)))
    # Ask for all the services to stop.
    sv.stop()

if __name__ == "__main__":
  tf.app.run()
```

In the parameter server current host:

```
    python trainer.py  --ps_hosts=localhost:2222   --
worker_hosts=localhost:2223,localhost:2224   --job_name=ps -task_index=0
    he first
```

In the worker host number one:

```
    python trainer.py  --ps_hosts=localhost:2222   --
worker_hosts=localhost:2223,localhost:2224   --job_name=worker -
task_index=0
```

In the worker host number two:

```
    python trainer.py  --ps_hosts=localhost:2222   --
worker_hosts=localhost:2223,localhost:2224   --job_name=worker --
task_index=1
```

Summary

In this chapter, we have reviewed the two main elements we have in the TensorFlow toolbox to implement our models in a high performance environment, be it in single servers or a distributed cluster environment.

In the following chapter, we will review detailed instructions about how to install TensorFlow under a variety of environments and tools.

10
Library Installation and Additional Tips

There are several options to install TensorFlow. Google has prepared packages for many architectures, operating systems, and **Graphic Processing Unit** (**GPU**). Although the execution of machine learning tasks is much faster on a GPU, both install options are available:

- **CPU:** This will work in parallel across all processing units of the processing cores of the machine.
- **GPU:** This functionality only works using one of the various architectures that make use of the very powerful graphic processing unit that is CUDA architecture from NVIDIA. There are a number of other architectures/frameworks, such as Vulkan, which haven't reached the critical mass to become standard.

In this chapter, you will learn:

- How to install TensorFlow on three different operating systems (Linux, Windows, and OSX)
- How to test the installation to be sure that you will be able to run the examples, and develop your own scripts from thereon
- Aboutt the additional resources we are preparing to simplify your way to programming machine learning solutions

Linux installation

First of all, we should make a disclaimer. As you probably know, there is a really big number of alternatives in the Linux realm, and they have their own particular package management. For this reason, we chose to use the Ubuntu 16.04 distribution. It is undoubtedly the most widespread Linux distro, and additionally, Ubuntu 16.04 is an **LTS** version, or **Long Term Support**. This means that the distro will have three years of support for the desktop version, and five years for the server one. This implies that the base software we will run in this book will have support until the year 2021!

You will find more information about the meaning of LTS at https://wiki.ubuntu.com/LTS

Ubuntu, even if considered a more newbie-oriented distro, has all the necessary support for all the technologies that TensorFlow requires, and has the most extended user base. For this reason, we will be explaining the required steps for this distribution, which will also be really close to those of the remaining Debian-based distros.

At the time of the writing, there is no support for 32 bits Linux in TensorFlow, so be assured to run the examples in the 64 bits version.

Initial requirements

For the installation of TensorFlow, you can use either option:

- An AMD64-based image running on the cloud
- An AMD64 instruction capable computer (commonly called a 64 bit processor)

On AWS, a well suited ami image, is code ami-cf68e0d8. It will work well on a CPU and if you so wish, on GPU images.

Ubuntu preparation tasks (need to apply before any method)

As we are working on the recently-released Ubuntu 16.04, we will make sure that we are updated to the latest package versions and we have a minimal Python environment installed.

Let's execute these instructions on the command line:

```
    $ sudo apt-get update
    $ sudo apt-get upgrade -y
    $ sudo apt-get install -y build-essential python-pip python-dev python-
numpy swig python-dev default-jdk zip zlib1g-dev
```

Pip Linux installation method

In this section, we will use the pip (pip installs packages) package manager, to get TensorFlow and all its dependencies.

This is a very straightforward method, and you only need to make a few adjustments to get a working TensorFlow installation.

CPU version

In order to install TensorFlow and all its dependencies, we only need a simple command line (as long as we have implemented the preparation task).

So this is the required command line, for the standard Python 2.7:

```
    $ sudo pip install --upgrade
https://storage.googleapis.com/tensorflow/linux/cpu/tensorflow-0.9.0-cp27-n
one-linux_x86_64.whl
```

Then you will find the different dependent packages being downloaded and if no problem is detected, a corresponding message will be displayed:

```
Collecting tensorflow==0.9.0 from https://storage.googleapis.com/tensorflow/linu
x/cpu/tensorflow-0.9.0-cp27-none-linux_x86_64.whl
  Downloading https://storage.googleapis.com/tensorflow/linux/cpu/tensorflow-0.9
.0-cp27-none-linux_x86_64.whl (27.6MB)
    100% |################################| 27.6MB 48kB/s
Collecting numpy>=1.8.2 (from tensorflow==0.9.0)
  Downloading numpy-1.11.1-cp27-cp27mu-manylinux1_x86_64.whl (15.3MB)
    100% |################################| 15.3MB 89kB/s
Collecting six>=1.10.0 (from tensorflow==0.9.0)
  Downloading six-1.10.0-py2.py3-none-any.whl
Collecting protobuf==3.0.0b2 (from tensorflow==0.9.0)
  Downloading protobuf-3.0.0b2-py2.py3-none-any.whl (326kB)
    100% |################################| 327kB 2.7MB/s
Requirement already up-to-date: wheel in /usr/lib/python2.7/dist-packages (from
tensorflow==0.9.0)
Collecting setuptools (from protobuf==3.0.0b2->tensorflow==0.9.0)
  Downloading setuptools-25.1.1-py2.py3-none-any.whl (442kB)
    100% |################################| 450kB 2.8MB/s
Installing collected packages: numpy, six, setuptools, protobuf, tensorflow
  Found existing installation: setuptools 20.7.0
    Not uninstalling setuptools at /usr/lib/python2.7/dist-packages, outside env
ironment /usr
Successfully installed numpy-1.11.1 protobuf-3.0.0b2 setuptools-25.1.1 six-1.10.
0 tensorflow-0.9.0
```

Pip installation output

Testing your installation

After the installation steps we can do a very simple test, calling the Python interpreter, and then importing the TensorFlow library, defining two numbers as a constant, and getting its sum after all:

```
$ python
>>> import tensorflow as tf
>>> a = tf.constant(2)
>>> b = tf.constant(20)
>>> print(sess.run(a + b))
```

GPU support

In order to install the GPU-supporting TensorFlow libraries, first you have to perform all the steps in the section the GPU support, from Install from source.

Then you will invoke:

```
    $ sudo pip install -upgrade
https://storage.googleapis.com/tensorflow/linux/gpu/tensorflow-0.10.0rc0-cp
27-none-linux_x86_64.whl
```

> TIP: There are many versions of pre-packaged TensorFlow.

They follow the following form:

```
    https://storage.googleapis.com/tensorflow/linux/[processor
type]/tensorflow-[version]-cp[python version]-none-linux_x86_64.whl
```

> TIP: Where `[version]` can be `cpu` or `gpu`, `[version]` is the TensorFlow version (actually 0.11), and the Python version can be 2.7, 3.4, or 3.5.

Virtualenv installation method

In this section, we will explain the preferred method for TensorFlow using the virtualenv tool.

From the virtualenv page (`virtualenv.pypa.io`):

> *"Virtualenv is a tool to create isolated Python environments.(...) It creates an environment that has its own installation directories, that doesn't share libraries with other virtualenv environments (and optionally doesn't access the globally installed libraries either)."*

By means of this tool, we will simply install an isolated environment for our TensorFlow installation, without interfering with all the other system libraries which in turn won't affect our installation either.

These are the simple steps we will follow (from a Linux terminal):

1. Set the `LC_ALL` variable:

```
$ export LC_ALL=C
```

2. Install the `virtualenv` Ubuntu package from the installer:

```
$ sudo apt-get install python-virtualenv
```

3. Install the `virtualenv` package:

```
virtualenv --system-site-packages ~/tensorflow
```

4. Then to make use of the new TensorFlow, you will always need to remember to activate the TensorFlow environment:

```
source ~/tensorflow/bin/activate
```

5. Then install the `tensorflow` package via pip:

```
pip install --upgrade
https://storage.googleapis.com/tensorflow/linux/cpu/tensorflow-0.9.0-cp27-n
one-linux_x86_64.whl
```

You will be able to install all the alternative official `tensorflow` packages transcribed in the *pip linux installation method.*

Environment test

Here we will do a minimal test of TensorFlow.

First, we will activate the newly-created TensorFlow environment:

```
$ source ~/tensorflow/bin/activate
```

Then, the prompt will change with a (`tensorflow`) prefix, and we can execute simple code which loads TensorFlow, and sums two values:

```
(tensorflow) $ python
>>> import tensorflow as tf
>>> a = tf.constant(2)
>>> b = tf.constant(3)
>>> print(sess.run(a * b))
6
```

After your work is done, and if you want to return to normal environment, you can simply deactivate the environment:

```
(tensorflow)$ deactivate
```

Docker installation method

This TensorFlow installation method uses a recent type of operation technology called containers.

Containers are in some ways related to what virtualenv does, in that with Docker, you will have a new virtual environment. The main difference is the level at which this virtualization works. It contains the application and all dependencies in a simplified package, and these encapsulated containers can run simultaneously, all over a common layer, the Docker engine, which in turn runs over the host operative system.

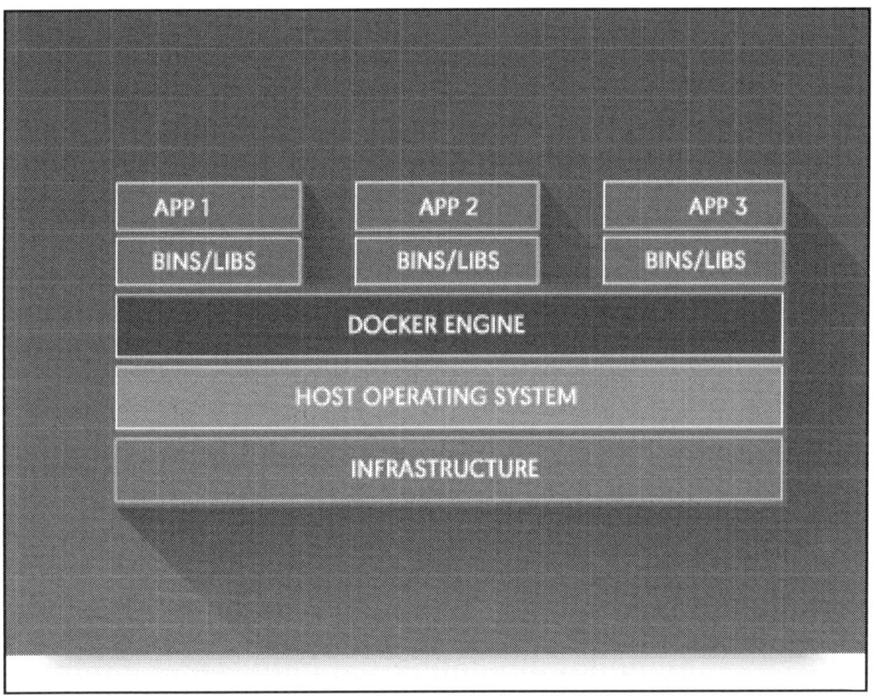

Docker main architecture(image source - https://www.docker.com/products/docker-engine)

Installing Docker

First of all, we will installdocker via the apt package:

```
sudo apt-get install docker.io
```

Allowing Docker to run with a normal user

In this step, we create a Docker group to be able to use Docker as a user:

```
sudo groupadd docker
```

> TIP: It is possible that you get the error; `group 'docker' already exists`. You can safely ignore it.

Then we add the current user to the Docker group:

```
sudo usermod -aG docker [your user]
```

> TIP: This command shouldn't return any output.

Reboot

After this step, a reboot is needed for the changes to apply.

Testing the Docker installation

After the reboot, you can try calling the hello world Docker example, with the command line:

```
$ docker run hello-world
```

```
$ docker run hello-world

Hello from Docker!
This message shows that your installation appears to be working correctly.

To generate this message, Docker took the following steps:
 1. The Docker client contacted the Docker daemon.
 2. The Docker daemon pulled the "hello-world" image from the Docker Hub.
 3. The Docker daemon created a new container from that image which runs the
    executable that produces the output you are currently reading.
 4. The Docker daemon streamed that output to the Docker client, which sent it
    to your terminal.

To try something more ambitious, you can run an Ubuntu container with:
 $ docker run -it ubuntu bash

Share images, automate workflows, and more with a free Docker Hub account:
 https://hub.docker.com

For more examples and ideas, visit:
 https://docs.docker.com/engine/userguide/
```

Docker Hello World container

Run the TensorFlow container

Then we run (and install if it was not installed before) the TensorFlow binary image (in this case the vanilla CPU binary image):

```
docker run -it -p 8888:8888 gcr.io/tensorflow/tensorflow
```

```
$ docker run -it -p 8888:8888 gcr.io/tensorflow/tensorflow
Unable to find image 'gcr.io/tensorflow/tensorflow:latest' locally
latest: Pulling from tensorflow/tensorflow

759d6771041e: Downloading [==================================================>          ] 48.31 MB/65.69 MB
8836b825667b: Download complete
c2f5e51744e6: Download complete
a3ed95caeb02: Download complete
b1a230d2f7d7: Downloading [=====================>                                ] 50.95 MB/117.2 MB
f4bd848af23b: Download complete
9ff2d28f3bea: Downloading [=========================>                            ] 34.13 MB/66.78 MB
de3ac9a732b6: Waiting
ba1ff7fd8338: Waiting
8b638dd1001b: Waiting
4c3f9ea22d7e: Waiting
```

TensorFlow installation via PIP

After the installation is finished, you will see the final installation steps, and Jupyter notebook starting:

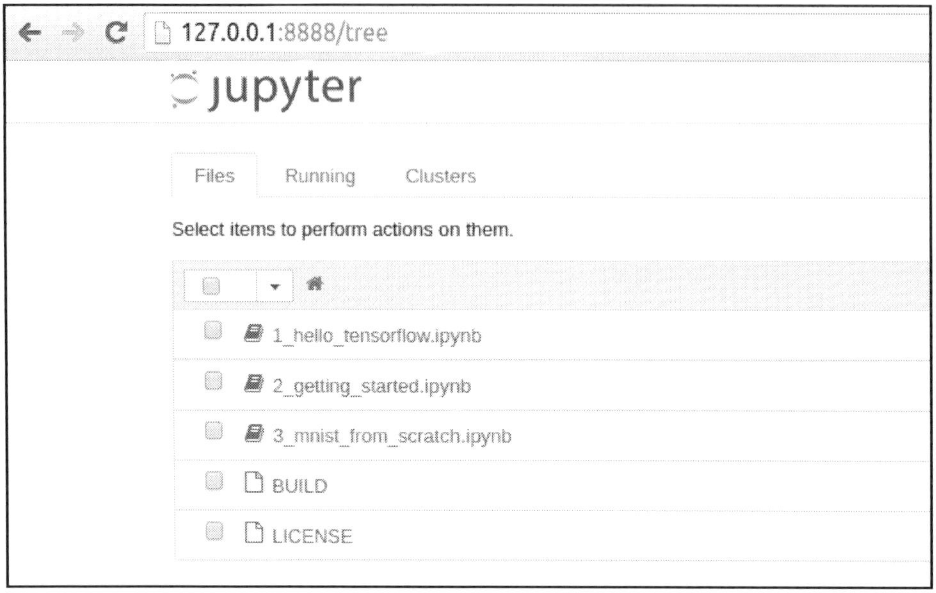

Many of the samples use the Jupyter notebook format. In order to execute and run them, you can find information about installation and use for many architectures at it's home page, `jupyter.org`

Linux installation from source

Now we head to the most complete and developer-friendly installation method for TensorFlow. Installing from source code will allow you to learn about the different tools used for compiling.

Installing the Git source code version manager

Git is one of the most well-known source code version managers in existence, and is the one chosen by Google, publishing its code on GitHub.

In order to download the source code of TensorFlow, we will first install the Git source code manager:

Git installation in Linux (Ubuntu 16.04)

To install Git on your Ubuntu system, run the following command:

```
$ sudo apt-get install git
```

Installing the Bazel build tool

Bazel (`bazel.io`) is a build tool, based on the internal build tool Google has used for more than seven years, known as Blaze, and released as beta on September 9, 2015.

It is additionally used as the main build tool in TensorFlow, so in order to do some advanced tasks, a minimal knowledge of the tool is needed.

> TIP: Different advantages, compared with competing projects, such as Gradle, the main ones being:

- Support for a number of languages, such as C++, Java, Python, and so on
- Support for creating Android and iOS applications, and even Docker images
- Support for using libraries from many different sources, such as GitHub, Maven, and so on
- Extensiblity through an API for adding custom build rules

Adding the Bazel distribution URI as a package source

First we will add the Bazel repository to the list of available repositories, and its respective key to the configuration of the apt tool, which manages dependencies on the Ubuntu operating system.

```
    $ echo "deb http://storage.googleapis.com/bazel-apt stable jdk1.8" |
sudo tee /etc/apt/sources.list.d/bazel.list
    $ curl https://storage.googleapis.com/bazel-apt/doc/apt-key.pub.gpg |
sudo apt-key add -
```

Bazel installation

Updating and installing Bazel

Once we have all the package source installed, we proceed to install Bazel via `apt-get`:

```
$ sudo apt-get update && sudo apt-get install bazel
```

This command will install Java and a big number of dependencies, so it could take some time to get it installed.

Installing GPU support (optional)

This section will teach us to install the required packages needed to have GPU support in our Linux setup.

Actually the only way to get GPU computing support is through CUDA.

Check that the nouveau NVIDIA graphic card drivers don't exist. To test this, execute the following command and check if there is any output:

```
lsmod | grep nouveau
```

If there is no output, see *Installing CUDA system packages*, if not, execute the following commands:

```
    $ echo -e "blacklist nouveau\nblacklist lbm-nouveau\noptions nouveau
modeset=0\nalias nouveau off\nalias lbm-nouveau off\n" | sudo tee
/etc/modprobe.d/blacklist-nouveau.conf
    $ echo options nouveau modeset=0 | sudo tee -a /etc/modprobe.d/nouveau-
kms.conf
    $ sudo update-initramfs -u
    $ sudo reboot (a reboot will occur)
```

Installing CUDA system packages

The first step is to install the required packages from the repositories:

```
sudo apt-get install -y linux-source linux-headers-`uname -r`
nvidia-graphics-drivers-361
nvidia-cuda-dev
sudo apt install nvidia-cuda-toolkit
sudo apt-get install libcupti-dev
```

If you are installing CUDA on a cloud image, you should run this command before this commands block:

```
sudo apt-get install linux-image-extra-virtual
```

Creating alternative locations

The current TensorFlow install configurations expect a very rigid structure, so we have to prepare a similar structure on our filesystem.

Here are the commands we will need to run:

```
    sudo mkdir /usr/local/cuda
    cd /usr/local/cuda
    sudo ln -s /usr/lib/x86_64-linux-gnu/ lib64
    sudo ln -s /usr/include/ include
    sudo ln -s /usr/bin/ bin
    sudo ln -s /usr/lib/x86_64-linux-gnu/ nvvm
    sudo mkdir -p extras/CUPTI
    cd extras/CUPTI
    sudo ln -s /usr/lib/x86_64-linux-gnu/ lib64
    sudo ln -s /usr/include/ include
    sudo ln -s /usr/include/cuda.h /usr/local/cuda/include/cuda.h
    sudo ln -s /usr/include/cublas.h /usr/local/cuda/include/cublas.h
    sudo ln -s /usr/include/cudnn.h /usr/local/cuda/include/cudnn.h
    sudo ln -s /usr/include/cupti.h
/usr/local/cuda/extras/CUPTI/include/cupti.h
    sudo ln -s /usr/lib/x86_64-linux-gnu/libcudart_static.a
/usr/local/cuda/lib64/libcudart_static.a
    sudo ln -s /usr/lib/x86_64-linux-gnu/libcublas.so
/usr/local/cuda/lib64/libcublas.so
    sudo ln -s /usr/lib/x86_64-linux-gnu/libcudart.so
/usr/local/cuda/lib64/libcudart.so
    sudo ln -s /usr/lib/x86_64-linux-gnu/libcudnn.so
/usr/local/cuda/lib64/libcudnn.so
    sudo ln -s /usr/lib/x86_64-linux-gnu/libcufft.so
/usr/local/cuda/lib64/libcufft.so
    sudo ln -s /usr/lib/x86_64-linux-gnu/libcupti.so
/usr/local/cuda/extras/CUPTI/lib64/libcupti.so
```

Installing cuDNN

TensorFlow uses the additional cuDNN package to accelerate the deep neural network operations.

We will then download the `cudnn` package:

```
$ wget
http://developer.download.nvidia.com/compute/redist/cudnn/v5/cudnn-7.5-linu
x-x64-v5.0-ga.tgz
```

Then we need to unzip the packages and link them:

```
$ sudo cp cuda/lib64/libcudnn* /usr/local/cuda/lib64
$ sudo cp cuda/include/cudnn.h /usr/local/cuda/include/
```

Clone TensorFlow source

Finally, we arrive at the task of getting TensorFlow source code.

Getting it is as easy as executing the following command:

```
$ git clone https://github.com/tensorflow/tensorflow
```

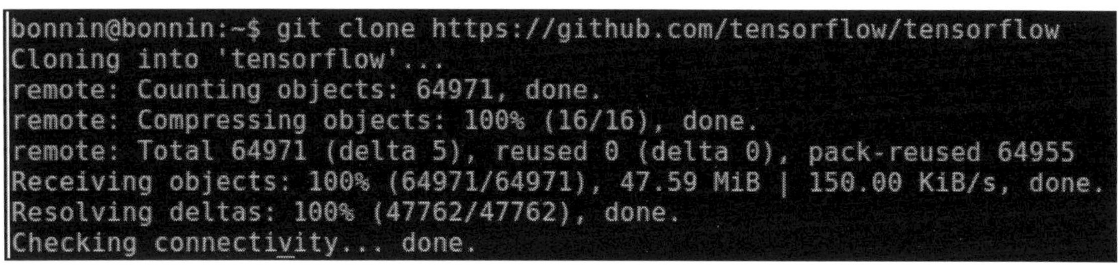

Git installation

Configuring TensorFlow build

Then we access the `tensorflow` main directory:

```
$ cd tensorflow
```

And then we simply run the configure script:

```
$ ./configure
```

In the following figure you can see the answers to most of the questions (they are almost all enters and yes)

```
$ ./configure
Please specify the location of python. [Default is /usr/bin/python]:
Do you wish to build TensorFlow with Google Cloud Platform support? [y/N]
No Google Cloud Platform support will be enabled for TensorFlow
Do you wish to build TensorFlow with GPU support? [y/N] y
GPU support will be enabled for TensorFlow
Please specify which gcc should be used by nvcc as the host compiler. [Default is /usr/bin/gcc]:
Please specify the Cuda SDK version you want to use, e.g. 7.0. [Leave empty to use system default]:
Please specify the location where CUDA  toolkit is installed. Refer to README.md for more details. [Default is
/usr/local/cuda]:
Please specify the Cudnn version you want to use. [Leave empty to use system default]:
Please specify the location where cuDNN  library is installed. Refer to README.md for more details. [Default is
/usr/local/cuda]:
Please specify a list of comma-separated Cuda compute capabilities you want to build with.
You can find the compute capability of your device at: https://developer.nvidia.com/cuda-gpus.
Please note that each additional compute capability significantly increases your build time and binary size.
[Default is: "3.5,5.2"]:
Setting up Cuda include
Setting up Cuda lib64
Setting up Cuda bin
Setting up Cuda nvvm
Setting up CUPTI include
Setting up CUPTI lib64
Configuration finished
```

CUDA configuration

So we are now ready to proceed with the building of the library.

If you are installing it on AWS, you will have to execute the modified line:

```
TF_UNOFFICIAL_SETTING=1 ./configure
```

Building TensorFlow

After all the preparation steps, we will finally compile TensorFlow. The following line could get your attention because it refers to a tutorial. The reason we build the example is that it includes the base installation, and provides a means of testing if the installation worked.

Run the following command:

```
$ bazel build -c opt --config=cuda
//tensorflow/cc:tutorials_example_trainer
```

Testing the installation

Now it is time to test the installation. From the main `tensorflow` installation directory, just execute the following command:

```
$ bazel-bin/tensorflow/cc/tutorials_example_trainer --use_gpu
```

This is a sample representation of the commands output:

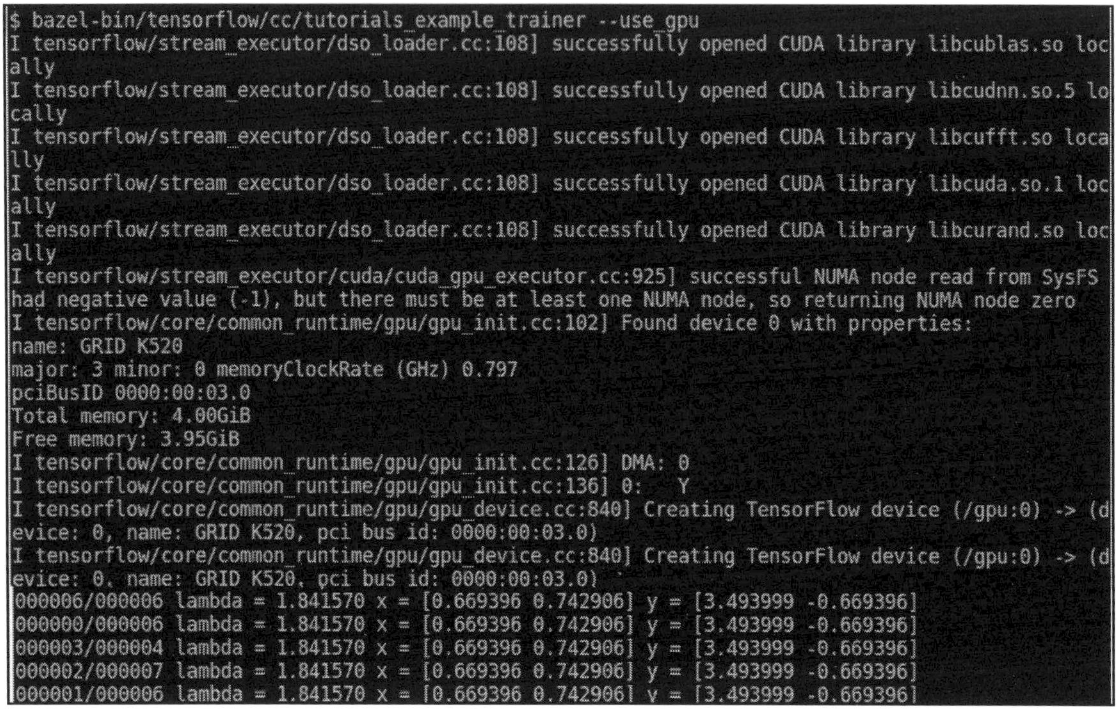

```
$ bazel-bin/tensorflow/cc/tutorials_example_trainer --use_gpu
I tensorflow/stream_executor/dso_loader.cc:108] successfully opened CUDA library libcublas.so loc
ally
I tensorflow/stream_executor/dso_loader.cc:108] successfully opened CUDA library libcudnn.so.5 lo
cally
I tensorflow/stream_executor/dso_loader.cc:108] successfully opened CUDA library libcufft.so loca
lly
I tensorflow/stream_executor/dso_loader.cc:108] successfully opened CUDA library libcuda.so.1 loc
ally
I tensorflow/stream_executor/dso_loader.cc:108] successfully opened CUDA library libcurand.so loc
ally
I tensorflow/stream_executor/cuda/cuda_gpu_executor.cc:925] successful NUMA node read from SysFS
had negative value (-1), but there must be at least one NUMA node, so returning NUMA node zero
I tensorflow/core/common_runtime/gpu/gpu_init.cc:102] Found device 0 with properties:
name: GRID K520
major: 3 minor: 0 memoryClockRate (GHz) 0.797
pciBusID 0000:00:03.0
Total memory: 4.00GiB
Free memory: 3.95GiB
I tensorflow/core/common_runtime/gpu/gpu_init.cc:126] DMA: 0
I tensorflow/core/common_runtime/gpu/gpu_init.cc:136] 0:   Y
I tensorflow/core/common_runtime/gpu/gpu_device.cc:840] Creating TensorFlow device (/gpu:0) -> (d
evice: 0, name: GRID K520, pci bus id: 0000:00:03.0)
I tensorflow/core/common_runtime/gpu/gpu_device.cc:840] Creating TensorFlow device (/gpu:0) -> (d
evice: 0, name: GRID K520, pci bus id: 0000:00:03.0)
000006/000006 lambda = 1.841570 x = [0.669396 0.742906] y = [3.493999 -0.669396]
000000/000006 lambda = 1.841570 x = [0.669396 0.742906] y = [3.493999 -0.669396]
000003/000004 lambda = 1.841570 x = [0.669396 0.742906] y = [3.493999 -0.669396]
000002/000007 lambda = 1.841570 x = [0.669396 0.742906] y = [3.493999 -0.669396]
000001/000006 lambda = 1.841570 x = [0.669396 0.742906] y = [3.493999 -0.669396]
```

TensorFlow GPU test

Windows installation

Now it is the turn of the Windows operating system. First, we have to say that this is not a first choice for the TensorFlow ecosystem, but we can definitely play and develop with the Windows operating system.

Classic Docker toolbox method

This method uses the classic toolbox method, which is the method that works with the majority of the recent Windows releases (from Windows 7, and always with a 64 bit operating system).

> TIP: In order to have Docker working (specifically VirtualBox), you need to have the VT-X extensions installed. This is a task you need to do at the BIOS level.

Installation steps

Here we will list the different steps needed to install `tensorflow` via Docker in Windows.

Downloading the Docker toolbox installer

The current URL for the installer is located at `https://github.com/docker/toolbox/releases/download/v1.12.0/DockerToolbox-1.12.0.exe`.

After executing the installer, we will see the first installation screen:

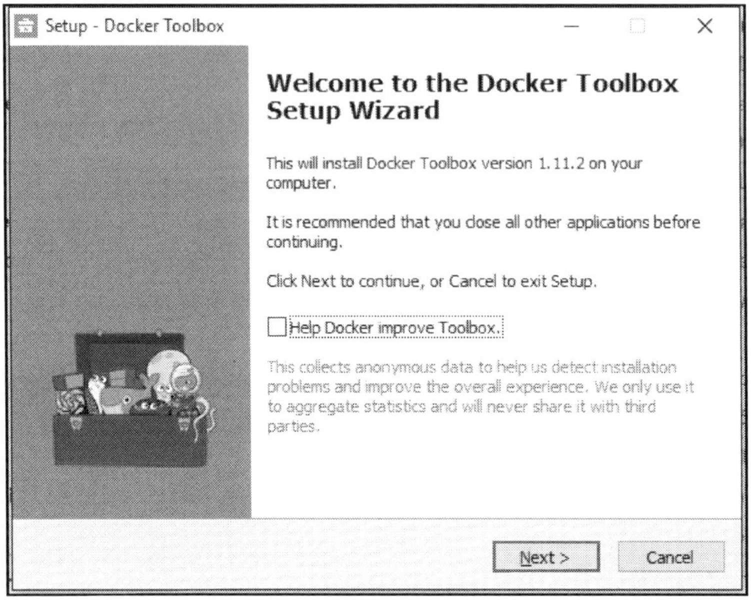

Docker Toolbox installation first screen

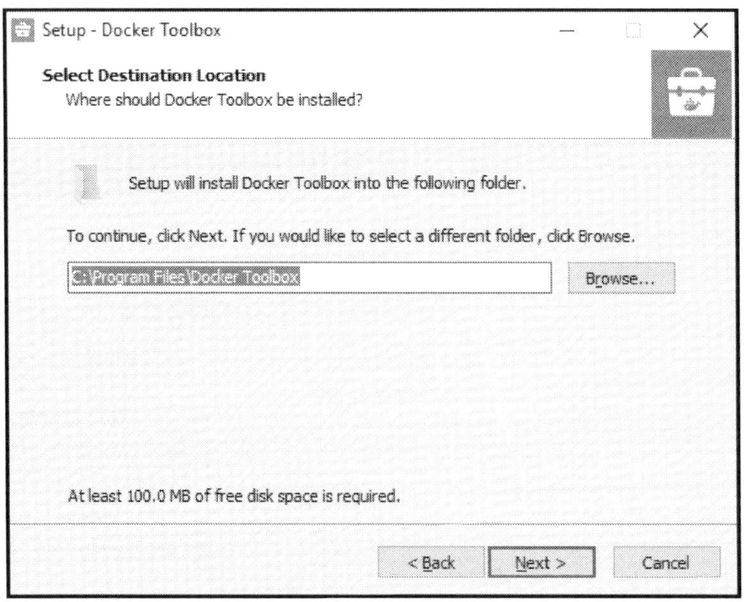

Docker toolbox installer path chooser

Then we select all the components we will need in our installation:

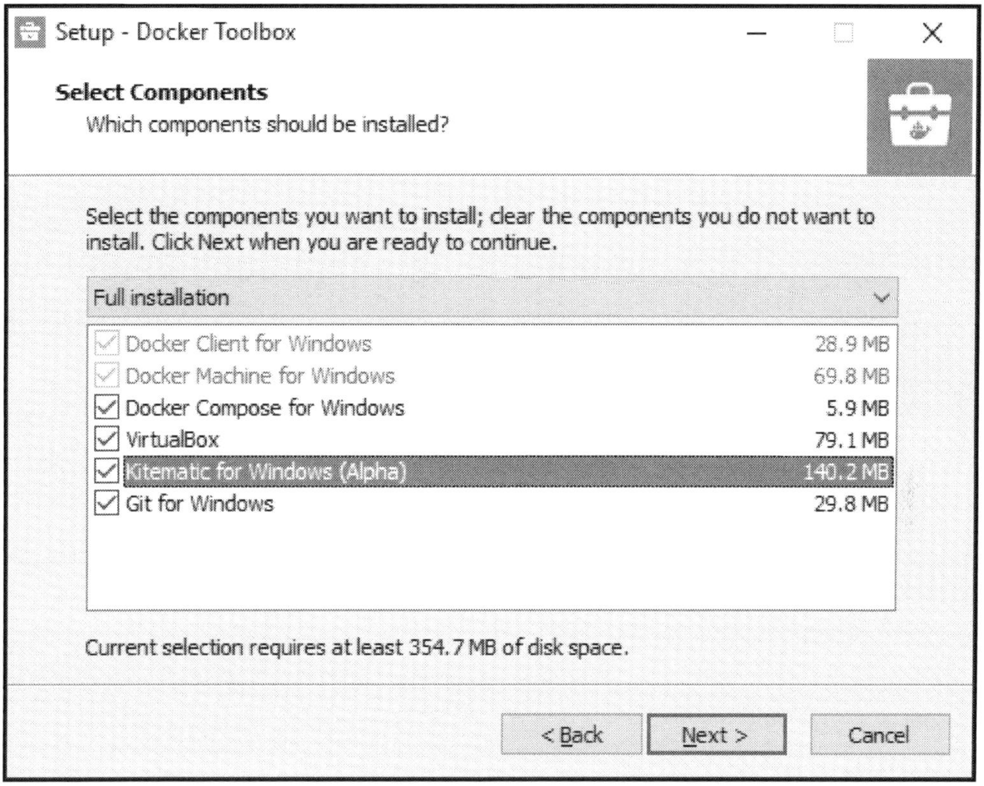

Docker Toolbox package selection screen

After various installation operations, our Docker installation will be ready:

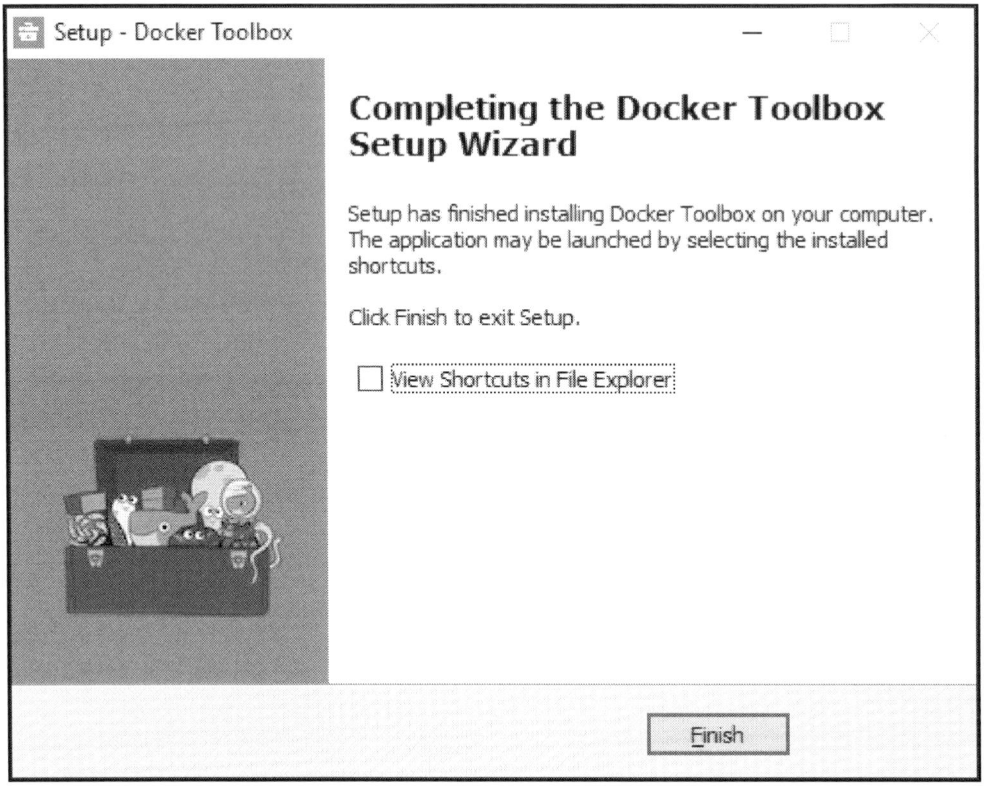

Docker toolbox installation final screen

Creating the Docker machine

In order to create the initial machine, we will execute the following command in the Docker Terminal:

```
docker-machine create vdocker -d virtualbox
```

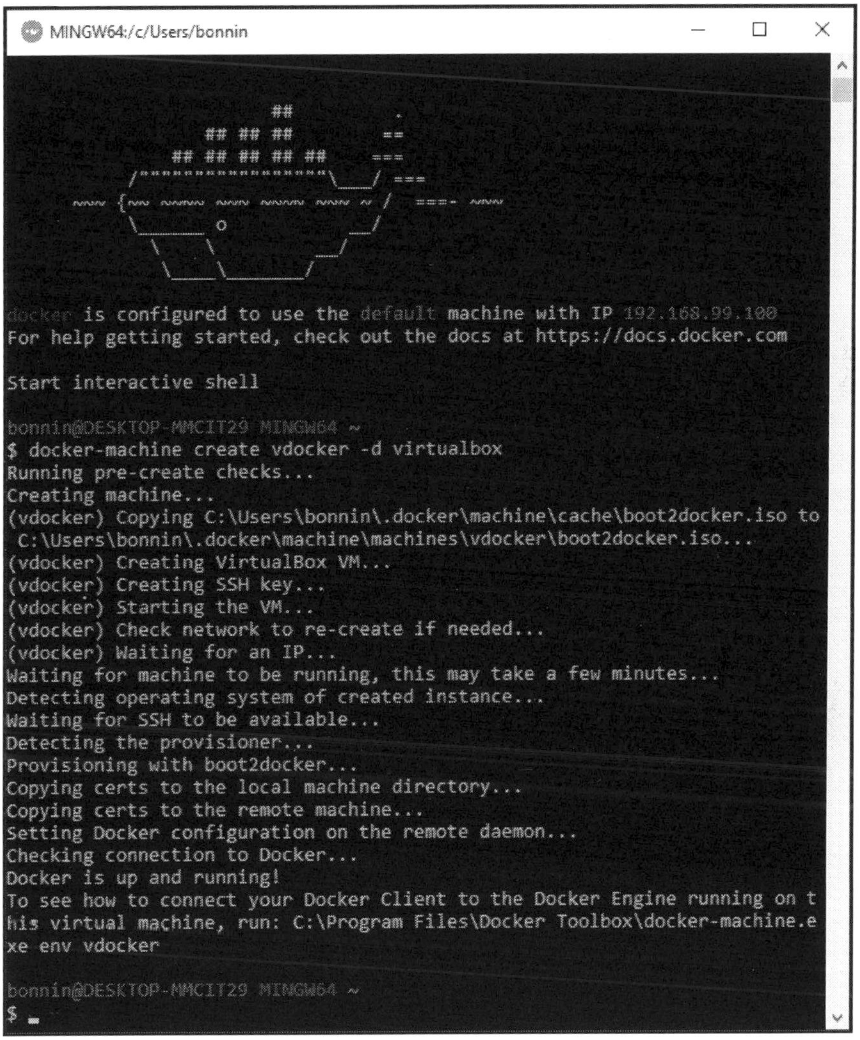

Docker initial image installation

Then, in a command window, type the following:

```
FOR /f "tokens=*" %i IN ('docker-machine env --shell cmd vdocker') DO
%i docker run -it b.gcr.io/tensorflow/tensorflow
```

This will print and read a lot of variables needed to run the recently-created virtual machine.

Then finally, to install the `tensorflow` container, we proceed as we did with the Linux counterpart, from the same console:

```
docker run -it -p 8888:8888 gcr.io/tensorflow/tensorflow
```

> TIP: If you don't want to execute Jupyter, but want to directly boot into a console, you run the Docker image this way:

```
run -it -p 8888:8888 gcr.io/tensorflow/tensorflow bash
```

MacOS X installation

Now let's turn to installation on MacOS X. The installation procedures are very similar to Linux. They are based on the OS X El Capitan edition. We will also refer to version 2.7 of Python, without GPU support.

The installation requires sudo privileges for the installing user.

Install pip

In this step, we will install the pip package manager, using the `easy_install` package manager which is included in the setup tools Python package, and is included by default in the operating system.

For this installation, we will execute the following in a terminal:

```
$ sudo easy_install pip
```

Then we will install the six module, which is a compatibility module to help Python 2 programs support Python 3 programming:

To install `six`, we execute the following command:

```
sudo easy_install --upgrade six
```

After the installation of the `six` package, we proceed to install the `tensorflow` package, by executing the following command:

```
sudo pip install -ignore-packages six
https://storage.googleapis.com/tensorflow/mac/cpu/tensorflow-0.10.0-py2-non
e-any.whl
```

Then we adjust the path of the `numpy` package, which is needed in El Capitan:

```
sudo easy_install numpy
```

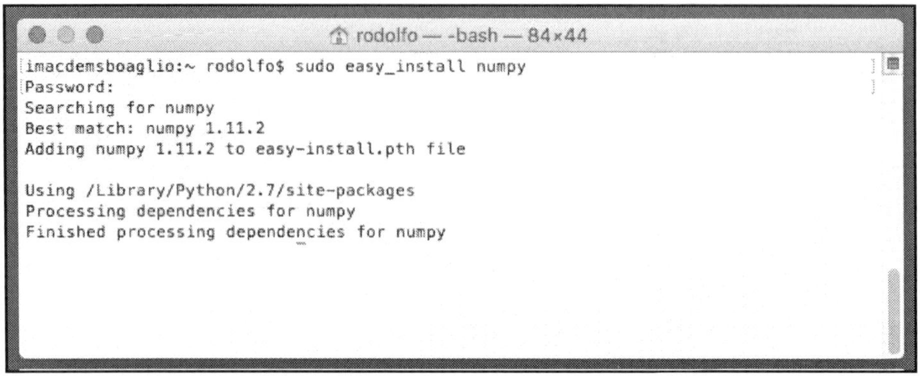

And we are ready to import the `tensorflow` module and run some simple examples:

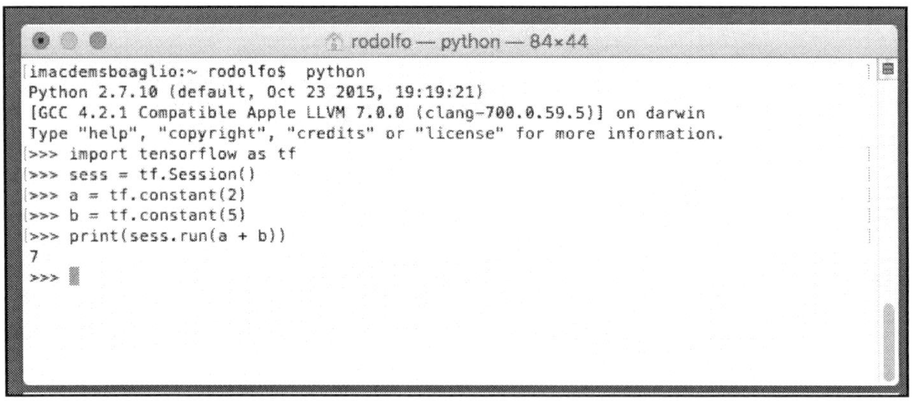

Summary

In this chapter, we have reviewed some of the main ways in which a TensorFlow installation can be performed.

Even if the list of possibilities is finite, every month or so we see a new architecture or processor being supported, so we can only expect more and more application fields for this technology.

Index

K

L

M

N

O

P

R

S

T

U

V

W

20016472R00157

Printed in Great Britain
by Amazon